The International Connection

The International Connection

Opium from Growers to Pushers

**Catherine Lamour
and Michel R. Lamberti**

Translated from the French
by Peter and Betty Ross

PANTHEON BOOKS

A Division of Random House
New York

All rights reserved under International and Pan-American
Copyright Conventions. Published in the United States by
Pantheon Books, a division of Random House, Inc., New
York. Originally published in France as *Les Grandes
Manoeuvres de l'Opium* by Les Editions du Seuil, S.A.
Copyright © 1972 by Les Editions du Seuil, Paris. English
translation first published in Great Britain as *The Second
Opium War* by Allen Lane, a division of Penguin Books
Limited, London.

Library of Congress Cataloging in Publication Data

Lamour, Catherine.
The International Connection

    Translation of *Les Grandes Manoeuvres de l'Opium*
Includes bibliographical references.
1. Opium trade. I. Lamberti, Michel R., joint author.
II. Title.
HV5816.L3313   364.1'57'0904   74-4775
ISBN 0-394-48411-8

Manufactured in the United States of America

First American Edition

Contents

List of Maps

Introduction:
The Political Problem

Most countries of the world have long since introduced anti-drug laws and taken steps to enforce them. But though constantly strengthened, the agencies concerned in suppressing the traffic have not succeeded in disrupting the rings set up by the operators who, despite severe setbacks, persist in an activity that brings in enormous profits. Thus it has proved impossible to stem the tide of drug addiction which, during the past ten years or so, has swept across the world to the detriment more especially of the highly industrialized countries.

By the turn of the century it had already become apparent that the control of drugs – particularly narcotics – called for international cooperation. Indeed the tragedy of the New York 'junkie' and the Parisian *camé* is far from being an exclusively French or American phenomenon. Its international character becomes immediately evident if we consider that the heroin they inject into their veins originated in the poppy fields of Laos, Burma, Afghanistan, Mexico and elsewhere.

But the fight against drug addiction, when conducted on an international scale, at once assumes political and economic dimensions. For surprising though it may seem, heroin, like coffee, copper, uranium and oil, is closely identified with national interests. This is particularly the case in those countries afflicted by drug addiction, whose addicts not only represent a considerable drain on the national exchequer but also, by their personal conduct, tend to disrupt social life beyond the limits acceptable to the establishment. It should not be forgotten, however, that in the poppy-growing countries national interests are also involved. Here the drug problem is by no means confined to its medical or criminal aspects, since opium represents a means, if not the sole means, of subsistence for large sections of the

Introduction

peasant population and is in addition a source of foreign currency for the State.

In these circumstances the fight against the abuse of narcotics, regarded by the afflicted countries as a socially beneficial measure, may, in the opium-producing countries, assume the aspect of an attack on the way of life and standard of living of considerable strata of the population. And whereas the countries in which heroin consumption is increasing wish to strike at what they consider to be one of the roots of the evil, namely poppy cultivation, the authorities in the producing regions cannot adopt this point of view without first considering its economic and political implications.

Today some hard bargaining is going on between the countries producing narcotics and those consuming them. In June 1971 the United States assumed responsibility for initiating and leading a large scale offensive against opium, its producers and traffickers. This 'great opium war' is being fought out on all kinds of terrain – in chancelleries, in the corridors and assembly rooms of international organizations, in jungle villages, in the slums and palaces of big cities. Circumstances dictate its nature, which may be diplomatic, economic or military, or again may take the form of law enforcement measures or of direct political confrontation. All these we propose to describe in this book, at the same time endeavouring to assess whether they hold out any prospect of restricting the growth of drug addiction throughout the world.

Hence we shall say little about addicts as such or the psychosocial conditions favouring the spread of addiction. Large numbers of excellent works have already been written on this subject. Our intention here is to examine the international aspect of the traffic in narcotics, the nature of the relationship between governments and traffickers, the very special role played by opium and heroin in the civil wars of south-east Asia, the hypocrisy that pervades international negotiations relating to this somewhat unusual merchandise and, finally, the economic, social and political conditions which might eventually put an end to the cultivation of the opium poppy.

This survey, the result of investigations carried out in Laos,

Thailand, Burma, Pakistan, Afghanistan, Turkey, Iran, the Lebanon and the United States, has been rounded off with information drawn from various sources – newspaper articles, United Nations publications and confidential reports emanating from government, police and intelligence agencies. It is impossible to mention here all those who agreed to supply us with information. Among the many who did so were representatives of the various national agencies concerned with the control of drugs, in particular the U.S. Bureau of Narcotics and Dangerous Drugs (B.N.D.D.), officials of all nationalities, soldiers, peasants, traffickers of every description, whether active or retired, ardent advocates of capitalism, communist functionaries, and persons who expressed no definite political opinions.

Some of these informants tried to mislead us, some demanded payment for what they divulged while others agreed to speak only on the express condition that they remain anonymous. We are as grateful to them as we are to all the others, since by their attitude they often, if unwittingly, helped to shed light on some particular aspect of this strange Opium War.

Paris 1972

Part 1

The Drug's
Supply Routes

Of all the drugs that are known and distributed throughout the world, heroin is the most dangerous because it creates in those who use it a condition of physical and psychological dependence which quickly makes them its slave. This circumstance is distinctly advantageous to the trafficker since it means that he can count on a stable market as well as on supply channels which enable the drug or the raw materials needed for its preparation to be secretly conveyed to the place of consumption. That is why the fight against the traffic in narcotics has for many years been regarded primarily as a matter of law enforcement.

Nevertheless there is no denying that, despite the constant strengthening of the agencies concerned with drug control, the amount of heroin diverted into the market has continued to grow, as has the number of addicts. Even after severe setbacks a ring of traffickers will generally re-emerge somewhere else. Such are the profits to be derived from the trade in drugs that if one gang is broken up, its place is immediately taken by another.

Having come round to the view that law enforcement pure and simple is not enough to resolve the drug problem, the authorities in the United States – the country hardest hit by drug addiction – have now decided to attack the production of heroin at the actual source.

1 'Drugs' and 'Addicts'

What are 'drugs' and what are 'addicts'? Before these words are used, they need to be stripped of the pejorative – or at least emotive – connotations attaching to them in the mind of a public whose opinion has been too well conditioned. Indeed, as a result of carefully orchestrated propaganda, the taker of drugs is as often as not associated with 'long-haired hippies' or trouble-makers of whatever kind who threaten to disrupt the social order. Similarly, addicts and traffickers, the consumers and pedlars of drugs, are indiscriminately condemned.

The term addict is no more applicable to one who makes occasional use of drugs than is the term alcoholic to one who sometimes over-indulges in strong liquor. According to Dr Dale C. Cameron, a true addict is one who devotes 'substantial amounts of time and energy . . . to obtaining, thinking about, using or discussing the drug', or who 'tends to respond to different life situations and personal moods by taking drugs'.[1] He can then be said to be psychically dependent on the drug. Some people are more prone than others to fall into such a condition of psychical dependence. And in this respect some drugs are more dangerous than others.

The existence of a term as imprecise as 'drug' has made possible the use of convenient generalizations which blur the necessary distinction between cannabis (and its derivatives, hashish and marijuana), cocaine, opium (and its derivatives, morphine and heroin), the amphetamines, the barbiturates and the hallucinogens. Thus the general public has become firmly convinced that progression from the first whiff of hashish to the first shot of heroin is as automatic and inevitable as it is depraved. Yet all experts on the subject insist that in the

1. Dr Dale C. Cameron, 'Abuse of Alcohol and Drugs: Concepts and Planning', *W.H.O. Chronicle*, January 1971.

majority of cases it is not drug addiction which gives rise to psychological or psychiatric disorders. Rather it is individuals suffering from such disorders who tend to become drug addicts. 'It may be safely stated that many individuals who are attracted to drugs have personal problems', declares a report of the U.S. National Institute of Mental Health.

Until recently these were voices crying in the wilderness. And, while part of the already inadequate police forces responsible for drug control were expending their efforts in running to earth hashish and marijuana traffickers, that deadly poison, heroin, was arriving by the suitcaseful in the big cities of Europe and America.

This book concerns itself with heroin to the exclusion of all other drugs – not that the habitual use of mood changers and synthetic hallucinogens is devoid of danger, for it may well lead to serious psychological disturbance if not to irremediable physiological damage. But of all the drugs used throughout the world – and there are plenty of them – heroin is the most dangerous. For, apart from another opium derivative, morphine, it is the only one that makes helpless victims of those who take it, inducing in them a state of physical dependence which, beyond a certain stage, becomes irreversible. Until now all attempts at detoxication have proved disappointing. A person 'hooked' on morphine or heroin cannot do without it except at the cost of the almost unbearable suffering that is the result of the withdrawal syndrome. Here lies the trap. The heroin addict has become a creature exploited for the benefit of international gangs who, in the streets of New York, obtain a million dollars for one kilogramme of heroin whose raw material – ten kilogrammes of opium – has cost them at most five hundred dollars.

Since their resources, however large, are always inadequate, the national and international agencies responsible for the suppression of the traffic in narcotics have decided to give first priority to the battle against heroin, thereby implicitly postponing the tracking down of other drugs.

The argument now raging in regard to marijuana and hashish will no doubt soon die a natural death, while the use of these two mood changers, like that of tobacco and alcohol, will gradually gain acceptance. Given the knowledge that twenty-four million Americans have tried marijuana at least once and that eight million smoke it regularly,[2] we may now assume that those who oppose its unrestricted use are fighting a losing battle similar to that waged over Prohibition in the thirties. The Netherlands have already taken the first step in this direction with the announcement that, in future, the smoking of marijuana will be treated as a minor offence and punished accordingly, and that only traffickers will be subject to prosecution. A study carried out by an American official body, the National Institute of Mental Health, has recommended that similar measures be adopted in the United States. The authors of the study write: 'No ill-effects on health have been observed in subjects using marijuana in moderation. Violent reactions seldom occur.' And they go on to say: 'There is no proof for the assertion that marijuana leads to the consumption of other drugs.'[3] After a year of research a commission set up by Congress reached very similar conclusions. On 22 March 1972 it submitted a report advocating the easing of restrictions on marijuana for private and personal use. At the same time it recommended that those engaged in selling this product for gain should remain subject to prosecution – which, be it said in passing, is not altogether devoid of casuistry. Having declared that the American public's view of the 'ill-effects' of marijuana 'derived more from the imagination than from its actual effects', the official commission concludes: 'The effects of marijuana are not sufficiently harmful to justify the application of penal law to the behaviour of individuals in private.'

But of all the signs heralding a less repressive attitude towards the cannabis derivatives, hashish and marijuana, the most significant is the view expressed six weeks after his retirement

2. Report to Congress by the National Commission on Marijuana and Drug Abuse.
3. National Institute of Mental Health, second report to Congress, *Marijuana and Health*.

by John Finlator, known as 'Supernarc'[4] when co-director of the famous Bureau of Narcotics and Dangerous Drugs, an organization engaged in an intensive and world-wide struggle with drug traffickers. On 2 February 1972 Finlator proclaimed himself a supporter of a militant group advocating a more liberal approach to the use of marijuana. Many years of experience, he said, had taught him that repressive criminal laws would never solve America's drug abuse problems; when marijuana was banned in the thirties, there were no more than fifty thousand smokers in the whole of the United States, yet forty years later, according to the National Commission on Marijuana, no fewer than twenty-four million Americans had used it at least once. He continued:

I believe that society must accept the fact that there is such a thing as 'recreational' use of drugs. Obviously I don't believe that people should be permitted indiscriminate use of all drugs. Many have such a deleterious effect both on the user and on society as a whole, as to preclude their use. But drugs such as cigarettes, alcohol and marijuana are different. Their potential of harm is limited and falls within that area which people of this country have apparently decided is acceptable. We may discourage their use, as is currently the practice for cigarette smoking, and I support these efforts. But who would seriously suggest criminal penalties for those who smoke cigarettes or drink alcohol? Yet both these drugs have far more proven harmful effects than marijuana.

My views are also based on a pragmatic belief that the many priorities facing law enforcement officials today cannot permit the allocation of energy and resources to be utilized for the enforcement of the marijuana laws. Today we must redirect our efforts towards the more debilitating drugs. From my vantage point I predict that eventual legalization with government control similar to that used for alcohol is inevitable. When the country decides to honestly deal with the marijuana question, perhaps then we can begin to make some progress in the battle against drug abuse in the United States.

4. 'Narcs' are the special police attached to the Narcotics Squads. See *Washington Post*, 13 February 1972.

Heroin addiction is not a new phenomenon. Diacetylmorphine, an alkaloid obtained by heating a mixture of morphine and acetic acid, was first produced commercially in 1898 by the German firm of Bayer. At the time it was hailed as a major discovery, in the belief that heroin, while possessing analgesic properties ten times greater than those of morphine, would not induce the same condition of physical and psychical dependence. It soon found wide use in Europe and more especially in the United States where, up till 1923, it was more or less freely available.

After the First World War there were at least 200,000 morphine and heroin addicts in the United States. During the forties this figure declined steadily, falling to 20,000 by the end of the Second World War,[5] only to rise again to 50,000 in the early sixties, as a fresh 'epidemic' got under way. By 1969 the number of addicts was estimated at 250,000, a figure which, according to statistics prepared by the B.N.D.D., had more than doubled by the beginning of 1972 and was expected to have risen to 800,000 before the year was out. Fifty per cent of the addicts – upwards of 300,000 – live in New York.

In Europe the general public, though familiar with the word heroin, has no sense of direct involvement. By contrast, the United States have fallen prey to a veritable psychosis. Americans are afraid. Afraid that heroin addiction may strike their own family, afraid of being attacked in the street by an addict suffering from withdrawal symptoms. So long as heroin remained the appurtenance of the Black and Puerto Rican ghettos and the plaything of a few famous names in the worlds of jazz and show business, no one was unduly worried. Quite the contrary.

For the Blacks it was a means of escape, deflecting them from violence and affording a temporary respite from their frustrations and wretched living conditions. In fact the drug

5. During the Second World War shipments of opiates to the United States, even for legitimate purposes, were gravely impaired by the almost total disruption of communications with Europe. After the cessation of hostilities some time elapsed before the gangs were able to reorganize their rings.

provided one means, among others, of oppressing minority groups.

At the beginning of the seventies Blacks predominated among heroin addicts: in New York they constituted forty-seven per cent of such persons, twenty-seven per cent being Puerto Rican and only fifteen per cent white. Most of the latter, however, were aged between eighteen and twenty-five, and were sometimes even much younger. From that time onwards no one in America would have been surprised to learn, as we did from a nurse in a New York hospital, that on the previous day a boy of thirteen had died of an overdose, and that his fourteen-year-old brother was undergoing a course of detoxication.

Heroin first assumed the aspect of a national problem when it began to wreak havoc among the children of sedate middle-class families living in the smart suburbs of the larger American cities. This is a comparatively recent phenomenon, as is evident from a glance at the list (already extremely long) of articles on this subject that have been appearing in American periodicals since the sixties. Even during the period 1960–65, drugs are a constantly recurring topic – proof that the war in Vietnam, although it may have hastened the process, cannot be held solely responsible for the growth of drug addiction in the United States. Between March 1965 and March 1966 there was an appreciable increase in the number of articles on this subject, but it was not until February 1970 that the list became really extensive. The *Readers' Guide*[6] of that year contains two columns of such self-explanatory titles as, 'Drugs raise a Specter', 'Booming Traffic in Drugs: the Government's Dilemma', 'Heroin and Crime in the Streets', 'Drug Abuse: newest and most dangerous challenge' . . . Between March 1970 and February 1971 no fewer than fifty-six leading articles were devoted to the spread of addiction among the young.

This is not the place to analyse and assess the reasons why there should have been a further upsurge of drug addiction since the sixties, more especially amongst young people. Numerous

6. Annual list of all articles published in the American Press.

experts, doctors, psychologists and sociologists have concerned themselves with the problem. But they have only partially succeeded in mastering a highly complex phenomenon which is closely linked with a critical phase of our civilization.

According to Dr Dale C. Cameron,

Drug-taking often appears to be associated with rapid socio-economic change. If so, it may be related to a weakening of cultural controls as old patterns of living are replaced by new . . . The extent and rapidity of mass communication and of transportation now enable many persons in one part of the world to learn quickly of the doings of others in distant places.[7]

Though this explanation may well be correct, perhaps it does not go to the heart of the matter.

Obviously the United States are more affected than any other country by the new wave of drug addiction, since they hold the world record where addicts are concerned. But in 1972 their position was no longer as lonely as it had been three years earlier. The demand for narcotics is steadily increasing, with a corresponding expansion of the market available to international traffickers. Throughout Europe there has been a staggering rise in the number of heroin addicts. France alone now has 20,000.

Before the period 1966–68 the drug had made no noticeable inroads in that country. A study conducted by the French Ministry of Health[8] suggests that, if the present rate of increase is maintained, there could be more than a hundred thousand heroin addicts by 1976. Hardest hit were the Paris region and the large southern towns such as Marseilles and Nice, but other provincial centres including Strasbourg, Besançon and Dijon were also affected. Addiction, mainly confined to the young, began to manifest itself among the working class at

7. Dale C. Cameron, 'Abuse of Alcohol and Drugs: Concepts and Planning', *W.H.O. Chronicle*, January 1971.
8. This study presupposes that, over the next five years, the number of heroin addicts will show an annual increase of fifty per cent at the very least. The forecast should, of course, be seen as forming a basis for working hypotheses. It takes no account of the intensification of police counter-measures which, in 1972, appear to have stabilized the situation.

the end of 1970. A survey carried out in April 1971 by the I.F.O.P. (Institut français d'opinion publique) to discover what tht French felt about drugs, revealed that in urban areas ten to fifteen per cent of young people between the ages of fifteen and twenty-five – in all some 600,000, or one Frenchman in every hundred – would at some time be likely to experiment with drugs.

Although until quite recently the number of addicts in England was officially estimated at no more than 2,500, the authorities now admit to five thousand. West Germany, where the problem is now acute, used to be distinctly reticent about statistics, at least prior to 1971. The peril is also making itself felt in certain countries of the Third World hitherto untroubled by heroin addiction – in Thailand, South Vietnam, Iran, and, to a really dramatic extent, in Hong Kong where, out of a population of four million, 120,000 are heroin addicts.

If he is to satisfy his craving for this white powder an American heroin addict must have at his disposal some thirty to a hundred dollars a day, or ten thousand to thirty-six thousand dollars a year. In the United States the average wage does not exceed ten to twelve thousand dollars a year. At best this amount will hardly suffice to meet the requirements of the addict, since he rapidly falls victim to the phenomenon of tolerance, in other words, he must absorb ever larger doses of the drug if he is to attain the desired state of euphoria. More and more money has to be found. At the same time he finds it harder and harder to work. All he wants to do is remain quietly in a corner and 'float'. At the outset, when he first begins injections, a five dollar dose is enough to procure a 'flash', a sort of orgasm that takes place the moment the heroin injected into the bloodstream reaches the brain. He is then pervaded by a wonderful sense of well-being, of intense relaxation which may last from four to five hours. 'You feel as if you're floating,' we were told by Stan, a patient in a New York treatment centre. 'You don't notice the hostile faces in the crowd any more. You forget your problems; it's extraordinarily peaceful.'

But the body very quickly forms habits. Fewer than ten per cent of those who indulge in heroin manage to control their intake. What began as a pleasure sooner or later – depending on the individual – becomes a physiological need. This is what is known as being 'hooked'. The addict's life becomes a hell in which everything revolves round a single obsession – 'H' or, as it is sometimes called, 'horse', 'joy-powder' or 'junk' . . . Find a pedlar, the money to pay him, mix the white powder with water, heat in a spoon, inject. Next the 'flash' and, at last, a few hours of peace. Then begin all over again.

When deprived of the drug the addict suffers agonies. After eight to twelve hours he breaks out into a sweat, and his eyes and nose begin to run as though he had a heavy cold. He is racked by aches and pains, his body twitches uncontrollably and his limbs are subject to severe and painful cramps. Sleep becomes impossible and he experiences alternate surges of heat and cold. This physical discomfort is accompanied by an indescribable sense of anxiety. After the first day the symptoms get worse. The subject runs a high temperature and suffers from vomiting and diarrhoea. Nothing can soothe him but a good shot of heroin or morphine.[9]

The 'withdrawal syndrome' is not the only consequence of drug addiction. The addict loses all interest in food. He eats badly and irregularly so that he becomes anaemic and loses weight. His resistance to infection is lowered. The generally poor conditions in which he lives expose him to the risk of tuberculosis. Thus heroin addiction is a kind of slow suicide and many addicts hope that death will be the outcome of their adventure. When one of them dies of an overdose there is no means of telling whether or not he met his end accidentally. It is simply the logical culmination of a suicidal way of life.

Although usually quiet and peaceful, a heroin addict can become dangerous when deprived of the drug. He will stop at nothing to obtain a dose but will steal, assault passers-by, even commit

9. For further information on the effect of drugs, see L. Olivenstein, *La Drogue*, Éd. Universitaires, Paris, 1970.

murder. It has been calculated that at least fifty per cent of the crimes committed in the big American cities are directly linked with the abuse of hard drugs. As soon as you arrive in New York you are warned against carrying too much money, but at the same time advised not to carry less than ten dollars. For if, when attacked by an addict, you have nothing to give him, the chances are that you will get hurt. In the United States robberies committed by addicts amount to some two billion dollars a year. If to this we add the money allocated by the American government to the fight against the traffickers and to the treatment of addicts (more than three hundred million dollars), as well as the millions expended by those addicts who are still earning their living in a more or less normal way, we arrive at the astronomical total of four billion dollars devoted to heroin.[10] And this sum does not include the social cost of drug addiction in terms of shattered careers, the frightening spread of infectious diseases and, worst of all, the death rate. In 1971 alone 1,259 people died in New York as a result of an overdose of heroin. Each year drugs claim more victims between the ages of fifteen and thirty-five among the inhabitants of New York than do traffic accidents or the war in Vietnam.

Writing on 1 February 1971 in the American periodical *Newsweek*, Stewart Alsop described New York as being in a state of siege. Because of the growing number of addicts and the consequent increase in robbery, no sane person would choose to remain in the city if his means permitted him to do otherwise. New York, Alsop went on, was being killed by heroin, and other American cities were on the death list.

In time, unless the malignancy be brought under control, New York will be a shell . . . inhabited only by the very poor and a tiny handful of those rich enough to insulate themselves from the surrounding sea of fear . . . *Any* measure, no matter how radical, which holds out *any* promise of controlling the heroin malignancy, must be taken, and soon. It must become an overriding first priority for American policy . . . to control the production and distribution of this city-killing drug.

10. Congressional Sub-Committee estimates.

This anguished outburst fairly reflects the state of mind of the average American to whom the problem of heroin has become almost an obsession. A Gallup poll carried out in March 1971 revealed that drug addiction had moved up from seventh to third place in the list of national problems held to be of major importance.

Moreover the position is rapidly deteriorating because large numbers of addicts have found they can obtain the drug by becoming 'pushers', in other words by retailing heroin in the streets. When addiction has reached a certain stage, an addict finds it more expedient to place himself at the service of a trafficker than to steal women's handbags. In return for selling an agreed quantity of heroin he will receive a daily dose free of charge. This gives rise to a form of proselytism that is far from altruistic. For the more converts they make, the more white powder these 'dead heads', as they are often called in New York, are able to procure for their own use. Most of the heroin pedlars in the New York streets are themselves addicts. Speaking to a journalist from *U.S. News and World Report* in June 1971, Myles J. Ambrose, former U.S. Customs chief, stated that 'we have still not hit the peak of drug consumption in the United States'. Asked when he hoped to see a falling curve, Mr Ambrose replied:

That depends on the amount of drugs available. One can't become a drug addict if one doesn't find the narcotics. To my mind there is no doubt that there is a direct relationship between the number of addicts and the amount of drugs on sale in the market.

If what Mr Ambrose says is true, the failure of the campaign against addiction launched by President Nixon in June 1971 is a foregone conclusion. For the world's annual output of opium is sufficient to keep America's 500,000 addicts supplied for half a century.

Depending on the year, the amount of opium harvested throughout the world varies between 2,000 and 3,000 tons, of which no more than half is destined for the pharmaceutical industry.

The Drug's Supply Routes

The rest finds its way onto the black market and into the hands of traffickers who supply the opium smokers and heroin addicts.

The traffickers may draw their supplies from two different sources:

1. Countries where the cultivation of the poppy is legal but where part of the crop, despite State control, slips through the hands of the authorities.

2. Countries where the cultivation of the poppy is in principle forbidden but which lack the material and political means to enforce the regulations, even should they wish to do so.

Turkey, the third largest producer in the world, belongs to the first category. Until the government's decision to ban the cultivation of the poppy as from 1972, twenty-five per cent of the opium produced was channelled on to the black market, whereas by rights the entire output should have been purchased by the State. It is a problem not confined to Turkey alone. An investigation undertaken by the Strategic Intelligence Office of the B.N.D.D. produced the following figures for 1971:

	Production sold on the legitimate market, in tons	Production sold on the black market, in tons
Turkey	150	35–50
India	1,200	250
Pakistan	6	175–200
Iran	150	?
U.S.S.R.	115	?
People's Republic of China	100	?
Yugoslavia	0·83	1·7
Japan	5	—
Golden Triangle (Thailand–Burma–Laos)		750
Afghanistan		100–150
Mexico		5–15

Contrary to what might be supposed, the 'leakages' are not proportionate to the quantities legally produced, nor to the area under poppy cultivation. Rather they depend on the degree of administrative efficiency in the country concerned and the ability of the authorities to exercise adequate control over the peasants at harvest time.

However not even the strictest control can prevent the diversion of part of the crop, given the difference in price paid on the legal and illegal markets. Proof of this may be seen in the case of India whose system of State control is regarded as exemplary by all the international agencies, yet where leakages amount to eighteen per cent of total production. In Yugoslavia seventy per cent of production would appear, from the above table, to elude the controls, while Pakistan, with a legal production of six tons of opium, is shown as having contributed nearly two hundred tons to the traffic.

In countries belonging to the second of the categories mentioned above, the production of opium is illegal. Clearly, then, they will have no official body responsible for the control of a product which, in principle, does not exist. The entire crop, clandestinely harvested, is channelled on to the illicit market. According to the B.N.D.D. the contribution of these countries to the traffic amounts to between 850 and 1,000 tons.

These figures are disputed by some American Congressmen, notably by Robert H. Steele who alleges that the Golden Triangle alone produces over a thousand tons of opium, or two-thirds of the world's illicit production.

Other regions, about which no information whatever is available, produce opium in appreciable quantities – Nepal, for one, and probably Syria and Iraqi Kurdistan as well. There have also been reports of poppy-fields in South America. It has often been maintained that the cultivation of the poppy presupposes very special geographical or climatic conditions. This is not the case. All that is required is an ample supply of cheap manual labour, since the harvesting demands a great deal of painstaking work.

A number of countries where opium is not a traditional crop could, if they so desired, cultivate the poppy, as indeed Japan has recently begun to do. Thus opium production, which tends to rise in accordance with demand, could be very greatly increased. There are numerous indications that the poppy is now being grown in several Latin American, and perhaps also African, countries where it has not hitherto been known. It follows that the traffickers are unlikely to be faced with an immediate shortage of opium. So far as the heroin merchants are concerned the problem is not one of opium supplies, but rather of establishing and maintaining networks and supply routes for the conveyance of the end-product of the consumer.

2   Turks and Corsicans: the Traditional Route

When, after days of observation, the French police burst into the wash-house cum laboratory where Joseph Cesari was illegally manufacturing the highest grade heroin in the world, he turned round and, taking off his white smock, remarked in calm, even tones: 'Well, my lads, you can thank me for the fine haul you've made!'

This happened on Thursday, 8 October 1964, near Aubagne, a small town on the outskirts of Marseilles. The French Narcotics Squad had caught red-handed one of the very few chemists capable of manufacturing heroin to a purity of ninety-eight per cent. Joseph Cesari – Jo to his friends – had for years enjoyed the confidence of the various gangs in the Marseilles underworld. It was to him they entrusted the simple but very delicate operation of converting morphine into a white powder, fine as French chalk and insubstantial as icing sugar – heroin.

The process is not, apparently, a complex one provided the chemist adheres to the formulas. It can even be carried out in a bathroom with the most rudimentary apparatus. To obtain impure heroin in solution a mixture of base morphine and acetic acid is heated for six hours in a double boiler at a temperature of 85° C. There follow a number of purification processes during which the heroin is first precipitated in the form of crystals and eventually turns into a fine powder soluble in water; the whiter the product, the more it is appreciated. The operation calls for meticulous care. And it can be dangerous. If the proportion of morphine to acetic acid is incorrect or the temperature too high or too low the laboratory may be blown up; alternatively the resulting product may have a coefficient of purity of less than eighty per cent. In that event it will not be acceptable to the American market for which it is primarily

17

intended. In addition acetic acid is an extremely corrosive substance which attacks both the skin and the lungs. Again, únless he takes the utmost care, the chemist runs a grave risk of heroin poisoning or, indeed, of becoming an addict. In the circumstances he never works more than fifteen days a month.

Joseph Cesari was extremely careful to safeguard not only his health but his own person. It took more than two years of shadowing, surveillance and inquiries to catch him in the act, although the Marseilles Narcotics Squad had long been convinced of his guilt.

Joseph Cesari was born in Bastia on 2 January 1915. After 1960, he had led a life of luxury hardly in keeping with his previous occupations. He had been a barman, a wartime sailor, a grocer and a bar manager and had then gone back to sea. In 1954 he disappeared from circulation, to reappear in 1960 as a pig farmer. In 1962 he bought a magnificent estate near Aubagne. He employed a large domestic staff, owned six motor cars and frequented the most expensive clubs and restaurants in Marseilles.

Though Cesari often spent several days away from home, it was impossible to keep track of his movements. He did not travel by rail or by air, nor did he stay at hotels. He was, however, known to associate with notorious criminals such as Jean Mebbia, who had been implicated in the smuggling of ninety-two kilogrammes of heroin concealed in a refrigerator, and Achille Ecchini, compromised by the discovery of 115 kilogrammes of base morphine hidden in a consignment of goat-skins. It was further known that, on leaving home, he sometimes set off along the by-road to Aubagne and then vanished into thin air. But no one could ever discover where he turned off, for he was almost impossible to follow. A crafty and suspicious man, he employed every conceivable ruse to shake off possible pursuit. For instance, after driving at full throttle he would stop abruptly, get out, wait till all other cars were out of sight and then set off again slowly. In town he would make several circuits of a block, turn into a cul-de-sac and emerge again before finally parking his car.

It was only after two months of observation and 'tailing' that members of the Narcotics Squad discovered Cesari's bolthole, a driveway that ended at a large villa, the 'Clos Saint-Antoine'. It was difficult to keep a check on the man's comings and goings since the back of the house gave on to woodland in which he used to hide his car. A narrow, unmade path enabled him to enter and leave the house unobserved. For four weary days the police kept watch on the villa. Crouching in prickly bushes, they were far from comfortable. Moreover the hunting season was at its height and, as if that were not enough, the Foreign Legion was exercising in the area. Thus on the night of 8 October two figures might have been seen erupting from the bushes and taking to their heels, 'out-sleuthed by a couple of hounds', as they later remarked to their colleagues.

The decision to seize the villa was taken as soon as the police felt sure that the laboratory was actually in use. Outside the building a strong vinegary smell betrayed the presence of acetic acid. When they began their search the police discovered a hundred kilogrammes of heroin ready for dispatch and an almost equal quantity of base morphine, either unprocessed or in course of processing. Cesari, whose equipment was relatively sophisticated, was then producing forty kilogrammes of heroin a week, as against the fifteen or twenty kilogrammes manufactured by most other laboratories.

Joseph Cesari was sentenced to seven years' imprisonment. A few months after his release he resumed his activities and was again arrested in March 1972, just as he was about to start work on a fresh batch of base morphine. A few days later he hanged himself in his cell. Between his first and second arrest the law had been changed and he now faced a maximum sentence of twenty years.

This haul marked a red-letter day in the history of the war against the traffickers. The Marseilles Narcotics Squad had scored a resounding victory, for it was the first time in twenty years that a laboratory had been uncovered by the French police. But at the same time the episode illustrates the extraordinary difficulties confronting the men responsible for suppressing the traffic in drugs. To procure the arrest of a person presumed

19

to be guilty, it is not enough to accumulate evidence; there also has to be proof.

'The utmost patience is needed,' we were told by M. Gevaudan, Assistant Director of the French Criminal Investigation Department.

A suspected person has to be shadowed, which is both difficult and time-consuming. Detailed information must be accumulated concerning his bank accounts, telephone calls and personal contacts. Out of the hundred or so people he meets, one or two may be party to an as yet uncommitted crime in the planning of which he himself spends no more than a few hours a month. The rest of the time he lives and behaves normally. If you are to get results, all this means keeping a first-rate dossier of suspect characters and infiltrating your people into the underworld. You have to have specially trained men. It's a huge task and costs both time and money.

For their part the big gangs are extraordinarily well organized. They have world-wide contacts, political protection and vast financial resources. And their ingenuity is inexhaustible. Fake humps, fake pregnancies and even corpses have been known to be used for the conveyance of heroin. Again, the vehicle may be hollow heels, shoulder pads, dolls or tins of food. Before crossing the Turkish-Syrian frontier, one smuggler even went so far as to feed camels with small plastic bags filled with morphine. Then it was simply a matter of waiting until the beasts delivered themselves of the packages, helped along if needs be by a dose of laxative.

No sooner have the police made fresh dispositions than the gangs think up ways of circumventing them. Hence the rules governing the cat-and-mouse game between police and villains are constantly being revised. And, though sympathy may be wanting, a kind of mutual respect has nevertheless grown up between the racketeers and those who hunt them. Both sides are aware of each other's qualities. Speaking of Cesari, one of the policemen who helped to arrest him told us:

There was no one like him. He was a self-taught man. He'd never had chemistry lessons. It was his half-brother Dominique Albertini who taught him the rudiments of the business. He then filled in the gaps himself by carrying out experiments on his own. He was a connoisseur of works of art and limited editions, and there were some rare pieces in his Aubagne villa. We were always on very courteous terms. After his arrest he even suggested that we should come in with him and start up a new laboratory.

For the traffickers the palmy days began after the First World War. The wave of drug addiction that broke over the United States was not without its effect on Europe. People seeking oblivion from the post-war upheavals and the miseries of the slump in the thirties joined the ranks of those who, having been wounded in the war, had become addicted to the morphine or heroin used to alleviate their pain. Despite the Harrison Act of 1914[1] which imposed severe restrictions on the use of narcotics in the United States, one American in four hundred was addicted to an opium derivative. Like the law prohibiting the sale and consumption of alcohol, the Harrison Act was to prove a goldmine for American gangsters. Business steadily improved but did not reach really vast proportions until after the Second World War. Between 1947 and 1948 a savage struggle divided the five 'clans' of the New York Mafia who were unable to agree on the attitude to be adopted towards drugs.[2] There were those who believed that the traffic, if developed astutely, could be a source of huge profits. Others thought the risk too great, fearing that the political backing they could count on for certain of their transactions might not extend to this project, which was not only dishonest but very dangerous. Moreover their other enterprises might be jeopardized. The latter school of thought was defeated after months of bloody internecine strife.

But by 1957 the repressive measures taken by the police had

---

1. The Harrison Act laid down severe penalties for consumers of narcotics. The import, refining, purchase and sale, and even free gifts of opium, coca leaves and all their derivatives, were very strictly controlled. However the Act was not fully enforced until 1923.

2. The subject of Mario Puzo's American best-seller, *The Godfather*. It would seem that this struggle was resumed at the beginning of 1972.

21

wrought such havoc in the ranks of the Mafia that the clans again foregathered and decided to abandon the traffic. Not everybody respected this agreement. But from then on the various elements of the Mafia avoided in so far as possible all direct contact with the merchandise. Rather, they provided the brains and the money, leaving the task of distribution and retailing within the United States to Puerto Ricans, exiled Cubans and Blacks.

It is a noteworthy fact that, generally speaking, the traffickers always belong to peripheral and closed ethnic groups. For a considerable period the traffic in the United States was conducted by the Italians, who were later joined by Cuban exiles, Puerto Ricans and Blacks. In France the traders are Corsican, in Italy Sicilian, in Germany Turkish and in Asia 'Overseas' Chinese who call, and continue to think, themselves Chinese, although not resident in China. All this is perfectly explicable. Certain elements in these groups, driven into exile by destitution or political upheaval, and faced with unemployment, seldom have any choice but to become adventurers or rogues. Thus we may find colonies of Corsican exiles in northern Italy or south-east Asia. The solidarity born of shared misfortune induces the members of such groups to observe the law of silence, for example the famous Sicilian *omerta* which, under a different name, obtains among Corsicans and Chinese alike. Their strength lies in the fact that they make their own laws and see that they are enforced. The Mafia is based on the principle of *'sonna cosa nostra . . .'* (that's our own business). Anyone who fails to submit to this regime forfeits the support of the group. Those who betray it, die.

For more than a quarter of a century the drug followed the classic route from the Middle East to the United States by way of France. The Middle East provided the opium, sometimes raw, sometimes in the form of morphine. The process of converting the raw material into heroin was carried out in France, at first in Paris and later in Marseilles. According to the American authorities, who carried on a lively dispute with the French on the subject, eighty per cent of the ten to thirteen tons of heroin consumed in the United States each year was manufactured in Marseilles and originated in the poppy fields of Turkey.

Before being transformed into morphine in Syria, Turkish opium passed through the hands of several middlemen. Three to five kilogrammes of opium was the most that the individual peasant could safely offer for sale on the illicit market. This meant that the trafficker at international level had to have recourse to persons capable of collecting up to a thousand kilogrammes, or enough opium to yield a hundred kilogrammes of heroin. Since reasons of secrecy obviously precluded any one agent from travelling round the countryside calling on several hundred Turkish peasants, a number of intermediaries had to be employed, each of whom would buy in small lots direct from the growers. They had, of course, to be familiar figures in their respective districts, so that their comings and goings would arouse no comment. They in turn resold the merchandise to the broker who bought parcels of three hundred to a thousand kilogrammes for the account of a financier in Istanbul or Ankara. Next came the smuggler who transported the goods into Syria along little known paths. If he did not happen to be hand-in-glove with a customs official, he might employ an ex-soldier to guide his caravan through the minefields laid by the Turkish government on the Turkish-Syrian border. Having arrived in Syria he delivered the consignment to the man responsible for transforming the opium into base morphine. This operation presents few problems. All that is needed is seclusion and a wash-boiler in which to heat the opium mixed with water. But the liquid must not reach boiling point, otherwise the morphine may be destroyed. The solution is precipitated by means of quicklime in order to separate the vegetable elements from the two alkaloids to be isolated – morphine and codeine. Filtration and the addition of ammonium chloride produces a crystallized powder the colour of milk chocolate. This is base morphine.

The next stage in the journey depended on the location of the accomplices. The base morphine might be shipped direct

to Marseilles from Aleppo. Situated only twenty-four kilometres from the Turkish frontier, this port was known to be
the main centre for the storage of Turkish opium and its trans-
formation into morphine. Or again, since Lebanese financiers
often had a finger in the pie, the morphine might be conveyed
to Beirut, a place which offers a number of advantages. It is
a free port and for this reason merchandise in transit is not
subject to customs clearance. There are no restrictions on the
transfer of currency, and the Lebanese banks, like the Swiss
guarantee the secrecy of accounts – a highly important safeguard where traffickers are concerned.

Until quite recently morphine was conveyed to Marseilles
mainly by sea. In a cargo vessel there are at least thirty thousand
potential places of concealment and it is virtually impossible
to find hidden merchandise unless a tip-off has been received
from an informer.

More often than not the morphine was packed in waterproof
bags, secured to a buoy with a luminous marker, and thrown
overboard. During the night or at dawn smugglers disguised as
fishermen arrived to haul in their unusual catch. In March 1971
the traffickers experienced a setback when a genuine fisher-
man from Port-Saint-Louis-du-Rhône, a small village outside
Marseilles, netted 359 kilogrammes of morphine floating beneath the surface of the water. Soon afterwards a yacht with
two Turks and a Frenchman on board, 'out for a day's sailing',
was stopped and examined at the point where the contraband
had been discovered.

But for the most part the base morphine arrived without
misadventure at its destination, namely Joseph Cesari's laboratory. After manufacture the heroin was dispatched to the
United States, either direct or through Canada or Mexico. The
chain between the Turkish producer and the New York consumer consisted of no fewer than eighteen links.

In the mid-sixties the manner in which opium was conveyed
from Turkey to France underwent certain changes. Turkish
traders so reorganized their affairs as to dispense with inter-

mediaries. They began to manufacture base morphine themselves, shipping it either from large ports such as Istanbul or
Izmir, or from smaller and more inconspicuous fishing centres
– Bandirma, for instance, to the north of Izmir. The vessels
were invariably Turkish.

Gradually the sea route was superseded by overland transport.
Already in 1972 seventy per cent of the morphine consigned to
Europe travelled by road; the port of Marseilles had now become easier to control, since Algerian independence meant that
fewer ships called there. By contrast the number of cars and
trucks shuttling between Turkey and Europe had constantly increased. In 1972 no less than 700,000 Turkish nationals were
employed in West Germany and hence there was a continual
movement of travellers by rail, road and air between the two
countries. In addition Turkey now exports large quantities of
fruit, vegetables and meat. And smugglers can usefully take
advantage of the facilities afforded by the agreement on international road transport (T.I.R.),[3] in accordance with whose
terms a truck bound, say, for Germany from Turkey or Iran
is examined and sealed by customs before departure. It can
then cross the intervening frontiers undisturbed and will not be
re-examined until it reaches its destination. In spite of the
admitted and obvious advantages such an agreement offers to
smugglers of all kinds, it is virtually impossible to rescind
without gravely impeding the carriage of perishables whose very
name implies the need for rapid transportation. Nor would it be
reasonable to expect the thousands of sheep's carcases dispatched each year by refrigerated truck to be individually
inspected. Yet any one of these carcases could easily accommodate five kilogrammes of morphine.

The traffic takes two main routes from Turkey to Europe, both
of which pass through Bulgaria and Yugoslavia. According to
unconfirmed reports received by the B.N.D.D., the morphine
is sometimes transferred to a different truck in one or other of
these two countries. Thus if, as a result of a tip-off, Interpol
agents happen to intercept the first vehicle as it leaves eastern

3. *Transport international routier.*

Europe, their search for narcotics will yield nothing. It is diffi-cult to say whether or not there is any collusion between smug-glers and local authorities in these two countries. According to a document entitled *The American Secret Services*[4] drawn up by the C.I.A. in December 1971, 'Bulgaria is the new center for directing narcotics and arms trafficking between Western Europe and the Near East.' The document goes on to state that:

> If a narcotics smuggler is caught in Bulgaria, he reportedly pays a small fine for the violation and then is given the opportunity to re-purchase his seized shipment of narcotics for a certain percentage of its estimated value. The apprehended smuggler thus loses only a small part of his courier's fee and a few hours of his time.

In the same context it is further alleged that the Bulgarians sometimes resell the drugs they have seized or, again, that they actually organize the traffic, using trucks with Bulgarian registration plates. Certain advantages also accrue from the presence of a large Turkish colony at Skopje in Yugoslavia.

On leaving that country, the drug may proceed either to the south of France via the Adriatic and northern Italy or by way of Vienna to Munich and sometimes also to Stuttgart. This second route is the more popular, for the Franco-Italian fron-tier, although crossed by some five million vehicles a year, has become too hot for the Turks, particularly since March 1972 when a Turkish senator was caught with 145 kilogrammes of morphine in his car. He had come from Istanbul and was on his way to Lyons to buy, so he said, a hat for his daughter's wedding.

Munich has become the chief European centre for morphine. The presence there of a vast Turkish colony means that the merchandise can be unobtrusively stockpiled against future orders. Smugglers use the recreation areas of the Black Forest for their assignments. Driving a car registered in a French frontier district, the 'excursionist' mingles with the many thous-

4. Its content was revealed in *The Washington Post* of 28 April 1972 by Jack Anderson who, in his column 'The Washington Merry-Go-Round', makes a speciality of divulging confidential government reports.

ands who cross the border every Sunday. He is met by another 'excursionist', this time from Munich, whose bags contain morphine which eventually finds its way to Marseilles. For that city still remains the heroin capital. No one, not even the French authorities, would seriously consider denying the specialized role played by Marseilles in the drug traffic. It has come to be a byword, like Montémilar nougat or Dundee marmalade. To find out why, we must go back some fifty years.

The notion of manufacturing heroin did not come to the French underworld as it were out of the blue. Rather, the suggestion was made by certain clans of the American Mafia who, after the First World War, saw a promising market for the product in the United States. Until the International Convention of 1931, the manufacture of morphine, heroin and other opium derivatives was virtually unrestricted in Europe. This was no longer the case in the United States where the Harrison Act was already in force. At that time Paris was still the hub of Europe. The French racketeers bought narcotics from a number of European pharmaceutical concerns and smuggled their purchases into the United States. After 1931 they made use of their contacts in the industry to recruit chemists and set up secret laboratories in the Paris region. One of their employees was Albertini, Cesari's half-brother. The opium and morphine arrived from Turkey, Greece and Yugoslavia on board the Orient Express whose attendants were frequently implicated in the traffic.

Until the mid-fifties Paris remained the focal point of operations. But since half the opium and base morphine arriving from Turkey came by ship to Marseilles, common sense dictated the transfer of operations to that city.

It might be pertinent to ask why, from 1970 onwards, the conversion of morphine into heroin has not been carried out in Germany. Most of the raw material is consigned to the Federal Republic, where the presence of laboratories might reasonably be expected. But despite painstaking investigations on the part of the German Federal authorities, nothing of the kind has been discovered – at least up to the middle of 1972. Moreover the B.N.D.D's European experts told us that they had received no reports indicating the existence, or suspected existence, of any laboratories except in Marseilles.

Why does Marseilles retain its monopoly? A great deal of ink has been expended on this question, notably in a virulent letter of protest addressed to the French government on 19 November 1971 by fifty American Congressmen. They declared that,

France has long been a major trans-shipment and processing point for opium produced in other countries. By virtue of her key-position in the processing of and traffic in narcotic drugs [she] can either continue half-hearted apathetic efforts or rise to the challenge and make an all-out commitment to stamp out the narcotic drug abuse which is paralyzing cities around the world . . . Not one heroin processing laboratory has been closed since 1969 . . . The number of narcotic agents, now totalling fifty, currently stationed in Marseilles, a major processing and trans-shipment center, is grossly insufficient.

This representation was made a few days after the beginning of the Delouette affair. Roger Delouette had been arrested in an American east coast port while taking delivery of a Volkswagen minibus containing forty-three kilogrammes of pure heroin. He alleged that he was under orders from the French Secret Service or, more precisely, the Intelligence and Counter-Intelligence Branch (S.D.E.C.E.). In response to French denials, the American Press recalled the˙ S.D.E.C.E's involvement in the presumed murder of the Moroccan left-wing leader, Mehdi Ben Barka, in 1965. It also quoted the evidence of a former S.D.E.C.E. agent, Pierre Thyraud de Vosjoli,[5] who had served in Washington until 1963. During the war between Algeria and France, Vosjoli maintained, the S.D.E.C.E. had been responsible for the assassination in Switzerland of Algerian nationalists; he further accused them of having had a hand in the death of Enrico Mattei, the Italian oil magnate, whose interests in Algerian oil clashed with those of France.[6]

5. See *Washington Post*, 30 April 1972.
6. Mattei's private aircraft crashed in mysterious circumstances in October 1962.

Again, the *Wall Street Journal*,[7] a paper not given to flights of fancy, recalled that three members of SAC,[8] a somewhat similar organization, had been implicated in a case of heroin trafficking.

It was not the first time that the Americans had pointed an accusing finger at France. In August 1971 John Cusacks, European director of the B.N.D.D., in an extremely outspoken interview with a Marseilles journalist,[9] stated that there were 'eight to ten illegal laboratories functioning in Marseilles, these being financed by three or four big shots in the drug traffic, who operate with complete impunity'. However he subsequently withdrew this statement.

In a world-wide study of narcotics[10] two American Congress-men, Morgan M. Murphy and Robert H. Steele, further declared that 'over the past ten years, every narcotics case in Marseilles has involved one or more of four Corsican families: the Venturi brothers (Jean and Dominic), Marcel Francisci, Antoine Guerini and Joseph Orsini'.

While conceding the tremendous efforts made by France to fulfil the terms of the Franco-American agreement of 26 February 1971, the U.S. authorities incline to the view that the really vital task of prosecuting the bosses has not been accomplished. They are convinced that the links – established during the turbulent periods of the Resistance and the Algerian war – between certain politicians and criminals have ensured political protection for the latter, thus enabling them to act with impunity.

It is true that members of the French underworld took an active part in the Resistance[11] and that the services they rendered might possibly have involved a *quid pro quo*. Some of

---

7. 20 December 1971.

8. The Service d'Action Civique, a Gaullist strong-arm organization.

9. Marc Ciomei of *le Méridional*.

10. *The World Heroin Problem, Report of Special Study Mission*, 27 May 1971, p. 8.

11. Barthel'emy Guerini was actually awarded the *Légion d'honneur* for his wartime exploits. See Eugène Saccomamo, *Bandits à Marseilles*, Éd. Juillard, Paris 1968.

them – the Guerini brothers, for instance – were closely associated with the Socialist Party and helped to contain the power of the Communist Party in south-east France after the Second World War. Others, like Marcel Francisci, sided with the Gaullists and, at the end of the fifties, were invited to form an unofficial police force to combat the O.A.S. After the troubles of May 1968 a number of them were enrolled into SAC, the secret organization to which the party then in power entrusted its more unsavoury business. 'Where drugs are concerned,' a senior police official told us, 'the same names always keep cropping up. But while we have our suspicions we have no proof. It's legally impossible to take action against these people.' And as Monsieur Gevaudan, Deputy Director of the Criminal Investigation Department, explained:

We are blamed for not pulling in the big shots. The fact is that for years the drug problem in France has not been regarded as a priority. People here didn't go in for drugs, aside from the few initiates who took cocaine. But again you mustn't forget that it's exceptionally difficult to lay one's hands on the big operators. They may organize and finance the business, but they themselves never come in contact with the stuff. Only the smuggler and the man who takes it over from him actually handle it. Hence arrests are seldom made above the third level. And those fellows don't talk. It's not like in America. Under French law cooperation doesn't mean a lighter sentence.

Moreover things are not as simple as made out by the two Congressmen who held up the names of Guerini, Venturi, Orsini and Francisci as butts for American public opinion. While these may have been names to conjure with in the Marseilles of the fifties, a great deal has since happened in the Vieux Port. One of the Guerini brothers, Mémé, former 'pope' of Marseilles, is now in jail serving a twenty-year sentence. In any case he was never directly involved in the traffic, but was content to draw a percentage on all 'business' transacted in the town. Dominique Venturi and his brother Jean run 'clean' commercial undertakings, as do the Orsini brothers, while Marcel Francisci's main interests would appear to lie in gambling. According to the B.N.D.D., the two Orsinis and Francisci play a vital part in the import of base morphine from Turkey and the export of heroin to the United States.[12] There may well be good grounds for this supposition. Nevertheless it would seem that in France the structure of the gangs concerned with drugs is, in fact, extremely indeterminate; it does not always correspond to the American notion of the gang as a pyramidal organization. The groups vary in size and efficiency. Some are very small. When, for instance, a trafficker by the name of Ambrosino was arrested in 1971 for attempting to smuggle thirty kilogrammes of morphine from Germany into France, it transpired that the syndicate consisted of only three persons, aged fifty, sixty and seventy.

Since the middle of 1971 the police in Marseilles have been considerably strengthened. The Narcotics Squad now has over seventy members. Until 1970 there were only seven of them and their faces, according to an American official, were 'as well-known to the crooks as Brigitte Bardot's'. The squad now also has a large number of vehicles at its disposal. These improvements have had fruitful results. Six laboratories were discovered in 1972 alone.[13] The first of them had already been abandoned and the third had not yet gone into production. The second was occupied by Joseph Cesari, while the remaining three belonged to the Long brothers. The arrests that followed led to an appreciable increase in the price of heroin in Marseilles and New York.

However the French police admit that there may be at least ten – and perhaps even twenty – laboratories still operating in the south-east of France. What is the explanation?

'Searching for a lab is like looking for a needle in a haystack,' we were told by a French police official.

Any house will do, provided it's secluded enough. And there are thousands of such houses between Marseilles and Nice. Again, a cellar, laundry or garage will serve just as well. There are only two or three clues that may lead to the discovery of a laboratory's

12. Senate Committee on Government Operations against Organized Crime and Illicit Traffic in Narcotics, Washington, 1964.

13. Between 1964 and 1972, no more than six laboratories had been discovered in the area.

whereabouts – an abnormally high consumption of electricity, polluted water in the drains and the strong smell of vinegar given off by acetic acid. But electricity meters are read only once a quarter. By the time we get the figures the operators will have had ample opportunity to clear out, the more so since the equipment they need is so minimal that it can be removed within twenty-four hours. The 'chemists' have sometimes been known to bypass the meter and draw their supply direct from the mains. Nor do they always pour the polluted water down the drain. In most cases they run it off into the garden through a hose. That leaves traces, of course, but you won't see them until you've found the house. Lastly, you can't detect the vinegary smell of acetic acid except at close quarters. Obviously we keep a careful check on the sales of the product, but acetic acid is used in a great many industries and offenders often arrange to buy their supplies from bona fide users. Most of the labs are used just once – that is, for as long as it takes to prepare a consignment of about sixty kilos of heroin. Cesari was the only one to set up a relatively sophisticated and permanent plant. After his arrest, no one was going to make the same mistake again.

But the real strength of the Marseilles racketeer derives from the existence of the criminal underworld and its complex network of accomplices. A dependable man can always be found to carry out the simpler tasks. Being a port and hence open not only to immigrants but to influences of all kinds, Marseilles has been notorious for prostitution and smuggling for a century or more. Its racketeers first made their fortunes by trading in American cigarettes. There are reputedly more than thirty thousand people who are prepared to carry out discreetly one small service or another in return for a suitable reward. In the local idiom this is known as *la gâche*. The golden rule of every Marseilles barkeeper is to keep his mouth shut and refuse to cooperate with the police. A Narcotics Squad inspector, who was stationed in Marseilles but came from another part of France, told us of his misadventures. The civilian drivers placed at his disposal used all kinds of ruses to make him miss assignments between racketeers at which he had hoped to make arrests. They would make long detours, or enter small side-streets irretrievably blocked by a large truck, or else set him down at the wrong corner. While not actually in league with the criminals concerned, these drivers had no wish to be the accomplices of the police.

The following anecdote admirably illustrates this frame of mind. In the course of a once very popular French television series, 'The Invisible Camera', a handcuffed man was seen standing in a Paris street. Approaching a passer-by the man showed him his handcuffs and in a low voice said: 'Look! I'm in a bit of a spot. Do you think you could help me?' With an expression of intense dismay the other at once began to raise a hue and cry which culminated in the arrival of the police. Next, the scene moved to a street in Marseilles. When the handcuffed man made the same appeal to a passing Marseillais, the latter glanced rapidly to right and left before replying out of the corner of his mouth: 'Come along quick, chum, we'll soon fix those!'

This, perhaps, explains why the Marseilles 'chemist' feels safer in his home town than in Munich, Liège or Amsterdam. Moreover, away from his normal habitat, he would almost certainly be picked up very quickly, if only because of his accent. Hence he is not readily exportable.

Again, it might be asked why chemists cannot be trained elsewhere in Europe, since the conversion of morphine into heroin appears to be so simple a process. However this is a case where appearances are deceptive, as the following examples will show. Wishing to test a device for the detection of the fumes emitted when morphine is converted into heroin, the police requested a professional chemist with a laboratory of his own to manufacture a batch of heroin. To their astonishment they found that, though he managed to create plenty of fumes, the chemist failed to produce any heroin. Another expert, asked to experiment with a formula discovered in Cesari's laboratory, was never able to achieve a purity of more than sixty per cent.

We might further ask what the Marseilles racketeers would do if the police succeeded in putting a stop to their activities in the region. Because of the huge profits at stake it is difficult to believe that they would simply abandon the traffic in heroin. Most probably they would accept a greater degree of risk and resume operations in some other part of Europe – Germany, for instance, the destination of the morphine, or Amsterdam, where the authorities have adopted a preventive rather than a repressive attitude towards drugs, or Brussels where, under Belgian law, three years' imprisonment is the maximum penalty for narcotics offences.

The wide differences in legislation[14] between the various European countries, as well as the relaxation of customs formalities within the European Economic Community, lend themselves all too readily to the creation of a 'common market' in drugs.

This is partly why the Americans have thought it wiser to adopt a policy aimed at cutting off the manufacturing centres from their sources of raw material. In Turkey they have conducted a vigorous diplomatic campaign to induce the government to ban the cultivation of the poppy. In this they have been successful and the 1972 opium harvest in Turkey was officially the last.[15] But a measure of this kind is unlikely to hold out any prospect of a definitive solution in the immediate future. Even assuming that the poppy will never again be cultivated in Turkey, we have to take into account the surplus stocks accumulated by the traffickers in that country and in France. According to an interview given to a Marseilles journalist[16] by a representative of the B.N.D.D., stocks of morphine in the Marseilles region amount to some seven or eight tons while there is probably enough raw material in Turkey to manufacture the same quantity again. This represents at least a year's consumption in the United States.

Even if the traffickers are cut off from their sources of supply in Turkey, they will still be able to obtain raw material else-

14. At the instigation of the French authorities there have been several meetings for the purpose of coordinating the drugs legislation of the various European countries. But progress is always very slow when it comes to adopting a common policy and modifying the law.

15. See Chapter 12.

16. Interview with Marc Ciomei for *le Méridional.* See *le Monde* of 5 March 1972.

where. In South-East Asia alone the world possesses inexhaustible opium reserves. Moreover four of Turkey's not so distant neighbours are major producers: Iran and India, both of which, in principle, exercise a strict control over production, and also Afghanistan and Pakistan. The bulk of the opium harvested in the latter two countries finds its way on to the illicit market, more especially in the Arab world. But it could equally well be diverted to Europe.

As a result of the measures adopted in Turkey a neck-and-neck race has begun between the traffickers and the international police agencies represented by Interpol and the B.N.D.D. The police hope to make a maximum number of arrests by taking advantage of the vulnerability of the gangs at a time when the latter are busy reorganizing their pipelines. As a B.N.D.D. man put it:

In their frantic desire not to lose the American market which, because of the compulsive nature of addiction, cannot tolerate any interruption of supplies, the European racketeers will certainly make tactical mistakes. The greater the difficulties facing the 'traditional pipeline', the fiercer the competition will be.

3   Competition from Asia

In 1969 American official organizations were unanimously of the opinion that 'eighty per cent of the heroin consumed in the United States comes from France and Turkey, fifteen per cent from Mexico and five per cent from South-East Asia'. Three years later that opinion no longer prevails. The all too modest estimate of five per cent could hardly remain unchallenged in view of the evidence, since come to light, that Asian heroin has been entering the American market in ever greater quantities. Indeed the chief of the American Bureau of Narcotics, John Ingersoll, tacitly admitted as much at an interview in 1971 when he said: 'Once we eliminate Turkey as a source of opium, the quantity of heroin reaching the United States will decrease by fifty per cent.' To what source, then, did he attribute the thirty-five per cent needed to make up the previous total? Presumably South-East Asia, since a secret report issued by his organization in August 1972 contains the admission that the amount of opiates arriving from Asia had been grossly underestimated.

More than half the opium illegally consumed throughout the world comes from the famous 'Golden Triangle', also known as the 'Three Frontiers region', for it is there that the borders of Laos, Thailand and Burma meet. Burma is the largest producer of opium in the world after India. But unlike that country, where production is not only controlled but in theory disposed of wholly through legal channels, Burma contributes at least six hundred tons of opium to the illegal market, enough to yield sixty tons of heroin and supply the American market for six to eight years. To this must be added the opium produced in Thailand and Laos, estimated at a minimum of 750 tons, though the figure of 1,000 to 1,200 tons suggested by Steele would seem to be nearer the mark.

Admittedly a very large proportion of this output is consumed locally in the various countries of south-east Asia where smokers are numbered in millions. The Intelligence Office of the B.N.D.D. estimates that, of the 750 tons of opium believed to be produced each year in the Golden Triangle, 450 are smoked or used for medical purposes by local tribes cultivating the poppy. Another two hundred tons are consumed in the non-producing areas of south-east Asia and are distributed as follows:

Hong Kong	120 tons
Malaysia–Singapore	30 tons
Philippines	10 tons
Macao	10 tons
Cambodia	1 ton
Vietnam	29 tons[1]

The remaining hundred tons are converted into heroin in Bangkok, Vientiane and Hong-Kong to supply not only the American servicemen stationed in South Vietnam, Okinawa, Thailand and the Philippines, but also the expanding market in the United States. A hundred tons of opium yields ten tons of heroin, an amount equal to the official estimate of annual consumption in the United States. Neither the American servicemen, whose numbers have steadily decreased since 1969, nor the local addicts could possibly absorb such quantities. Hence the publication of these figures is tantamount to an admission on the part of the B.N.D.D. that south-east Asia has become a major source of supply for the American market.

Up till 1962 the only products obtainable on the Asian market were refined opium and heroin no. 3, this last being smoked, not injected.

Throughout the period of French rule in Indo-China opium was smuggled from Laos into Vietnam for the consumption of

1. *Special Report no. 101*, Strategic Intelligence Office, B.N.D.D., Washington.

the many Chinese, Vietnamese and European smokers in that country. Another classic pipeline ran from the Golden Triangle to Hong Kong or Singapore by way of Thailand. Hong Kong, and to a lesser extent Bangkok, served as entrepôts for the whole of Asia. The former specialized in the manufacture of heroin no. 3, or purple heroin, for local consumption. Before being sold as a finished product the opium was subjected to a simple process. While still having the consistency of a soft brown paste, it was put in water and boiled. The vegetable detritus and other impurities then rose to the surface and were skimmed off. Next, the opium was shaped into one kilogramme blocks and laid out in the sun to dry. The traffic as a whole was almost entirely confined to south-east Asia, apart from a few modest shipments sent by Corsican colonists to their friends in Marseilles.

According to a report prepared by the Strategic Intelligence Office of the B.N.D.D.,[2] the first refinery capable of producing heroin no. 4 (which can be injected) was set up in Thailand in 1962 at the village of Mang Tang Wu, in the depths of the Three Frontiers region. Its output was seven kilogrammes a month, almost all of which went to Hong Kong. The following year several other small refineries began manufacturing heroin no. 3 and no. 4 in this area. Most of them, however, soon ceased production for want of experienced chemists.

The so-called refineries in the Three Frontiers region are for the most part little more than *ad hoc* affairs. They are housed in wooden sheds, often beside a tributary of the Mekong, and are more reminiscent of a do-it-yourself workshop than a small factory. Their equipment is extremely primitive: copper vessels, metal filters with bamboo rims, strainers, plastic or rubber tubing, and some kind of heater. They even lack the stills found in French laboratories.

The opium processed in the Golden Triangle seldom contains more than ten per cent morphine. This alkaloid is extracted by heating the opium with chlorate of ammonia and slaked lime. The base morphine is shaped into blocks bearing the producer's

2. *Special Report no. 107*, Strategic Intelligence Office, B.N.D.D., Washington.

trade mark. The best known brand is '999', which comes from Laos, the number implying a purity of 99·9 per cent. For the most part the degree of purity found in Asian base morphine does not exceed fifty per cent, as compared with the Turkish product which may often rate seventy-five per cent.

The manufacture of raw heroin involves the acetylation of base morphine. Depending on the amount of care devoted to this operation, the powder produced will be either white and of extremely high quality – heroin no. 4, or pinkish-brown and of lower quality – no. 3 or purple heroin. One part of acetic acid is capable of producing one part of heroin no. 4, or six parts of heroin no. 3.

Most of the chemists in the Golden Triangle are Chinese. Until 1970 many of them were without any professional experience and had learnt their job as they went along. A mistake made during the acetylation process, or the incorrect use of chloroform or ether, would as often as not result in the appearance of by-products, compelling the chemist to switch from the manufacture of heroin no. 4 to no. 3, if not to abandon the operation altogether. In Laos we met a former chemist who admitted that the mishandling of the acetylation process had resulted in losses of raw material amounting to tens of millions of dollars.

To obtain heroin no. 3, base heroin is processed with hydrochloric acid, water, strychnine, caffeine (to facilitate its absorption by the body) and barbitone (to obviate the risk of fatal intoxication). Hence the actual heroin content of this grade does not exceed fifteen per cent. If, on the other hand, the chemist wishes to manufacture no. 4, the base heroin is dissolved in alcohol, mixed with animal black, boiled and filtered. This process is repeated several times, after which the solution is dehydrated by evaporation. The powder thus obtained contains ninety-five per cent heroin, a coefficient that can be raised to ninety-six per cent by further processing with alcohol, ether and hydrochloric acid.

The presence in Vietnam of American servicemen, whose numbers steadily increased from 1965 onwards, opened up new prospects for the local traffickers. In the Golden Triangle refineries sprang up like mushrooms and at the same time better-qualified chemists were recruited in Hong Kong. Hitherto the product had been of indifferent quality, manufactured for an under-privileged and under-paid clientele such as the Hong Kong dockers and the labourers of Bangkok. The laboratories were now adapted to cater for the tastes of the American G.I.s who demanded white heroin. According to the B.N.D.D. eight new refineries producing nothing but heroin no. 4 were already in operation by the beginning of 1971. Though at first indifferent in quality, the product rapidly improved. By August of the same year the B.N.D.D's Intelligence Office had already located twenty-nine refineries operating in the area of the Golden Triangle, fifteen of which were thought to be manu-facturing heroin no. 4.[3]

So long as the Americans continued to maintain large num-bers of troops in Vietnam, a proportion of the heroin was dis-patched to Vientiane, the capital of Laos. From there it pro-ceeded to Vietnam, not infrequently aboard a military aircraft, for a great many Laotian and Vietnamese officials were involved in the traffic.

Since the withdrawal of the last American combat units in August 1972, the bulk of the merchandise has been re-routed through Thailand, reaching Bangkok by road or rail, and also by air as and when the necessary accomplices are available. At Bangkok it is loaded on to inshore trawlers which may carry it as far as Hong Kong or else drop it overboard in waterproof bags to be picked up by larger vessels bound for Hong Kong, Singapore, Japan or the United States.

Hong Kong is not only an entrepôt for the traffic but also the world's worst black spot as regards the consumption of opiates. Official figures show a total of 80,000 addicts in a population

3. *Special Report no. 107*, Strategic Intelligence Office, B.N.D.D., Washington. According to a C.I.A. report in June 1971 the Golden Triangle then contained twenty-one refineries of which only seven were producing heroin no. 4, mainly for export to Hong Kong, Saigon, Japan and the United States.

of four millions. Of these, some 60,000, or at least one person in seventy, are heroin addicts. According to other estimates, less official perhaps but nevertheless emanating from the British police, a more realistic count would be 100,000 heroin and 20,000 opium addicts; i.e. a quarter of the total number of addicts in the United States, in a territory whose population is comparable to that of Norway. It has been further estimated that enough raw material is brought into Hong Kong annually to manufacture five tons of heroin and twenty tons of smoking opium, all of it is intended for local consumption.

Hong Kong is a city built on opium. At the end of the eighteenth century the British realized how much they would gain by exchanging opium – then extensively and cheaply produced in British India – against the tea, silk and other Chinese merchandise for which they had hitherto paid in silver. They therefore began introducing ever larger amounts of the drug into China, despite the ban that had been placed on its importation in 1729 by the Emperor Yong Čheng. During the eighteenth and early nineteenth centuries addiction spread rapidly throughout that country and finally assumed such alarming proportions that the Chinese felt impelled to arrest the British merchants in Canton and demand the destruction of their opium stocks. Anticipating the loss of a source of considerable revenue, the British dispatched a military expedition in order to force the Chinese to open several of their ports to unrestricted European trade. The Opium War broke out in July 1839 and ended in August 1842 with the signing of the Treaty of Nanking which confirmed the cession of Hong Kong to Britain. From then on the British colony was the hub of the opium trade which grew at a spectacular rate. It was on this traffic that Jardine & Co., one of the largest firms in Hong Kong, laid the foundations of its fortunes. By 1868, when the government at home placed restrictions on the trade, British sales of opium to China amounted to nearly 200,000 cases a year, while the country's opium smokers numbered over a hundred million.

Until 1946, the year in which the British forbade the use of opiates in the colony so as to conform to international agreements, opium addiction was regarded in Hong Kong as nothing out of the ordinary. Indeed, cynicism apart, it might almost be described as a necessity. In a town where money-making has been the colonists' chief aim in life, there is no other way for a poverty-stricken population, constantly swollen by the influx of immigrants from China, to forget the hopelessness of its lot. Tens upon thousands of its inhabitants live crowded aboard damp, unhealthy junks or in appalling shanty-towns. When they are rehoused, which is seldom, others come to take their place. The fact of being cooped up on a minute piece of territory from which there is no escape save by boat or aeroplane adds to the general feeling of anxiety that permeates all sections of the community.

Opium, by bringing forgetfulness to the colonized, ensures peace for their masters. The ban abruptly placed upon it in 1946 without a supporting medical programme compelled addicts to have recourse to heroin, less obtrusive in use because it gives off no smell. The heroin no. 3 smoked in Hong Kong looks like semi-refined sugar. The pinkish-brown powder is placed on a small piece of aluminium foil fashioned into a shallow bowl. It is then heated with a match, the smoke being inhaled through a piece of rolled-up cardboard or a matchbox lid until all the powder is consumed. This is called 'chasing the dragon'. No one really knows whether the term alludes to the resemblance the spiralling smoke bears to a dragon's tail, or whether the 'dragon' stands for the nightmare of poverty which is chased away. In the port of Hong Kong sixty per cent of the dockers 'chase the dragon' at least three times a day, squatting behind a pile of sacks or hidden in a doorway. In this way two thirds of their wages go up in smoke. The remaining third barely suffices to feed them. They have neither hearth nor home and most of them, having broken with their families, sleep rough on the quays.

In Hong Kong drugs represent extremely good value if the user is a European. Five pipes of opium cost the equivalent of 15p, and 20p will secure a dose of heroin. To meet his needs a heroin addict spends some £25 to £40 a month. But the average wage in the colony is less than £60 and the war in Vietnam has almost doubled the price of heroin. Before that, a heroin addict could 'float' all day long for somewhere between 25p and 80p.

Although the British authorities maintain that drug addiction has now been stabilized, it would still seem to be spreading, especially among the young. In the poorest families many of the children, who do not go to school, spend their days on the streets where they take to drugs. And in 1972, to the concern of the British community on the Peak, it was discovered that amphetamines and heroin had actually made their way into English schools.

Not only is Hong Kong a free port, an international banking centre and a nodal point on the world's air routes, it is also one of the hubs of the international traffic in narcotics. The refined opium or base morphine arrives there mainly by sea. Frequently a cargo vessel will drop anchor in international waters so as to be beyond the reach of the Hong Kong police. At night, or even during the day, if the port happens to be particularly busy, one of the colony's ten thousand junks will put out to collect the merchandise. At other times the consignment is attached to a float and deposited somewhere out at sea. Again, a coasting vessel may set it ashore on one of the dozens of small islands which form part of the territory. For the most part the cargo is not carried in the vessel itself, but is towed at the end of a line which only needs to be cast off if a police launch should appear on the scene. Once it has reached the quayside, the merchandise, now in the form of small parcels, is spirited away in baskets containing vegetables or shellfish.

Obviously the authorities cannot search the three thousand or so ocean-going vessels entering Hong Kong roads each year. In any case this would be incompatible with the colony's role as a free port, on which its prosperity to some extent depends. Moreover the authorities believe that the traffickers confine themselves to a maximum of two major deliveries a month so that the chances of detection are considerably reduced. In 1971, when heroin consumption was estimated at five tons, the harbour police seized only two lots of base morphine, one of eighty kilogrammes and the other of three hundred. Yet seizures over the past few years indicate that the traffickers are perfectly prepared to smuggle in large quantities at a time – say, a minimum of one ton of opium or a hundred kilogrammes of morphine.

Another factor favouring the racketeers is the corruption that prevails, not only among the Chinese members of the Hong Kong police, but also among their British colleagues.[4] Moreover, it would appear that the government does not always evince an excess of zeal. 'Everybody in Hong Kong, including the British authorities, is there to make money,' we were told by a prominent local banker. 'So long as someone else's business doesn't interfere with your own, you don't mind what he does.'

Since opium and its derivatives can be brought into Hong Kong with such ease, it follows that little more difficulty will be experienced in shipping them out on board vessels bound for Japan, Indonesia, Korea, South America or the United States. But the popularity of Hong Kong does not rest on these advantages alone. The colony's banking facilities make it possible to transfer money freely and unobtrusively to any place in the world. Further advantages are offered by the proximity of the Portuguese colony of Macao where the market in gold is free and uncontrolled. Payments in gold need not pass through a bank account and, indeed, the gold smuggler and opium smuggler are, as often as not, one and the same man.

There has been a great deal of conjecture as to whether there is a 'Mr Big' or a 'Mr Fatty' controlling the whole of the traffic in Hong Kong. According to Mr Donning, chief of the colony's Narcotics Bureau, there is not just one Mr Big, but several:

In Hong Kong, there are seven crime syndicates engaged in cut-throat competition, none of whom hesitates to denounce each other and filch each other's business and cargoes. If they don't actually do each other in, it's only so as to avoid bringing the police down on their heads.

4. In an interview with Patricia Penn, a Hong Kong journalist, on 23 August 1971, Charles Sutcliffe, the colony's Commissioner of Police, said: 'I would be the first to admit that there is a corruption problem in the police. But at the same time it must be emphasized that this problem is found at all levels in the community here, and does not only affect the forces of law and order.'

Popular rumour has it that one of the big bosses is a very well-known Chinese personality and a prominent member of the leading charitable organization in Hong Kong. Officially this tycoon's immense fortune is founded on sharks' fins, a delicacy to which the Chinese – that is, ninety-eight per cent of the colony's population – are admittedly very partial.

It is generally held that in Asia the traffic in narcotics is the monopoly of the Chou Chao community from the Swatow district, on the borders of Fukien and Canton provinces in south-east China. It is difficult to determine the extent to which the group is closed to Chinese from other parts of the country. (After all, even Corsicans are not as exclusive as is sometimes maintained.) But there is no doubt that in south-east Asia the traffic is organized by a Chinese 'Mafia' consisting of Overseas Chinese – in other words individuals who, having emigrated at various times from the Chinese mainland, continue to speak Chinese, eat Chinese food, and keep themselves to themselves. Today their network embraces a dozen or so of the larger cities in Asia.

It is far from easy to keep track of their financial dealings. They have a highly specialized system of monetary exchange peculiar to themselves, whether racketeers or not. Deliveries are seldom paid for cash down or by bank transfer. A man bringing a consignment to Bangkok, for example, may be given a note written by a Mr Wang on a scrap of paper no larger than a postage stamp, authorizing him to collect from a Mr Chang, a native of the same part of China, the sum of x thousand dollars. Mr Chang may well be an obsequious grocer or restaurateur in Singapore, New Delhi, London or Paris who has no connection whatever with opium or heroin trafficking. On being presented with Mr Wang's scrap of paper, he will hand over the sum in question, even though he may have to borrow money for the purpose. Months later, perhaps, he will pay for a delivery of pickled fish from one of his Asian suppliers with a scrap of paper drawable on Mr Wang in Bangkok. The result is an unofficial and highly complex financial network, based not only on mutual trust between members of the same community but also on the law of retaliation should that trust be betrayed.

In south-east Asia no case has been recorded of trafficking in opium or heroin other than under Chinese control. Admittedly a number of highly placed politicians in various Asian countries are in collusion with the traffickers, as we shall presently see. But their function is mainly to provide protection or to help with transport arrangements. The men handling the financial side and the conversion of opium into heroin are invariably Chinese. They are sometimes called 'five passport Chinese' for, besides possessing a Hong Kong and possibly a British passport, they will have had little difficulty in acquiring, at the going rates, those of Laos, Thailand, Cambodia and Malaysia.

It is perhaps surprising, in view of their remarkable business acumen, that the Chinese racketeers should have failed to embark on the large-scale production of heroin no. 4 until 1969, by which time several hundreds of thousands of American servicemen had already been in Vietnam for two years. This delay proved disastrous, for by the time the traffickers were in a position to supply the market, the withdrawal of American troops had already begun. Both the B.N.D.D. and the Laotian intelligence agencies[5] are of the opinion that, by the beginning of 1972, the Chinese racketeers were left with very considerable stocks of opium and heroin on their hands. Hence it was only logical that they should follow in the wake of their departing customers and sell their wares in America.

But the reorganization of the traffic took time. It also presented a number of problems. While pondering their solution the racketeers diverted part of their merchandise on to the local market, with the result that Thailand and South Vietnam have experienced a spectacular increase in heroin addiction. This running sore is one of the many legacies of the war in south-east Asia.

In the United States the distribution of heroin is handled exclusively by American gangs, linked in one way or another with the Mafia. Hence, if the Chinese racketeers were to enter the American market, they must not only contract with strangers but also take them on trust. By the middle of 1972,

5. Interview with General Kbhamu; cf. Chapter 9.

this threshold had still not been crossed, which no doubt explains why there have as yet been no really large seizures of merchandise arriving direct from Asia. The biggest to date was made on 11 November 1971 in a New York hotel, when B.N.D.D. agents arrested Domingo S. Canieso, an attaché from the Philippine Embassy in Laos, and Siu Tsien Chou, a Chinese Nationalist from Bangkok. The pair were carrying at least twenty kilogrammes of heroin packed in plastic bags bearing the brand name 'Double U.O. Globe'.

This arrest underlines the difficulties attendant on agreements between Asian and American traffickers. A number of seizures have revealed that there are generally two couriers for each delivery – a representative of the American buyers, and a Chinese to keep an eye on him. Some arrests have been made with the aid of a computer into which aircraft passenger lists have been fed to reveal that two people, one an Asian, have several times travelled, apparently as complete strangers, to the same destination aboard the same aircraft.

It has sometimes been suggested that the large Chinese community in the United States might facilitate contacts between Americans and Asians. Experts on Chinese affairs dispute this on the grounds that the Chinese living in America belong to the Toi Shan and Chung Shan communities from south-west Canton and as such have no established links with the Chou Chao. On the other hand B.N.D.D. agents are in no doubt whatever that the traffickers will ultimately find some kind of a workable solution. For not only are the rewards too alluring, but the rupture of the Turkish pipeline has posed the very urgent problem of alternative sources of supply. The Americans want the goods and the Chinese have a surplus. Both sides know that they must not trespass on each other's territory. In the circumstances agreement cannot be far off.

According to members of Congressional committees investigating narcotics, large quantities of Asian heroin are already reaching the United States by way of South America and sometimes even Europe. So vast are the sums involved that a racketeer's profits will hardly be affected if one of his couriers, instead of travelling direct from Bangkok, has to be routed through Paris or Frankfurt. Hence a close watch on the ports and airfields of the West Coast will not alone suffice to stem the anticipated flood of Asian heroin. Even now it is comparatively easy to find in Amsterdam so-called Chinese heroin which has come, not from Communist China as its name implies, but from Bangkok, having been smuggled into Holland in small quantities by tourists, sailors and airline personnel. 'Amsterdam could become another forwarding centre,' we were told by a B.N.D.D. agent in Washington.

The Dutch take a non-repressive attitude towards addicts, tackling the problem from the treatment angle. We don't deny that this choice is well-founded. But since the law is more lenient in the Netherlands, word has gone round among addicts that this is where to come and stay and do their buying. Consequently there's a constant coming and going of people, all of them potential smugglers. We're afraid that one of these days not base morphine but semi-refined heroin no. 2 will be shipped from Hong Kong to Amsterdam. The final conversion process would be carried out in Europe. Less skill would be called for, and fewer chemicals such as acetic acid. In this way things would be less risky for the chemist.

Like their French predecessors, a number of discharged American soldiers may elect to remain in south-east Asia, and some may decide to traffic in narcotics, as did Henry W. Jackson, who was arrested in 1971. This ex-serviceman, having settled in Bangkok, sent consignments of heroin to the United States with the connivance of serving soldiers who stowed away the merchandise aboard aircraft and troopships.

Before very long we may well see a renewal of the ties between the Marseilles underworld and the 'Chinese Mafia', a connection which has tended to lapse since the departure of the French administration from Indo-China.[6] Though the Corsican racketeers in Saigon and Vientiane have experienced numerous vicissitudes since the withdrawal of the French Expeditionary Corps, many feel unable to tear themselves away from the

6. See Chapter 8.

former cólony. They continue to be on excellent terms with their erstwhile accomplices the Chinese who, when the French left, took the lion's share of the traffic.

In view of the probable cessation of Turkish supplies it would seem only logical for the French underworld, rather than forfeit its role as intermediary, to seek dominance over a new southeast Asia–France–America supply route in place of the traditional one from Turkey.

No doubt the American racketeers would prefer to dispense with an intermediary they can only regard as superfluous. But the French are materially favoured by the lasting and well-tried relationships within the 'Corsican–Chinese underworld', as it used to be known in Indo-China, no less than by the presence on the spot of Corsican ex-colonists familiar with their partners' traditions and habits. According to a usually well-informed source, a meeting attended by leading figures in the Marseilles underworld took place in August 1970 at the Continental Hotel in Saigon. On that occasion it was decided to make two morphine shipments a month to Marseilles.

At the time of writing it is still too early to say whether anything will come of these transactions. What is certain is that opium and heroin from south-east Asia, some of which is already reaching the United States through the medium of troops serving there, will take the place of Turkish opium and its derivatives on the American market.

4   The Latin-American Connection

For many years America was the only consumer of heroin and today she remains the chief market for the drug. Hence, despite a growing European clientele, the traffickers' main concern is to smuggle the product into the United States.

The steady improvement in the techinques employed by the law enforcement agencies means that the traffickers are forced to adapt their own techniques and supply routes accordingly, a tendency which has become very much more marked since 1969. For this there are at least two reasons. The countries hit by addiction, prompted and led by the United States, have launched an offensive of unprecedented dimensions against the racketeers. Again, improved methods of communication and the vastly increased number of people travelling from one country to another have provided fresh openings for the international gangs. It is easy enough for them to find someone 'clean' who is prepared, for a suitable reward, to see a bag or parcel through to its destination. Indeed, so great are the profits to be made from transactions in drugs that it matters little if a courier, in order to cover up his tracks, has to travel all the way round the world before delivering the merchandise. Nowadays travelling to the ends of the earth is so commonplace that anyone may do so without attracting undue attention.

For more than a quarter of a century heroin shipped from Europe entered the United States through New York. But since that city has grown too hot for the traffickers they have tended to eschew direct deliveries in favour of a series of transshipments. The heroin, refined in French laboratories, is first consigned to Italy, Spain or a country in northern Europe for onward transmission to Canada or one of the many countries in South America. From there it is conveyed by various stages to the United States. In the late sixties a traveller or vehicle

50

coming from Colombia or Brazil was *ipse facto* less suspect than one arriving from France. This is no longer the case. In the meantime Latin America has become an entrepôt for seventy per cent of all heroin consignments, whether from Europe or Asia, destined for the United States.

It is less hazardous to smuggle the white powder through one of the dozens of townships scattered along the Canadian and Mexican borders than through New York. Even better facilities are offered by the small ports, tourist resorts and the hundreds of private or disused airfields on the West Coast and the Gulf of Mexico. The innumerable islands in the Caribbean provide ready-made staging posts between Europe and the United States. A French national visiting Martinique or Guadeloupe is not subject to customs formalities since both these West Indian islands are French *départements*. From there it is comparatively easy to send the heroin by coasting vessel to Puerto Rico. Once it has reached this American possession the merchandise can enter the United States without passing through customs.

This was the method used by Marcel Boucan, the owner of the lobster boat *Caprice des Temps*, who was arrested in March 1972 in Marseilles as he was about to sail for Guadeloupe with 425 kilogrammes of heroin concealed in the hull of his vessel. The cargo was apparently destined for Miami.[1] In May of the same year a French gang was arrested at Valencia after loading a Citroen car containing 128 kilogrammes of heroin aboard a cargo vessel bound for San Juan in Puerto Rico. Heroin from the Netherlands is most often routed by way of the Dutch West Indies – Aruba, Curaçao or Bonaire. If sent from Great Britain the drug usually goes by way of the British West Indies – Anguilla, Barbados or Saint Lucia.

Corruption is so widespread in the Latin American countries as to have become almost an institution. Any one of them may be the recipient of a cargo, but three in particular play a leading role in the traffic, namely Paraguay, Panama and Mexico.

1. In 1972, according to Myles Ambrose, a former U.S. customs chief, Miami was the main entry point for hard drugs entering the United States.

The Drug's Supply Routes

In Paraguay contraband is a well-established tradition. It has long been common knowledge that General Stroessner, who has ruled the country with an iron hand since 1954, secured the allegiance of his fellow generals by granting them valuable privileges, including the licence to bring in with impunity contraband such as cigarettes, radios, electrical apparatus, watches and spirits. These goods, secretly flown into Paraguay from the United States by light aircraft nicknamed 'Mau Maus', and sometimes even by DC3s, are subsequently resold at considerable profit throughout Latin America. Two hundred private landing grounds, situated in the vast *haciendas* owned by the dictator's henchmen, enable the operations to be carried out unobtrusively. But these pirate aircraft can, if needs be, depart from the airport of Asunción, the capital city, on payment of the traditional bribe, or *mordida*.

It soon dawned on the *contrabandistas* of Paraguay that they would do better if they did not fly empty when leaving for the United States on a buying spree. The cargo – marijuana, cocaine, heroin – was ready to hand.

Paraguay's part in the drug traffic first made the headlines in the American Press with the Auguste Ricord affair. A veteran of the Marseilles underworld faced with a death sentence for collaborating with the Nazis, Ricord had taken refuge in Argentina after the Second World War. In 1968, following some brushes with the police, he left that country and settled in Paraguay. There he opened a motel and restaurant, the *Paris-Nice*, which sported a huge replica of the Eiffel Tower above its entrance.

The interception of three Mau Maus entering the United States revealed that Ricord, from his base in Paraguay, was operating a vast ring of traffickers specializing in narcotics. The merchandise arrived by sea from Brazil or by air from France or Spain where Ricord had accomplices. From the investigation it transpired that he had been dealing in heroin ever since 1963. Between 1967 and 1972 he had been responsible for smuggling 5·5 tons of heroin into the United States.

In March 1971 the Americans, armed with this evidence, demanded Ricord's extradition. They were convinced that Paraguay, which was receiving U.S. military aid to the tune of some ten million dollars a year, could hardly turn down such a modest request and a military aircraft was sent to Asunción to pick up the malefactor. But despite the utmost American pressure, Stroessner decided that Ricord should serve his sentence in Paraguay. Installed in a comfortable cell where he was allowed to receive all the visitors he wished and have meals sent in to him from his restaurant, Ricord continued for over a year to conduct his affairs as though nothing had happened. It was not until 14 August 1972, after the United States had threatened to cut down their aid to Paraguay, that the Asunción Court of Appeal finally issued an extradition order. On 3 September Ricord was imprisoned in New York.

According to Jack Anderson, the *Washington Post* commentator, so many of the leading Paraguayan military are deeply embroiled in the heroin traffic that General Stroessner could do nothing about it even if he wanted to. In a sensational article Anderson disclosed the names of some of these individuals; for example,

Stroessner's trusted chief of investigative police, Pastor Coronel . . . General Andres Rodriguez . . . commander of 3,000 American-equipped troops based near Asunción. His troops stand guard over contraband warehouses . . . Air Force chief, General Vicente Quinonez, who supervises Asunción airport and dozens of smaller fields . . . The interior secretary and his right-hand man, National Police Chief, General Francisco Britez[2]

and many other strategically placed persons.

Mau Mau aircraft from Paraguay, stopping to refuel at Panama airport, found a ready collaborator in the person of its manager, Joaquim Him, at least until 1971 when he was arrested in the United States-controlled Canal Zone.

Panama has been associated with all types of contraband ever since its colonization, when Spain arrogated to herself a trade monopoly, buying raw materials from her colonies for next to nothing and charging them high prices for her own manufactures. This inequitable state of affairs soon led to the

2. cf. *Washington Post*, 24 May 1972.

development of an alternative trading system, backed by the English. Panama was one of its centres, for the isthmus was so narrow that goods could be easily transported to the Pacific coast and thence to the countries west of the Andes. The Atlantic coast of central America, from Belize to Panama, was moreover a happy hunting-ground for English pirates and privateers such as Henry Morgan and Francis Drake, who plundered the Spanish galleons.

Today Panama is an important commercial centre. This small country has the largest merchant fleet in the world. Like Liberia, it lends its flag to large numbers of foreign vessels in return for certain financial advantages. In addition to six hundred Panama-registered ships carrying crews of all nationalities there are more than 12,000 ocean-going vessels passing annually through the canal which links Pacific and Atlantic. With two large and ten small ports, where customs formalities are reduced to a minimum, as well as a hundred or so small airfields, Panama provides an admirable staging post for traffickers. Moreover, since it is her ambition to become an international banking centre comparable to Switzerland, secrecy of accounts is scrupulously observed.

As regards narcotics, Panama faces a rosy future. Not only is she a highly convenient stopping place for light aircraft from South America, but the steady growth of her trade with Hong Kong has led to the import of a wide range of oriental goods, among which we might reasonably expect to find heroin.

These happy circumstances have been exploited to the full by the country's leaders. In a paper presented to a Congressional Sub-Committee investigating problems relating to the Panama Canal Zone, John Ingersoll, chief of the Bureau of Narcotics and Dangerous Drugs, declared that Panama was 'one of the most significant countries for the trans-shipment of narcotic drugs to the United States', and that one twelfth of all the heroin and cocaine entering America came by this route.[3]

On 8 July 1971 twenty-four year-old Rafael Richard, son of the Panamanian Ambassador to Formosa, was arrested at New

3. *Briefing Paper on the Republic of Panama*, 5 November 1971.

York's Kennedy Airport as he was about to bring seventy kilogrammes of heroin into the United States. He carried a diplomatic passport signed by the Panamanian Foreign Minister, Juan Tack, in person. But Rafael Richard, not being a diplomat, had no right whatever to such a passport. His uncle, Guillermo Gonzalez, arrested in New York while waiting to take over the consignment, was the personal friend and one-time bodyguard of Moises Torrijos, Panamanian Ambassador to Spain and brother of General Torrijos, 'supreme head of the Panamanian government'.[4] In the course of previous trips Messrs Richard and Gonzalez had already brought a total of nearly half a ton of heroin into the United States.

On 23 February 1972, a fact-finding commission was sent to Panama by the Congressional Sub-Committee dealing with problems relating to the Canal. Members of the commission stated that in their presence agents of the B.N.D.D. based in Panama had accused Moises Torrijos and Juan Tack of being implicated in the traffic.[5] These allegations were indignantly repudiated by the Panamanian authorities. Yet when Joaquim Him, then manager of Tocumen Airport, was surprised by the Americans in the Canal Zone and arrested, these same authorities did everything in their power to secure his release. Him had been charged with having dispatched more than a million dollars' worth of heroin to Dallas.

But information is of little avail if it cannot be acted upon. When these disclosures were made public in March 1972 by John Murphy, secretary of the Panama Canal Sub-Committee, they could hardly have come at a more inopportune time for the State Department. Washington was then about to resume the long interrupted negotiations for a fresh treaty on the Canal Zone whereby the United States would restore sovereignty to the Panamanians while retaining responsibility for defence and

4. General Torrijos had seized power by a *coup d'état* in 1968. In September 1972 the Chamber of Representatives elected a President of the Republic, but proceeded at once to grant plenary powers to Torrijos as 'supreme head of government for the period 1972–1978'.

5. Report of the Panama Canal Sub-Committee, containing a general survey of narcotics problems, 8 March 1972.

the movement of shipping. As ill luck would have it Juan Tack, an impassioned advocate of Panamanian rights, represented one of the chief obstacles to the conclusion of the agreement. Hence the State Department refused to comment on the accusations made by Murphy and his sub-committee beyond declaring them to be 'inappropriate'. In a report prepared by the Panama Canal Sub-Committee, the State Department was roundly slated for its lenient attitude towards highly-placed individuals in 'friendly' foreign governments who had been responsible for introducing drugs into the United States. But in the case of Panama, the report went on, this habitually 'moderate' attitude to the problem of narcotics had assumed extreme proportions; evidently it was to be left to Congress to find the answer to the question: Should the U.S. begin by negotiating a treaty involving a commitment of seventy years' duration and amounting to five thousand million dollars, or should they give priority to a business involving the illicit export of drugs to the United States?

South America is not only a transit area for narcotics. It is also a producer.

For centuries the leaves of the coca plant have been used as a stimulant in the countries of the Andes region. Indeed even today the Indians of Bolivia and Peru still try to forget their miseries by chewing these leaves whose juice also helps them to withstand fatigue and hunger. To judge by the quantities seized, cocaine is once more returning to favour, having suffered an eclipse since the vogue it enjoyed immediately after the Second World War. Seizures rose from 2·5 kilogrammes in 1960 to 436 kilogrammes in 1971.

The manufacturing process is simple and calls for no scientific qualifications. To produce one kilogramme of greenish paste all that has to be done is to scatter one of the lighter hydrocarbons on a hundred kilogrammes of well compacted leaves. By a simple chemical process the paste is transformed into cocaine hydrochloride. Even at this 'ex-factory' stage it will command a price of 8,000 dollars a kilogramme. By now the drug is a white, odourless powder that may be injected, inhaled or taken orally. Unlike morphine and heroin, cocaine induces psychological rather than physical dependence, and this may take an acute form. Again unlike heroin, which has sedative properties, cocaine is a very powerful stimulant under whose influence the user may commit acts of blind violence.

Cocaine is dearer and less easy to obtain than heroin. In New York it is regarded as a luxury drug, for a dose costs anything from seven to ten dollars, as compared with five dollars for heroin. But in the eyes of addicts its principal virtue is that it does not lose its stimulating properties when the subject is undergoing treatment for opiate addiction. Indeed one American professor predicted that, if the vendors succeeded in slightly lowering their prices, there would be a wave of cocaine addiction by the end of 1971. European traffickers who use South America for a staging post are showing an increasing tendency to effect two-way operations; on the outward journey they carry heroin and return with cocaine for the European market.

In a restricted document issued in May 1972 the C.I.A. produced statistics, based on earlier B.N.D.D. figures, to show that Mexico was producing twenty to twenty-five per cent of the heroin consumed in the United States. It would seem that the poppy is also cultivated in Colombia and Ecuador and has recently been introduced in Nicaragua.

Mexican legislation is relatively stringent. It provides not only for prison sentences of two to nine years but also for the automatic expropriation of peasants who grow the plant. In June 1972 a television programme on this subject created a considerable stir in the United States.[6] It showed that these laws were rendered virtually inoperative by the corruption which, in Mexico, is the very cornerstone of the existing social order. In a one-hour documentary, which included interviews with traffickers, Jay MacMullan, the producer, demolished the myth of U.S.–Mexican cooperation with regard to drugs. For instance a trader in marijuana said that in the small town of Mazatlan he had chosen the police for his suppliers because they offered

6. *The Mexican Connection* broadcast over the C.B.S. Television Network, Sunday, 25 June 1972. Producer Jay MacMullan.

better quality and a wider choice at lower prices. 'The Mexican police,' he went on, 'would come and wait for our aircraft in their official cars and wearing uniform. If necessary they would block the road at two points to make a temporary landing strip.'

Another of Jay MacMullan's stories concerned the general commanding the Sinaloa military district who, in return for a handsome consideration, was asked to close his eyes to the existence of poppy fields in a certain valley. When he refused to do so this particular valley was withdrawn from his jurisdiction and made part of another military district.

But the most interesting part of the programme was devoted to an experiment conducted by MacMullan himself. Having borrowed a small aircraft piloted by an experienced marijuana smuggler, he proceeded to demonstrate how easy it was to enter the United States from Mexico without being detected.

The frontier between the two countries is over three thousand kilometres long. For 1,900 kilometres it follows the Rio Grande, which can be crossed at night without too much difficulty. Over the remaining 1,100 kilometres there are large expanses of desert. By flying low over these areas, pirate aircraft elude the radar screen, which in any case is far from effective. They then touch down either on disused airfields dating back to the Second World War, or else simply in the desert. Sometimes, too, cargoes are dropped by parachute at pre-arranged points. A round trip of only a few hours may bring in as much as fifty thousand dollars. And nothing could be easier than finding a pilot in the person of an adventurer or an ex-USAF flyer from Vietnam. According to American Federal agents, at least ten aircraft cross the frontier illegally every night carrying marijuana, heroin or cocaine.

The situation is not fundamentally different on the Canadian side. For how protect a frontier, almost 5,000 kilometres of which runs through an almost unpopulated countryside?

Again, can the U.S. authorities really be expected to search all the sixty-five million cars and trucks, the 360,000 aircraft (now increasingly 747s, each carrying 350 passengers) and the 150,000 vessels arriving in the United States every year, not to speak of the thousands of private yachts shuttling between the Caribbean and the shores of America or cruising up and down the Californian coast? Moreover, in the neighbourhood of Miami alone there are no less than eighty-two airstrips capable of receiving small passenger aircraft. Of the tens of millions of people who enter and leave the United States each year, only a few thousand carry drugs. They represent less than one hundred thousandth of the total passenger traffic. Hence it is hardly surprising that seizures made by the law enforcement agencies in the consumer countries as a whole do not, according to their own estimates, exceed ten to fifteen per cent of the merchandise transported. Indeed, nothing is likely to stop the traffic so long as those who organize it are in a position to earn profits which can only be described as fabulous.

5   Counter-measures – a Drop in the Ocean

'America has the largest number of heroin addicts of any nation in the world . . . The problem has assumed the dimension of a national emergency . . . If we cannot destroy the drug menace in America, then it will surely in time destroy us.' Thus President Nixon on 17 June 1971, before a television audience of millions. The speech marked a turning-point in the official American attitude towards drugs. Thereafter the battle against narcotics was regarded by Washington as one of the most urgent items in the American political programme, and concrete measures were put in hand so as to convince the country that the Republican administration was not simply making empty promises.

At this time the Bureau of Narcotics and Dangerous Drugs, set up in 1968, disposed of no more than six hundred agents and a budget of fourteen million dollars. By the end of 1972 its numbers had almost trebled, while there had been a fivefold increase in the sums placed at its disposal.[1] During the same period another organization specializing in the suppression of narcotics, the Customs Bureau, saw its budget increased from eighty-nine million dollars to a hundred and ninety million. Of these, nine millions were earmarked for the salaries of over nine hundred new agents.

The function of the Customs Service is to intercept traffickers the moment they attempt to enter American territory. The B.N.D.D. has wider responsibilities, extending into the international field, its task being to trace the supply routes back to the point where the opium leaves the hands of the poppy-growers. It is therefore the Bureau of Narcotics which, through its agents abroad, cooperates with other police forces all over

1. In 1972 the B.N.D.D. comprised 1,600 agents and its budget amounted to seventy-four million dollars.

the world. Indeed in some cases it virtually takes over from the local police – *de facto* if not *de jure* – either because of the latter's incompetence or because their resources, compared with those of the B.N.D.D., are derisory. Though a national agency, the Bureau plays an international role, which is why the traffickers often confuse its agents with those of Interpol.

Set up in 1923 with headquarters in Paris, the International Criminal Police Commission (Interpol) is, however, simply a data bank at the disposal of the world's police forces. It is not concerned solely with drugs[2] nor does it play any active role. Such is not the case with the B.N.D.D. Not only has this agency created a world-wide network of representatives and informers; it has also secured technical and financial aid for a number of countries and has itself helped to equip their police, in whose investigations it may, subject to prior agreement, sometimes intervene. Thus the B.N.D.D. is America's spearhead in the battle against narcotics. It is also the only organization specializing in the suppression of the drug traffic which has sufficient resources to plan its activities on a global scale. And so the United States, yet again arrogating to themselves the role of 'universal watchdog', have assumed the direction of the campaign being waged against drugs by the countries of the west.

Until very recently law enforcement agencies were largely dependent on their contacts for the information that would enable them to make arrests. Today, despite the introduction of new techniques, 'tip-offs' still remain of paramount importance. Where drugs are concerned, luck is seldom on the side of the police. For whereas the trafficker knows more or less where the danger lies and what it is likely to be, the police are working virtually in the dark. They know neither the identity nor the whereabouts of the traffickers, who are among the élite of the underworld. Hence arrests are rarely made except as the result of information provided by criminals collaborating with the police. 'No one can muscle in on drugs unless he can provide the boys in the racket with first-class references,' we were told by a French police official. 'He'll have to satisfy them that he's

2. Drugs account for no more than thirty per cent of the information collated on world-wide criminal activities by Interpol.

got what it takes and that he knows how to keep his mouth shut if arrested.'

The police and customs can count for information on a variety of circumstances such as rivalry between gangs anxious to rid themselves of competition, dissension within the ranks of an individual gang, or a criminal's wish to 'retire from business' on favourable terms. Again there are addicts who 'grass' so as to obtain the drugs they want. But the best way of obtaining 'tip-offs' has always been to pay for them. The B.N.D.D. has injected new life into the system by considerably raising the rate. When sums of fifty thousand dollars are being offered, informers are not likely to be wanting.

But information is not enough. There must also be proof. It is the task of the 'undercover narc', or narcotics agent, to provide it. The technique is deceptively simple and involves the surreptitious introduction of a police officer into the haunts of the traffickers where he will pose as a buyer or seller of drugs in order to catch the crooks red-handed. Though the principle is simple enough, its application may be fraught with danger and difficulty. Men must first be trained for this clandestine work. Having familiarized themselves with the customs and unwritten laws of the circles they are to frequent, they must do all that lies in their power to gain access to the higher echelons. While it is comparatively easy to catch a 'pusher' operating in the street, or even a small wholesaler, it is much more difficult to track down the big wholesaler, let alone the financier controlling a ring. At this level no overlapping is allowed and no precaution neglected. According to a B.N.D.D. man, it is virtually impossible to infiltrate the Mafia, since an agent inevitably gives himself away when asked to reel off the names of his Sicilian cousins.

For the past few years the police have ceased trusting to flair alone. They have acquired some highly sophisticated equipment by exploiting modern technological inventions, many of which are the fruits of research connected with the war in Asia. For instance, to intercept airborne smugglers flying in under the radar screen at treetop level, the police use aircraft that are equipped with the latest electronic sensors, already tested by the army in Vietnam and Laos. Or again, if the drug is brought in by sea, aboard a high-speed launch or sailing boat, the police seek to intercept it by using even faster launches and, best of all, helicopters. Since 1970 the customs have been operating a computer linked to more than a hundred and fifty of their posts on the Mexican and Canadian borders and at the principal American airports. The installation of a further hundred and fifty terminals was planned for 1972. Each time a vehicle crosses the frontier its number is recorded by a computer which immediately produces a card giving details of the owner. This goes to join several million others in a central card index. Every week between 250,000 and 300,000 individuals are thus 'processed' without their knowledge in the space of a few seconds. Since its inception this system has led to the arrest of some four hundred traffickers and the seizure of 4·5 tons of marijuana, 15 kilogrammes of heroin, 4 kilogrammes of cocaine and over a million doses of amphetamines.

The radio communications system linking the customs officers to each other and to their headquarters is one of the most up-to-date in the world. A customs man operating anywhere inside the United States can be instantly contacted. An electronic device is now being developed which will be capable of detecting, without the owner's knowledge, whether a suitcase contains heroin or has a false bottom.

While the B.N.D.D. does not lag behind the Customs so far as gadgetry is concerned, it continues to rely primarily on undercover personnel. In the opinion of its chiefs the training of agents is of paramount importance. Since its formation the B.N.D.D. has trained some twenty thousand people, including several hundred overseas teams. Besides being taught how to identify different kinds of drugs, they receive instruction in banking procedure, karate and marksmanship.

All told, these efforts have been productive. In 1971 the Customs Bureau confiscated five times more heroin than in 1968, a quantity representing a market price of 691 million dollars. In the same year the Bureau of Narcotics seized over 1,900 kilogrammes, an increase of more than 138 per cent on 1970; its agents also arrested 3,512 traffickers. The B.N.D.D.

has carried out some truly spectacular operations. One of these, 'Eagle', was the first to bring about the total destruction of a major ring. On 20 and 21 June B.N.D.D. agents struck in Puerto Rico and in three American cities. In all they arrested a hundred and thirty members of a gang of Cuban exiles specializing in heroin and cocaine. In February 1971 Operation 'Flanker', carried out simultaneously in Hartford, New York, Philadelphia, Baltimore, Detroit, Chicago and New Orleans, led to the apprehension of 179 traffickers, including a prominent member of the New York Mafia. In March 1972 information provided by B.N.D.D. agents enabled the French police to arrest the owner of the *Caprice des Temps*. Finally, in May 1972 the Bureau, in collaboration with Interpol and the Belgian and French police, arrested five international racketeers who were about to smuggle 130 kilogrammes of heroin into the United States.

Yet despite these successes and the deployment of men and equipment on an unprecedented scale, drugs continue to find their way into the United States. When asked by a journalist whether he thought the traffic in narcotics was increasing or decreasing, Myles Ambrose, a former U.S. Customs chief, replied that in 1972 there appeared to be no shortage of heroin on the American market. We may well ask why, despite the commitment of vast resources and the repeated blows inflicted on the traffickers, the authorities have failed to bring about any reduction in the quantity of drugs on offer in the United States. There are, however, several factors militating against the law enforcement agencies: the growing number of amateur traffickers; the enormous profits made by the racketeers who are thus never short of accomplices; and, finally, the rivalry dividing the two big American organizations, the Bureau of Narcotics and the Customs Bureau.

Speaking to a journalist from the *U.S. News and World Report* in July 1971, Myles Ambrose declared that 'over the past four years there had been a "fantastic" growth in amateur trafficking'.

Small-time smugglers, sometimes competing with the professional racketeers, sometimes working for them, have appeared on the scene in their tens of thousands. They may be tourists, hippies or students returning, perhaps, from Asia or the Middle East with heroin or marijuana for their own personal use. Some, however, tempted by the incredibly low prices in the producing countries, will also bring back supplies for friends and acquaintances, thus making a comfortable profit. Obviously the amounts involved are not very great. But these small parcels, if seen as a whole, would form a mountain of heroin and an even larger mountain of marijuana.

In Kabul, India, Thailand and Pakistan, we encountered large numbers of these amateurs. Some may simply conceal, say, 100–250 grammes of heroin, three to four kilos of hashish or a small bottle of THC[3] in their luggage or clothing. The more enterprising wear boots with false heels, made to order by local craftsmen, or else have their footwear resoled with sheets of hashish which look deceptively like leather or black rubber. The profit on five kilogrammes of hashish bought in Kabul and resold in New York is enough to pay for the round journey. Hundreds of kilos of heroin have also been smuggled out of Vietnam through the U.S. Army Post Office; obviously, when half a million G.I.s were in the area, the American authorities could not possibly examine every parcel.

This ant-like activity is of relatively recent date and the police are helpless in the face of it. Informers and undercover agents are of little or no avail. The only effective answer would be to increase the customs checks.[4] But with dozens of Boeing 747s in service, each capable of disgorging 350 passengers, and with events such as World Fairs attracting hundreds of thousands of visitors, it would scarcely be feasible to search every traveller. The United States authorities had long been aware that the Munich Olympics in September 1972 would serve as a rendezvous for traffickers, both amateur and professional. The World Fair at Montreal had already shown that such people take

3. THC, or tetrahydrocanabinol, is the active ingredient in marijuana and can be concentrated in solution.
4. It was mainly to combat this type of traffic that the Customs installed an electronic detection system. Its value is debatable. While the detection rate is high (400 in one year), seizures have been negligible (15 kilogrammes of heroin).

65

advantage of these international gatherings to transact their business.

There is another factor which favours both categories of smuggler, namely, the high value of heroin in relation to its volume. Moreover it is very easy to hide. One kilogramme of pure heroin takes up no more room than a shaving roll. After dilution it will provide at least twenty thousand addicts with ten doses apiece.[5]

The traffickers' business methods are described by Robert H. Steele, a Congressman who has been in the forefront of the battle against narcotics.

It was a normal and routine business transaction [he writes]. The investor was interested only in the tremendous return on his investment money. For the purchase of a number of shares in the project – and no questions asked – he was offered, for his one hundred thousand dollars, a minimum profit of nearly two million dollars. His risk: the possible loss of his money. The 'broker' presented the investor with ten shares. The investor was told that he could expect a return on his investment in about six months. The 'broker' also advised the investor that his shares were negotiable and that, if the investor suddenly found himself in a financial bind, the 'broker' would buy back the shares for eighty cents on the dollar . . . This particular business transaction demonstrates one of the many procedural advances made over the past ten years by illegal drug traffickers . . . Although they are criminals in every sense of the word, they use established business practices and legal instruments in the conduct of their illegal trade. They have a reputation for making huge sums of money . . . and can easily find investors seeking a relatively quick profit requiring the payment of no taxes.[6]

We have only to consider the retail price of heroin to realize that there will always be someone prepared to incur the risks involved in trafficking. Pure heroin arriving in New York is invariably adulterated before it reaches the consumer. Each middleman mixes it with lactose or quinine to increase the volume and hence his profits. By the time it reaches the street

5. A heroin addict consumes on average 50–75 mg. heroin daily.
6. *Vista*, March/April 1972.

	Weight	Buying Price[1]	Selling Price	Expenses[2]	Profit
Opium					
Producer to first middleman	10 kg.		180	x[3]	180 – x
First middleman to agent	—	180	250	—	70
Agent to Istanbul exporter	—	250	280	—	30
Crossing of Syrian border	—	280	650	90	280
Cost of conversion of opium into base morphine	—	650	850	60	140
Morphine					
Crossing of Lebanese border	1 kg.	850	1,000	50	100
Refining of morphine in Lebanon	1 kg.	1,000	1,200	50	150
Transport to Beirut (couriers and accomplices)	—	1,200	1,500	75	225
Beirut–Marseilles (couriers)	—	1,500	2,000	100	400
Commission to local agent in Marseilles	—	2,000	3,000	200	800
Conversion to heroin in Marseilles	—	3,000	4,000	150	850
Heroin					
Marseilles–New York (couriers)	—	4,000	7,000	500	2,500
Entry into U.S.	—	7,000	12,500	1,000	4,500
American wholesalers	—	12,000	22,500	—	10,000

1. 1970 price in dollars.
2. Bribes, travel and conversion.
3. Seed and labour.

the heroin has been 'cut' no less than eight times and in the process the weight has risen from one kilogramme to five. As a B.N.D.D. agent told us, 'It's no longer heroin they're peddling, but lactose.' The little bag, bought at a street corner in New York, seldom contains more than five milligrammes of pure heroin. The cost is approximately five dollars, which means that the addict is paying a dollar a milligramme for his fix, or the equivalent of a million dollars per kilo of heroin.[7]

The ten kilogrammes of opium used in the manufacture of this kilo will have been sold by the Turkish or Thai peasant for 500 dollars at the most. Between producer and consumer the value of the merchandise has gone up two thousand times. This demonstrates how it is possible for a 'financier', with 100,000 dollars available for investment, to obtain a twentyfold increase on his outlay.

Admittedly these sums represent the cumulative profit of middlemen too numerous to be detailed here. But it would seem that the profit margin steadily increases, reaching a peak at the point of sale. The initial selling price of heroin after entry into the United States has risen from 12,000 dollars a kilogramme in 1970 to 20,000 dollars in 1973. The resale price to the first wholesaler is 28,500 dollars in New York, or 36,000 in Chicago. By 'cutting' his kilo with fifty per cent lactose the New York wholesaler doubles the volume of his merchandise which he resells at 38,000 dollars a kilo. The next vendor does the same, and so on all the way down the line.

A Turkish journalist, Ozgen Acar, set himself the task of tracing these increments stage by stage, from the Turkish producer to the first American buyer, in order to demonstrate the complexity of the process itself and the difficulty of assessing its profitability.[8]

---

7. The United Nations calculated that in 1971 the street selling price of heroin was 430,000 dollars a kilogramme. But at that time a dose sold for 5 dollars contained about 12 mg. of pure heroin. The stepping-up of law enforcement activities in 1972 affected the wholesale prices. To compensate for this, the pedlars reduced the heroin content to 5 mg. per five dollar bag.

8. *The Opium Report*, Ozgen Acar, Ankara, 1970.

Each year an average of some **twelve and** a half tons of heroin enters the United States where it is bought at 20,000 dollars a kilogramme and ultimately retailed at a million dollars a kilogramme. Bearing in mind the magnitude of these incentives, can it reasonably be hoped to stamp out the traffic on an over-all budget of 315 million dollars, the sum allocated for the purpose by the U.S. government in 1972?[9] In their struggle against the traffickers the agencies charged with the suppression of narcotics recall a David pitted against a Goliath.

The sums handled by the racketeers are such that no price is too high when it comes to buying a man's services. Their power lies in their ability to corrupt all, or almost all, those whom they approach. How many politicians, officials, magistrates or policemen can resist an envelope containing, perhaps, 150,000 dollars or more? A rhetorical question, no doubt, but observers are agreed that in every country concerned with the production, consumption, conversion or conveyance of opium and its derivatives, the traffic is protected, if not organized, by highly placed personages, to all intents and purposes beyond the reach of the law. If the traffickers did not have what one of them described as 'protection in political and administrative circles', they would, by their own admission, be unable to operate with any efficiency.

It need hardly be said that addiction and corruption go hand in hand, and the more widespread the addiction the worse the corruption. The traffickers want to protect and, in so far as possible, extend their market. 'It is, of course, true,' we were told by a European diplomat in Asia, 'that the drug racketeers have accomplices everywhere. But instead of castigating us, and/or the underdeveloped countries, for corruption, the United States would do better to put their own house in order.'

The case of New York in particular is significant. Corruption has always been rife in the New York police. During the prohibition era alcohol, and later on gambling, enabled the Mafia to

9. Even if this sum were doubled in 1973, as President Nixon proposed to Congress, it would suffice to treat no more than 250,000 addicts out of an expected 800,000.

distribute sizeable bribes among a body of men to whom over-scrupulousness in a society based on violence represented a risk incommensurate with their low rate of pay. Those who did not wish to sully their hands kept their eyes shut and, from the point of view of their own safety, it was just as well they did.

The men who wear blue uniform do not constitute a united and irreproachable whole. Joseph Fisch, head of a committee investigating corruption in New York State, tells of a complaint made by a policeman to the effect that one of his colleagues had threatened his life. Apparently the complainant had objected to malpractices within the force, whereupon he had been told: 'Watch out! That police badge of yours isn't a bullet-proof vest!'[10]

Corruption in the New York police was also investigated by a federal committee under Whitman Knapp. Its report, published in June 1972, aroused considerable interest. At least twenty detectives belonging to the New York police had accepted bribes from B.N.D.D. agents posing as traffickers. The sums involved ranged from a thousand to fifty thousand dollars. Two detectives had been paid six thousand dollars by a lawyer in return for agreeing to declare in court that his client was not a trafficker but a police informer.[11] Following these revelations the strength of the New York drug squad was reduced by sixty-four per cent in order to diminish the risk of corruption in a sphere where a bribe of fifty thousand dollars was by no means unusual. When a *New York Times* reporter asked a senior police official up to what level men could still be found who were prepared to accept a gift for services rendered, his only reply was to raise his arms wearily, as much as to say 'the sky's the limit'.

It is an open secret that pushers can operate with complete impunity in certain New York streets, more especially in Harlem. Amsterdam Avenue, between 96th and 155th Streets is well known to addicts as a place where a fix can be procured without difficulty at any hour of the day or night. The

10. 'The Institutionalizing of Police Corruption', *New York Review*, 1971.
11. *New York Times*, 15, 16, 17, 18 June, 1972.

Representative for that district, Charles B. Rangel, told us that he had once sat in his official car, plainly identifiable by its registration plates, and watched while a pusher calmly sold at least eight doses under his very nose. 'Because of police corruption,' Rangel added, 'we've reached the point where the whole judicial system is called in question.'

Evidence laid before various investigating committees has revealed that many of the police, sometimes the very ones entrusted with the suppression of the traffic, extort money from the traders or else become their protectors, to the extent even of providing them with cars and apartments. Not infrequently the police round off their monthly pay cheques by selling confiscated heroin, originally retained for the purpose of rewarding potential informers.

In New York the public's loss of confidence has reached the point of no return. If a ghetto-dweller reports a local pusher to the police, he is less likely to get their support than to be denounced by them to the pusher, who sooner or later will wreak his revenge. Thus, as the powder train of heroin grows ever longer fear has set in, and no remedy for this situation appears to be in sight.

The efficiency of the counter-measures within the borders of the United States and even beyond is threatened by the notorious and, indeed, tragi-comic rivalry between the U.S. Customs Bureau and the Bureau of Narcotics and Dangerous Drugs. The conflict came to a head in 1969 when a decision had to be made as to which of these two agencies should be empowered to conduct investigations outside American territory.

While the Customs Bureau professed itself fully competent to maintain relations with foreign police forces, the B.N.D.D. argued that an organization created for the sole purpose of dealing with drugs must be able to take an over-all view of the problems relating to supply, demand, detoxication and law enforcement, whether at home or abroad.

Relations have deteriorated to such an extent that the two agencies have virtually ceased to coordinate their activities or even exchange information. In 1970 President Nixon felt impelled to intervene in person, and in February of that year decided that the Bureau of Narcotics should be the only organization empowered to represent the United States on questions of drugs. Thenceforward the Customs were to have no hand in such matters unless previously authorized by the B.N.D.D.

The presidential memorandum laid down that all investigations into infringements of the drug laws, both inside and outside the United States, were to fall within the province of the B.N.D.D. The Customs Bureau was to do no more than keep watch on points of entry into the United States in such a way as to aid the B.N.D.D. in its efforts to contain illicit trafficking in drugs.

In spite of the presidential edict, the conflict between the two agencies has shown no signs of abating. When the Customs moved into a magnificent new building on Wall Street at the beginning of 1972, they refused to accommodate the Bureau of Narcotics in the same premises although this would have facilitated cooperation. As it is, cooperation does not exist. This situation has catastrophic results, as Congressman Robert H. Steele pointed out to a Congressional Sub-Committee in January 1972. It had seriously affected efforts to put important traffickers out of action. Steele had learnt from officials that in the previous twelve months numerous cases passed to the two agencies had come to naught through conflicts over jurisdiction. Many arrests had been made prematurely. Traffickers whose traces had been followed from Europe by the B.N.D.D. were apprehended the minute they entered the United States by customs agents who seized their drugs, and so the B.N.D.D. was unable to follow the goods to their ultimate destination, the big operators of Chicago and New York.

But when the Customs make a haul they take all the credit, even though they may have acted on information supplied by the B.N.D.D. The reverse also applies. Both are equally anxious to demonstrate their efficiency in order to justify their existing budgets and, if possible, have them increased.

Sometimes their differences take a tragi-comic turn. As a rule the undercover agents employed by the Customs try to sell drugs in order to unmask the buyers, while those of the

B.N.D.D. try to buy them in order to catch the wholesalers. Thus it is by no means unusual for a B.N.D.D. man to buy heroin – or flour – from a customs man. As Congressman Steele said, when B.N.D.D. informers or undercover agents in the guise of buyers are looking for suppliers and customs agents try and sell in the guise of traffickers, the rivalry between the two agencies could become lethal if their men were armed.

He also alleges that, on arriving at frontier posts, B.N.D.D. agents on duty are regularly held up by the Customs. This was confirmed by a French policeman who told us that, when on his way to New York in company with a member of the Narcotics Bureau, he was searched from head to foot.

'The absence of coordination', as it is euphemistically known in Washington, between Customs and B.N.D.D. has enabled large numbers of gangsters to slip through the net, either because information has not been passed on, or because an ill-considered arrest has prematurely given the game away. This rivalry between the two organizations has also had repercussions abroad, notably in France. A senior French official deplored the absence of centralization in the organizations responsible for suppressing the drug traffic in the United States. 'It makes international coordination difficult,' he told us, 'which is why so many cases are badly handled and come to nothing.'

Again, the director of Interpol, speaking before the United Nations Convention on Narcotic Drugs, made a public appeal to the two agencies in the hope of inducing them to resolve their interdepartmental squabbles.

For decades the state police and federal police in the United States have been similarly at loggerheads on questions of spheres of influence. Hence the problem is unlikely to be solved by the amendment laid before Congress by Steele in January 1971 in which he proposed to delimit yet again the respective responsibilities of the various American organizations concerned with the drug problem. Moreover it seems doubtful whether the National Narcotics Information Board, a coordinating body set up on 27 July 1972, will be any more effective. The participation of an additional agency in the hunt for traffickers would seem better calculated to promote rivalry than to diminish it.

The international law enforcement agencies harbour no illusions as to the possibility of stamping out the drug traffic. They know it to be an unattainable goal. We need only ask how many shipments succeed in slipping through the barriers for every one that is intercepted. According to the B.N.D.D., ninety per cent of all drugs dispatched arrive safely at their destination.

In fact these agencies do not set their sights too high. Their aim is to prevent the amount of heroin reaching the consumers from rising above the present level. Assuming they succeed, either the number of addicts will be stabilized or, if it continues to grow, consumption per capita will fall off as a result of the relative shortage of heroin. But this is no more than a makeshift solution. And apart from that there is no guarantee that it will prove effective. Increasing pressure on the demand for heroin would doubtless cause prices to rise and thus encourage the traffickers to run greater risks. Conceivably a number of potential addicts might be deterred by a sharp increase in the cost of narcotics. But those who were well and truly hooked would have no other choice but to step up their thefts to pay for their fixes. The result would be a fresh wave of crime, and American cities, more especially New York, would become little better than jungles.

Hence the government has gradually come round to the view that if, despite the many elaborate measures employed by the law enforcement agencies, traffickers continue to enter American territory, action must be taken at source, in other words where the raw materials for narcotic drugs are grown and processed.

In his speech of 17 June 1971 President Nixon declared:

Heroin, this deadly poison in the American lifestream . . . is a foreign export . . . No serious attack on our national drug problem can ignore the international implications of such an effort, nor can the domestic effort succeed without attacking the problem on an international plane – I intend to do that . . . I instructed our ambassadors to make clear to their host governments . . . that I consider the heroin addiction of American citizens an international problem of grave concern to our nation.

The battle against addiction is no longer confined to the United States, having spread to all other parts of the world. Law enforcement and the dismantling of smuggling rings are still indispensable tasks, but they must be conceived in global terms. Up till 1970 the B.N.D.D. had branches in twenty-three countries and employed some fifty agents on foreign duty. By 1972 it possessed 115 agents in forty-four different countries, and was planning to expand even further.

American diplomats have received strict instructions to encourage these countries to adopt a stiffer attitude towards the production and sale of opium. It is thanks to their efforts that Laos has now introduced a law forbidding both of these activities. Thailand, too, has responded by tightening up its legislation. Wherever possible the U.S. representatives have put pressure on governments to bring in more effective controls over opium production, if not to suppress it altogether. This, according to President Nixon, is a vital aspect of the battle. In his speech of 17 June he also said:

> It is clear that the only really effective way to end heroin production is to end opium production and the growing of poppies . . . I am asking the Congress to provide two million dollars to the Department of Agriculture for research and development of herbicides which can be used to destroy growth of narcotics-producing plants without adverse ecological effects.

American diplomats have been no less active in the council chambers of international organizations. They have pressed tirelessly for the revision and clarification of existing narcotics agreements. They have also succeeded in setting up a Fund for Drug Control financed by the member countries of the United Nations. But the new ground upon which America has now taken her stand has changed the character of the battle against addiction which, from being a simple question of law enforcement, has become a diplomatic problem of global dimensions.

While some countries are happy enough to join the American anti-drug crusade, the same cannot be said of certain others, where very considerable political and economic interests are at stake. Thus the outcome of this new opium war will depend very largely on the diplomatic weapons at the disposal of the United States, and on the manner in which they can be brought to bear on any country that obstinately refuses to fall into line.

Part 2

The Golden Triangle: Opium and the War

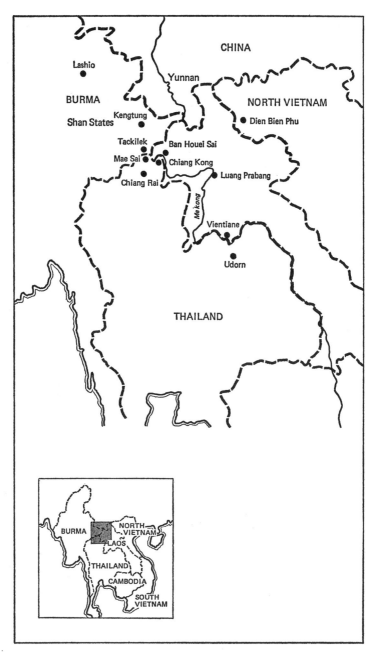

The Golden Triangle

The campaign launched by Washington to cut off illicit supplies at source might be expected to encounter fewest difficulties in countries that are largely dependent on American aid. Those that immediately spring to mind are Thailand, Laos and Vietnam where, since the early sixties, the United States have been conducting an anti-communist crusade involving the commitment of half a million young Americans in an interminable war.

Yet these three countries act as a conveyor belt for at least a quarter of the illicit opium consumed throughout the world. Not the least of the paradoxes arising out of the Vietnam War is that the region's traditional opium trade should have been provided with a new industry, the manufacture of heroin, whose customers were the G.I.s and, later, the ever-growing number of addicts in the United States. In 1971, on their return from a mission to Asia, two American Congressmen, Morgan M. Murphy and Robert H. Steele, proclaimed aloud what had hitherto been no more than a whisper, namely that ten to fifteen per cent of the American expeditionary force was known to take heroin.

After lengthy speculation as to whether Hanoi's strategy included the deliberate intoxication of American soldiers, the authorities were eventually compelled to admit that there was no need to look so far. Numbers of Vietnamese, Thai and Laotian personages who enjoyed the confidence of the Americans have been able to make fortunes out of this lucrative traffic by exploiting the general instability and corruption resulting from the war. This fact has been admitted in the highest American military circles.

Before tackling the opium problem, the Americans must first rid themselves of these unsavoury associates for whom the conflict in south-east Asia is just one means among many of lining their pockets. But in that case the United States would have to look elsewhere for assistance in slaying the communist hydra. Meanwhile the American government is faced with a choice of two evils, of choosing between one war and another.

6   Thailand: the Ineradicable Poppy

'Thailand is not at the beck and call of the United States, and her policy is wholly independent of foreign interference.' This statement, often heard in Bangkok government circles, would appear to be borne out by the Thais' keen sense of independence, their well-known pride and their jealous nationalism no less than by their occasional outbursts of bad temper *vis-à-vis* the United States. But a rapid survey of Thailand's history since 1945 reveals that successive governments in Bangkok have consistently followed Washington's lead. Broadly speaking, Thai policy has been to encourage the spread of private enterprise and to combat communist insurrection both at home and abroad. On the outbreak of the Korean War Thailand was the first to dispatch an expeditionary force of 4,000 men to fight alongside the Americans. Today she is alone in maintaining in South Korea a military contingent under the auspices of the United Nations Peace-Keeping Force. She is also one of the pillars of NATO's Asian counterpart, SEATO, whose headquarters were established at Bangkok in 1954 with a Thai as its first secretary-general. When the United States embarked on the war in Vietnam, Thailand sent troops there to fight the N.L.F. guerrillas. In her anxiety to help the 'free world', she became one of the first countries to offer to train Marshal Lon Nol's Cambodian troops. Ever since the beginning of the Second Indo-China War she has been safeguarding the Americans' rear by allowing them the use of five large bases from which their bombers set out to pound North Vietnam and Laos. The withdrawal of American fighting troops from South Vietnam did not detract from Thailand's strategic importance – quite the contrary, in fact, since the U.S. Air Force and Navy continued to support the ground operations thenceforward conducted by the South Vietnamese Army. In return for their loyal collaboration, the Thai authorities have received increasing military and economic aid from the United States. Part of that aid goes to sustain Bangkok's offensive against the guerrilla troops operating in the provinces of the south and the north-east.

This *entente cordiale* might give grounds for supposing that American efforts to eliminate heroin at source would encounter few difficulties so far as the Thais were concerned. But such was by no means the case. In 1972 the Bureau of Narcotics and Dangerous Drugs admitted the truth of the allegation made by certain members of the American opposition to the effect that Thailand was south-east Asia's main exporter of illicit opium, morphine and heroin. Indeed, Bangkok is a distribution centre not only for Thai opium but also for the major part of the vast quantity produced in Burma.

The Thais would have no real objection to the suppression of opium production in their country, a step which could have distinct economic advantages. But action against growers or traffickers would be likely to jeopardize the basic political objectives shared in common by Thailand and the United States.

Although a law was passed in 1958 forbidding the cultivation of the poppy, Thailand produces some 150 tons of opium a year, this being either smoked by the peasants or sold on the black market. The cultivators belong to tribes of Chinese or Sino-Burmese origin who inhabit the jungle-covered and often barely accessible hill country in the north and north-east. The most expert growers are the Meos, an independent and somewhat bellicose tribe, of whom there are some sixty thousand in Thailand. The Yaos number about twenty thousand and the Lissus and Lahus ten and fifteen thousand respectively. The Akhas, the most recent arrivals from China or Burma, number barely more than eight thousand. Opium production, of which these people have a virtual monopoly, is their principal commercial activity. Save for the sale of a few pigs, it is their sole means of earning money with which to buy the necessities of life.

As a rule the tribes live in villages perched like eyries on the mountain peaks. It took us at least ten hours under a broiling sun to reach an Akha settlement in the Meung Nam district. As we laboured up the steep path, our guide maintained a rapid, even pace, though bent almost double under a thirty kilo sack of rice. In common with most of the young men of his tribe, he had completely shaved his head save for a small plait at the back. The sun was about to set as we arrived in the village. Under the overhanging eaves of the large bamboo huts women were squatting on the ground sewing beads, coloured feathers and pieces of silver on to strips of cloth. These are used as trimmings for their unusual costume, consisting of a very short and full skirt, leggings, a cap and sometimes a small embroidered jacket, all made of a dark blue cotton material. The skin of men, women and children alike is streaked, indeed almost incrusted, with black grime. The Akhas are notorious for the filth of their persons, water being very scarce on the hilltops where they live. Every day the women go down into the valleys, carrying on their backs large hollowed-out bamboos, a journey of several hours to fetch a few litres for cooking and drinking purposes. It would never occur to anyone to use this water for washing.

A surprising number of cringing, emaciated dogs were roaming round the village in company with a herd of black pigs. One of these dogs was chased and surrounded by a bunch of urchins who killed it with an axe. Within minutes the remains had been thrown on to a blazing fire. There was a stench of burning leather as the fur and skin were consumed. Next the meat was dropped into a big cauldron to join the unnameable mixture already cooking there. After a dinner consisting of this stew – the Akhas' favourite dish – served with bamboo hearts and tea, the village chief, our host for the night, invited us to smoke opium as he himself was accustomed to do after the evening meal. While we reclined on bamboo mats, our heads comfortably resting on cushions, he prepared the pipes. Spearing a little ball of opium on the end of a long needle (known as a dipper), he slowly heated it at the flame of an oil lamp, pressing it from time to time against the glass funnel to produce an oblong shape. As soon as the paste was sufficiently soft, he quickly transferred it to the tiny bowl of a pipe whose long stem was made of chased silver. He then held the bowl over the flame, and, as the opium sizzled and burnt, he inhaled great lungfuls of the acrid smoke.

We had come there to attend the opium harvest. This takes place between January and March and goes on for several weeks, the fields being scattered about the hills, sometimes at a great distance from the villages. The opium is harvested a few days after the poppy has shed its magnificent white and mauve or purple petals, leaving a green seed pod the size of a pigeon's egg. The work not only requires great deftness of touch but has to be carried out in a limited space of time. In the evening whole families go out into the fields to tap the pods. A small and often very primitive three- or five-bladed knife is used to scarify the pod, either in a spiral or vertically, making many separate incisions from which a thick, white latex begins to ooze, gradually turning brown on exposure to the air. This is left to seep out overnight. At sunrise the peasants come out to collect the brown latex with the aid of scrapers of various sizes which they draw rapidly over the incisions made the night before. Each poppyhead yields a morsel of opium the size of a small pea which is placed in a box carried on a string round the neck. At the end of perhaps two hours' work the receptacle will be full of a brown muddy substance smelling of leaf mould.

Production methods are very different from those practised in India, Turkey or Pakistan where the poppy takes its place in the classic rotation of crops characteristic of a more advanced agriculture. Here in the hill country of Thailand, as in Laos and Burma, opium is cultivated in clearings burnt in the jungle.

The tribes lead a semi-nomadic existence. At the end of the rainy season, in November and December, the men and women fell trees which they allow to dry before burning them and chopping away the charred stumps. They then remove what remains of the ground cover. Their first crop may be rice, followed later by opium or maize. They know nothing about fertilizers, even those of animal origin, and their rotation of crops is purely arbitrary, yet their yields are good, for it takes several years to exhaust the soil. Then they move on and settle elsewhere, leaving behind them barren hilltops and deforested slopes. In a lightly populated region the forest can withstand such on-slaughts and will re-establish itself within the space of ten or fifteen years. But if the population increases and the peasants return too often to the areas they have despoiled, the land will become so degraded as to be irrecoverable.[1]

This is precisely what is happening in Thailand today. The introduction of western medicine has considerably reduced mortality among the tribal population which is therefore growing very rapidly. Moreover there has been a continuous stream of immigrants. The majority are of Chinese origin and have spent a longer or shorter period in Burma before making their way to Thailand. We came across whole villages of Lahus who, having entered the country illegally, were seeking to establish themselves there. They were looking for land in the Meung Nam district, a few kilometres from the Burmese frontier. But land is becoming scarce. Indeed the nomadic and unproductive form of agriculture practised by the tribes demands a vast acreage to support what is a relatively sparse population. In apparently uninhabited districts where getting from one village to the next involves a three-day march through the jungle, it comes as a surprise to learn that productive land is growing ever scarcer. Today the primary forests of northern Thailand have suffered severe damage. Thousands of acres are either completely denuded or else support a meagre growth of secondary forest on poor quality soil. Apart from the drain on her timber reserves, the destruction of the forests is having grave repercussions on Thailand's economy.

The removal of trees and ground cover in the northern hill country is seriously upsetting the country's drainage system. Rivers and streams whose course was formerly regulated by the vegetation have now become torrents. In the rainy season they cause disastrous floods in the paddy fields upon which the country's prosperity depends. The increasingly vociferous protests of the rice-growers in the plains are further embittering their already uneasy relations with the hill tribes. A great many dis-

1. The increase in poppy cultivation in response to growing demand has materially helped to increase the process. Opium is a crop that rapidly exhausts the soil.

cussions, meetings and conferences have been held to thrash out this problem. Invariably the conclusion has been that the cultivation of the poppy must be banned and the hill-dwellers induced to cease their wanderings and adopt some other form of agriculture. But these plans are always shelved because of the considerable political and economic difficulties involved.

As early as 1965 the Thai authorities had begun to proclaim the presence in the south and north-east of 'subversive communist movements', an omnibus term that embraced all local uprisings. Though these were less often due to the political agitation than to the exploitation of the Sino-Burmese tribes, they were used to justify Bangkok's demand for increased U.S. military and financial aid.

The brutal punishment meted out to Meo tribes who have persistently tried to regain the lands from which they have been evicted has created a climate favourable to communist propaganda. Deliberately turning their backs on the Thais who despise them, the hill tribes have established contact with those of their kinsmen who went to Laos to join the nationalist-progressive camp. Broadcasts in the Meo language from Communist China urge these people to rebel and endeavour to instil in them a sense of racial and political solidarity with the three million Meos living in South China. One of the inflammatory themes designed for the consumption of the hill-dwelling minorities, and more particularly the Meos, is that the Thai government intends to deprive them of their means of livelihood – in this instance the poppy – confiscate their lands and reduce them to penury. The fate of the Meos in Laos, where they have been massacred and dispossessed, can only lend verisimilitude to this argument in the eyes of their fellow tribesmen in Thailand. The latter, always at odds with the Thai plainsmen, are more than ever on the alert, so that the smallest incident would suffice to spark off an insurrection amongst those who have not already rebelled. Already the entire district along the Laotian border, from Chiang Kham in the north to Loey in the north-east, has been declared 'insecure' because of 'Red Meo' activity.

At one time the only weapons possessed by the Meos, Akhas and Yaos were crossbows or locally-made flintlocks. These primitive fire-arms, no less dangerous to the user than to the potential victim, are still to be found in every village. But the vast arms traffic that has grown up with the war in south-east Asia, has enabled them to buy more up-to-date weapons. We once spent the night in a Meo settlement on the banks of the Tekok, two days' march from Tha Ton. Some of the sentries posted round the village carried Japanese rifles of Second World War vintage, but others were armed with Garands, the American combat rifle, or the extremely modern M16 brought in from Laos. The last-named weapons had been bought for the equivalent of 150 dollars apiece from opium buyers and Chinese Nationalist soldiers who had settled in the district. In fact the tribes exchange the better part of their opium crops for arms and ammunition.

In this climate of revolt, actual or potential, the Thai authorities are obviously reluctant to enforce the ban on poppy growing, the more so since the hill tribes live in the frontier regions and are thus in direct contact with the areas occupied by the Pathet Lao. Moreover, in view of the American withdrawal from Vietnam, the Thais have every incentive to avoid a conflagration in their northern territories.

A rebellion that broke out in Tak Province shows how easily a trivial incident can blow up into an ugly situation. Mae Sot is situated on the border at a point where Burma forms a wedge in Thai territory. It is an inaccessible district covered with thick jungle and inhabited by Meo tribes. In 1969 the Thai government decided for strategic reasons to build a road linking Mae Sot and Uphang further to the south. The road-makers came upon some poppy fields and destroyed them. Thereupon the Meos reacted swiftly and violently. A Thai official was murdered at Kilometre 4. Work on the highway was suspended and was not resumed until several months later, this time under the protection of the army. In December the Meos shot and killed three workmen. As a reprisal the Thai labourers and the people of Uphang executed a Meo notable. Thereafter corpses piled up on both sides. Meo communist cadres arrived from Laos to help the tribes organize themselves into self-defence groups. Work on the road was again suspended and in April 1972 the region was declared an 'insurrectional zone'.

The same caution inhibits the Thai government from using modern chemical and biological weapons to destroy the poppy fields. American experience in Vietnam has demonstrated the effectiveness of defoliation, while agricultural researchers in Malaya have discovered a virus which attacks the opium poppy. But the use of such weapons to combat illicit opium production would undoubtedly play into the hands of those seeking to promote subversive activities. For without opium the tribes, who produce barely enough dry rice for their own needs, would be deprived of their means of livelihood. The Meos are unable to live comfortably below a certain altitude and hence they cannot be resettled in the valleys where the atmospheric pressure is too high for them. The only solution would be to find alternative crops capable of being grown in upland regions and producing a return comparable to that of opium. But such schemes present serious economic and technological difficulties.

Theoretically there are certain – if not very many – crops which could be substituted for opium without loss of income. But in practice each has a number of drawbacks which put it out of the running, at least in present circumstances. The poppy can be grown on any sort of terrain and calls for no investment other than the labour force, whereas most crops require level ground and may well demand the construction of expensive terraces. Moreover problems associated with the technicalities of production are not the only ones that have to be faced if opium is to be replaced with another crop. There is also the question of transportation. The tribes live in remote areas, far from the centres of consumption. A crop's value has to be very high in relation to its weight if the cost of several days' carriage, whether by man or mule, is to be covered. It would in fact be difficult to find a substitute for opium, of which a single kilogramme – as against several hundredweight of coffee or potatoes – provides a return of twenty dollars. Moreover the transportation of such produce would demand the prior construction of a road system, undoubtedly an extremely costly undertaking.

But given adequate transport and communications, there still remains the question of a stable market. The failure to find an answer to that question has, over the past few years, bedevilled most of the government's schemes, however unambitious, for the cultivation of alternative crops. 'One possibility is common flax,' we were told by an Australian expert.

Not only does it produce linseed oil but, better still, its fibres make excellent raw material for the manufacture of cigarette paper, postage stamps and bank notes. Unfortunately they haven't yet started making paper in Thailand. Ramie does very well on the slopes and its plaited fibre can be used for making handicraft products. But outlets for that sort of thing are very limited. They could also try fruit, even the kinds usually grown in temperate regions. But a tree takes several years to bear after planting. Also prices fluctuate violently from year to year, which is a bit discouraging for the growers.

A Meo peasant in the Chiang Mai district told us that he was prepared to grow anything, even if it brought in less money than opium. But he wanted an assured sale for his produce, and this is precisely what no one will venture to guarantee. Diverse products have been mooted – dehydrated mushrooms, camphor, essential oils, silk worms – all of which seem promising enough on paper. But it still remains to be shown who will buy these articles, at what price and for how long. In brief, the introduction of alternative crops presupposes a sustained effort on the part of the State in terms of investment marketing.

No such problems attach to opium for which the demand continues to increase – so much so that the peasants do not have to concern themselves with its sale. Rather it is the buyers who come to the villages to collect the product. While a few may be Thais, most are Haws, Chinese immigrants of several generations' standing. Like the tribesmen, the Haws, who resell the merchandise at a handsome profit, regard opium as a crop second to none from a commercial point of view and there is every reason to believe that they would do their utmost to prevent its suppression.

89

The traders travel from village to village at harvest time, buying opium from the tribesmen and selling them such necessities as salt, sugar, tea, footwear, candles, matches, oil lamps, torches, and cloth. Often it is simply a case of barter. The Haws, who originate from Yunnan, are a minority of a very special kind. They do not live in the plains but in large villages half way up the mountain slopes, and constitute an essential economic link between the hill-dwellers and the rice growers of the plains. While preserving their culture and their Chinese traditions, they have succeeded in establishing excellent relations with the tribes. Many of them have in fact married Meo, Akha or Lahu women. The semi-clandestine nature of the production and distribution of opium has further strengthened the bonds between these traders and the hill-dwellers. The latter in any case dislike dealing direct with the plainsmen, who cheat them and make fun of their gaudy clothing.

Admittedly the Haws also exploit the tribes by buying opium at a rock-bottom price, while charging the maximum for their own wares. According to a report issued by the Thai Ministry of the Interior, the Haw traders not only make a profit of thirty to a hundred per cent on the goods they sell to the villagers, but also anything up to a hundred per cent profit on the opium they resell to the Chinese wholesalers in the plains. The opium bought for 40–45 dollars a kilo in the hills is resold for 75–90 dollars to the merchants in Tak, Lampang or Chiang Mai. The Haws also lend money to the tribes or sell them goods on credit, thereby securing a pre-emptive right to future harvests. But because of their reluctance to go down into the plains, the hill-dwellers are very largely dependent on these middlemen. If other crops are to be substituted for opium, one of the first prerequisites would be the removal of the Haws who live in a state of virtual symbiosis with the mountain folk. Hence, however much time or money is spent on agricultural technology, transport facilities, the re-training of peasants or the search for domestic and foreign outlets for the proposed new products, it will still be necessary to dismantle the trading system operated by the Haws and replace it with one controlled by the State. But upheavals of this order would entail an expenditure of many millions of dollars, a sum that is far beyond Thailand's resources.

Some attempt has been made to reduce opium production. Schemes to assist such tribes as do not live too far from urban centres have been introduced at the instigation of the King who takes a personal interest in the problem of the highland minorities. While these programmes have had some measure of success, the net result is not very encouraging. For instance, in the Meo village of Dong Pui in Chiang Mai Province, poppy fields continue to flourish beneath the very walls of the royal family's summer residence. Various other modest projects have been put in hand, largely on the initiative of the Ministry of the Interior, but so derisory is the budget and so inadequate the staffing that little real progress can be expected.

The United Nations project, which received a great deal of publicity in the Thai Press in 1971, has raised many hopes – in the corridors of the U.N., if nowhere else. The administrators of the Fund for Drug Control decided to invest the initial two and a half million dollars at their disposal in Thailand. This sum was to be devoted not only to experiments in substituting other crops for opium and the provision of better equipment and training for the police, but also to research into the detoxication of opium addicts. However this was no more than a pilot project affecting two villages. In fact nobody on the spot harbours any illusions as to the practical significance of so limited an undertaking – not even, it would seem, the imperturbable Texan at present in charge of the technical side. This man pointed out that the 1970 preliminary report of the U.N. Commission on Narcotic Drugs (sponsor and administrator of the project) had held out little hope of finding substitute crops for the poppy capable of bringing in equal returns, and commented: 'That situation remains unchanged today'.

Officially American diplomats in Bangkok profess to be delighted with the United Nations experiment which, in the words of the experts, should 'provide valuable pointers to ways and means of tackling the major problems of crop substitution', the

91

results being all the more eagerly awaited in that Thailand is the only country where such an experiment is being carried out. In private, however, these same diplomats concede that, in view of the country's economic potential and the current political situation, there would seem to be little hope of any significant drop in opium production for the next fifteen years at the very least. To illustrate the kind of difficulty confronting the work of the United Nations from the very outset, one of them told us that the Thai government refused to permit the construction of roads in the area designated for the scheme, despite an American offer to foot the bill. For the Thais maintained that the building of roads in districts over which they had little control could only help the communists pursue their subversive activities by increasing their mobility.

The economic and political difficulties militating against the suppression of opium production are compounded by the even more complex problem of grappling with the traffickers. Those mainly responsible for conveying and refining the opium produced in Thailand and Burma are Chinese irregulars, better known as the K.M.T., who have settled in Thai territory. Employed as mercenaries by the Thai government in counter-guerrilla operations, their position, both military and political, is so powerful that they have now become a law unto themselves.

7

The K.M.T: a
New Secret Army

Between March and June the opium caravans come down from the borders of Burma, Laos and Thailand. The largest of them may transport up to twenty tons of opium carried by elephant or mule. They are escorted by between three and five hundred men equipped with modern weapons to fend off possible attack. Moving along jungle tracks they make their way to the more or less illicit settlements of the Chinese irregulars in north Thailand and western Laos. From there the opium goes by road to Bangkok, by air to Vientiane, or else to the local refineries where it is converted into base morphine and heroin.

This lucrative traffic is largely in the hands of the K.M.T.[1] These troops consist of the remnants of Chiang Kai-shek's Nationalist army, driven out of Communist China after the revolution of 1949. During the fifties the K.M.T. was used by the C.I.A. to seal off the Sino-Burmese border, and today it plays a vital part in the Thai government's counter-guerrilla operations in the mountainous regions of the north.

In October 1949 Chiang Kai-shek's army collapsed before the onslaught of the communist forces. The Nationalist troops in the south, fleeing before the advance of the People's Liberation Army crossed the Yunnan border and sought refuge in the countries of south-east Asia. Five thousand of them made their way to French Indo-China where they were disarmed and interned. In 1953 these men were sent to Formosa. In January 1950 a group of two hundred, soon followed by fifteen hundred others, settled in Burma, some ten kilometres from the Thai

1. Short for Kuomintang, meaning National People's Party, now in power in Formosa.

frontier. They ensconced themselves in the mountainous district of Mong Hsat from which the Burmese army was unable to dislodge them. The influx of refugees into Burma continued throughout 1951.

Part of this defeated army dispersed, and many of the Chinese soldiers became integrated with the local population, married Lahu, Yao or Shan women and took up – or perhaps reverted to – farming. But more than six thousand of them remained together as a military entity, their numbers being swollen by indigenous tribesmen. In 1952, having removed or assimilated thirty-four local hereditary chieftains, or *sawbwas*, this nationalist military formation, then numbering some 12,000 men, seized *de facto* power throughout the eastern part of the Burmese Shan States, an area bounded on the north-east by Chinese Yunnan, now communist, and on the east and south by Laos and Thailand. On the west the precipitous gorge of the Salween River formed a natural defensive barrier against the Burmese, a barrier all the more effective for the total absence of roads. Thus the new domain of the Chinese Nationalists formed an autonomous entity. Although under the terms of the Constitution the Shan States belong to the Union of Burma, Rangoon has never exercised any real control over the region, whose population is in a perpetual state of revolt against the Central Government.

As early as 1951 the C.I.A. began to show an interest in this forgotten army massed on the Chinese border. They hoped that it might serve as a deterrent to Chinese communist infiltration into south-east Asia, and even – why not? – as an instrument for reconquering part of the People's Republic. From then on the K.M.T. received secret consignments of American arms, ammunition and equipment, either through Formosa or direct from Bangkok. These items were dropped on to Mong Hsat from C46 and C47 aircraft which bore no markings. Later, a landing ground near the town was brought back into service, thus establishing a semi-clandestine link with Formosa. In 1951 Chiang Kai-shek's government sent in several hundred reinforcements.

These troops, then under the command of General Li Mi, did

not, however, restrict their activities to the organization of intelligence networks for the benefit of the Americans. On no less than seven occasions, between 1950 and 1952, they attempted to cross the Yunnan border and penetrate into Chinese territory.[2] Each time they were repulsed with heavy losses by the People's Liberation Army. At the end of 1952, having finally abandoned any idea of invasion, the K.M.T. decided to settle permanently in Burma. This was the cue for Rangoon to voice its protest before the United Nations, a protest which aroused world-wide indignation.

The Burmese authorities sought to repel the K.M.T. intruders by force of arms, but the attempt ended in total failure. Commanded by General Li Mi, the Nationalists, operating as the 'Anti-Communist Army of National Safety', crushed the Burmese forces. Moreover they used this attack as a pretext to cross the Salween, going on to capture the town of Mong Shu in late 1952. They even had the audacity to ally themselves with the Karen and Mon tribes who were rebelling against the Burmese government.[3] And it was now that an agreement was apparently reached between the Karens and the Nationalist Chinese whereby modern weapons were to be exchanged for the wolfram mined at Mawchi, a town under Karen control about 130 kilometres from Rangoon.[4] In company with Karen rebels, some seven hundred soldiers of the K.M.T. took the towns of Pagun and Panga barely fifty kilometres away from the Burmese capital. In making this deep thrust into Burmese territory the K.M.T. may have been prompted by the desire to secure landing-grounds capable of receiving large cargo aircraft and thereby speed up deliveries from Formosa.[5]

Confronted by this dire threat to its existence, the Burmese government launched a vigorous counter-offensive and, in March 1953, succeeded in pushing the K.M.T. back behind the Salween River. At the same time the Prime Minister, U Nu, lodged a

2. *Reporter*, 12 May 1953.
3. See Chapter 10.
4. *Reporter*, 12 May 1953.
5. *U.S. News and World Report*, 10 April 1953.

complaint before the United Nations, accusing the Formosan government of 'bare-faced aggression against the Union of Burma'. The Burmese were worried not so much by the presence on their soil of Chinese Nationalist troops as by the massive aid being received by them from the United States and Formosa. Moreover they feared that the activities of the Chinese Nationalists would ultimately provoke a retort from Peking and that Burma would become the scene of a second Korean War.

On 22 April 1953 the United Nations General Assembly censured the presence of K.M.T. troops in Burma and ordered them to lay down their arms and leave the country. Under the terms of an agreement concluded in Bangkok between representatives of Thailand, the United States, Formosa and Burma, two thousand K.M.T. soldiers were to be evacuated to Formosa in October 1953 by the Chinese Nationalist company, Civil Air Transport.[6] In fact the men in K.M.T. uniform who climbed aboard the aircraft bound for Formosa were local tribesmen, and the weapons they carried were museum pieces. All the modern equipment remained on the spot.

Enraged by this setback, the Burmese government launched a violent assault on the K.M.T. at the beginning of 1954. Mong Hsat was bombed and two thousand Nationalist troops were forcibly escorted to the Thai frontier. Yielding to international pressure and that of the Burmese army, Formosa agreed to repatriate 5,328 soldiers and 1,142 members of their families. There now remained some six thousand K.M.T. troops in the Shan States, but Rangoon alleges that reinforcements were subsequently sent in from Formosa. In addition the K.M.T. was recruiting among the indigenous tribes. By 1960 its strength had risen to ten thousand. Their patience exhausted, the Burmese embarked on a joint operation with the Chinese army in 1961. Though this was strenuously denied by U Nu, the Prime Minister, the Red Army is believed to have sent 10,600 men into Burmese territory. Whatever the case, its troops

6. The forerunner of Air America, a charter company operating for the C.I.A. in Laos.

96

undoubtedly sealed off the Yunnan border to prevent the K.M.T. from retreating into China.[7]

The operation drove large numbers of the K.M.T. to take refuge in Laos and Thailand. Most of them ended up in the Thai portion of the Golden Triangle, leaving behind in their camps a large quantity of arms and equipment of American origin. When these came to light Burma lodged a note of protest with the United Nations. Washington denied all responsibility for the consignments. For her part, Formosa agreed to repatriate a further contingent of Nationalist soldiers, officially disassociating herself with any who refused to comply. By the end of 1961 the six thousand or so K.M.T. men who had decided to remain in the Golden Triangle were no longer, at least in theory, receiving any aid, either from Formosa or from the C.I.A. This interlude was short-lived. The course of the Second Indo-China War was to provide these forsaken soldiers with a chance of resuming their trade.

The Chinese Nationalists in north Thailand are divided into three distinct groups. The 'Fifth Army' is commanded by General Tuan Shi Wen, more familiarly known as Lo Tuan or 'the old Tuan'. He is, in fact, a very old man. His headquarters are in Mae Salong, a village perched on a mountain top and surrounded by dense jungle. His force consists of some two thousand men. The 'Third Army', fifteen hundred strong and commanded by General Li Wen Huan, is based at Tam Ngop to the west of Chiang Mai, in extremely wild country. While the nucleus of both armies consists of Chinese ex-officers, the main body of the troops has been recruited locally among the Meos, Lahus, Lissus, Yaos and Shans. At the beginning of 1972 these two formations, hitherto at loggerheads, amalgamated under the command of General Tuan Shi Wen. A third, much smaller, group has its headquarters at Fang near the Burmese frontier. This is the 'First Independent Unit', a well-equipped force of four hundred men commanded by General Ma Ching Ko.

Having arrived in Thailand in complete disarray, the Chinese

7. *Birmanie*, Claude Moisy, Ed. Rencontre, *Atlas des voyages*.

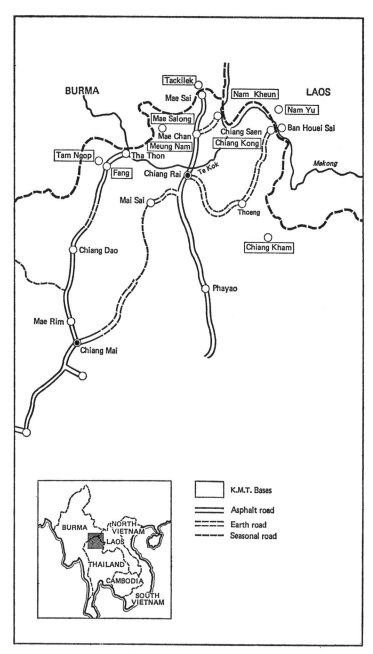

K.M.T. settlements in Thailand

Nationalists went through some difficult months in their new country of adoption. As a Chinese journalist put it in a Bangkok newspaper: 'Formosan aid had been completely cut off. The K.M.T. soldiers did not have enough land to produce even half the rice they needed. They were clothed in rags.'[8]

Abandoned by Formosa and the United States, the K.M.T. had to find some means of livelihood. They continued to traffic in opium as they had previously done in Burma, but on a very much larger scale. Before the arrival of the Chinese Nationalists in the Shan States – the 'opium storehouse' of Burma – Burmese opium was already finding its way to Thailand, but only in very modest quantities. The product was collected from the tribes by Haw, Burmese and Thai merchants, or by Shan rebels who conveyed it in small lots to the Golden Triangle. There it was sold to Chinese merchants whose families had been established in the region for many generations. But it was not until the arrival in Burma of the K.M.T. with its military organization that trade really began to flourish. The Chinese Nationalists found an accomplice in the person of General Phao, Chief of the Thai Police from 1951 to 1957, and the C.I.A's man in Thailand. From then on, opium was dispatched in large quantities to Chiang Mai and Bangkok. Meanwhile the K.M.T. was promoting poppy cultivation in the Shan States. When the main body of the Nationalist troops was compelled to flee to Thailand, the stage was set for the continuation if not the expansion of their activities there. They had maintained their contacts with local opium buyers in Burma. Moreover not all the Chinese Nationalists had left Burmese territory and some who had fled subsequently returned. Today there are perhaps three thousand of them living north of Tachilek. Thus the K.M.T. units in Thailand had at their disposal all the necessary intermediaries through whom to continue obtaining supplies in Burma. Since its troops controlled some forty kilometres of the Thai–Burmese frontier, the K.M.T. had little difficulty

8. C. C. Cheng, 'Northern Border Area', *The Bangkok World*, 7 November 1967.

in securing the lion's share of the traffic. It was also in collusion with highly placed personages in Bangkok whose cooperation was essential if the goods were to be passed on to other southeast Asian countries. These connections also explain the comparative ease with which the K.M.T. managed to establish itself in Thailand after its expulsion from Burma.

According to the American Bureau of Narcotics, the K.M.T. had gained control of eighty per cent of the opium traffic in the Golden Triangle by March 1972. The K.M.T. troops based in Thailand themselves go to Burma to fetch the opium. They do not buy direct from the growers but from Chinese Nationalists who have remained in the country or else from Shan rebels with whom they have agreements. Thus General Tuan Shi Wen's Fifth Army is associated with eleven groups in the Shan States, and the Third Army with seven others.[9]

Again, the Chinese irregulars take advantage of their position on the frontier to demand a levy from all competitors' caravans crossing their territory. In return they offer protection against attack, whether by rival traffickers, the Burmese army or the border patrols of the Thai police.

But the law enforcement squads, both Thai and Burmese, often prefer to keep their eyes shut in return for a few dollars per kilogramme of opium, rather than join battle with the Chinese Nationalists. Not always, however. On several occasions the K.M.T. has had brushes, not only with the Burmese Army, but also with elements of the Shan Liberation Army, and even with Chinese Nationalists across the border. For instance, in 1969 troops of Tuan Shi Wen's Fifth Army clashed with a band of Chinese operating in Burma. The latter had previously levied five Indian rupees per *joy* (1·6 kg.) of opium on the general's caravans passing through their territory, but had now decided unilaterally to increase the rate.

In July 1967 the Golden Triangle was the scene of a small-scale opium war. Chang Chi Foo, an independent trader of part-Shan, part-Chinese extraction, had become too powerful for the comfort of the K.M.T. which felt that its virtual

9. See Chapter 10.

monopoly was threatened. Worse still, he had concluded an agreement with no less a person than General Ouane Rattikone, Commander-in-Chief of the Laotian Armed Forces, whereby he was to make a very large delivery of opium to a heroin refinery under the general's protection at Ban Khwan on the Burmese–Laotian border. Chang Chi Foo announced his intention of crossing Chinese Nationalist territory in Burma without paying the customary levy. For its part the K.M.T. was unanimous in its determination to discourage such a dangerous precedent, and Chang Chi Foo was marked down for destruction. An ambush was laid by eight hundred Chinese Nationalists. This he successfully evaded and, having crossed the Mekong, arrived at Ban Khwan where he and his men took up defensive positions round a sawmill. When his pursuers arrived on the scene both sides opened up with mortars. But they were not allowed to fight to a finish. General Ouane Rattikone, outraged by the turn events had taken, dispatched five T28 aircraft which proceeded to bomb the two adversaries indiscriminately, leaving nearly two hundred dead on the field of battle. Chang Chi Foo and his men, who were fighting with their backs to the river, succeeded in recrossing the Mekong and reaching Burma. The opium, however, had to be abandoned. The surviving Chinese irregulars tried to escape by way of north Laos, but they were surrounded and captured by Laotian infantry. After a fortnight of negotiations the K.M.T. troops were permitted to return to Thailand, but not until they had paid General Ouane Rattikone a fine of eight thousand dollars. In all fairness to the Commander-in-Chief of the Laotian Army, be it said that this sum was shared out among the men who had captured the Chinese Nationalists. But the opium that had been abandoned in the sawmill at Ban Khwan – nearly half a million dollars' worth – was appropriated by the general himself.

This episode, despite the serious losses suffered by the K.M.T., finally assured its supremacy in the opium traffic. Chang Chi Foo, the main loser, could no longer hope to compete. Today the Shan rebel armies and the independent traffickers still buy opium from the tribes in the parts of Burma under their control, but they resell it to the K.M.T. which has a monopoly of outlets in Thailand.[10] In exchange the Chinese sell contraband weapons, more especially to the Shan rebels who use them in their fight against the Central Government. The K.M.T's only serious competitors are now the 'self-defence forces' (K.K.Y.), bands of mercenaries employed by Rangoon to contain the Shan rebellion.[11] The K.K.Y. also work on their own account — sometimes, it would seem, with the active connivance of the Thai Border Patrols.

At Kilometre 19, beyond Mae Chan on the asphalt road between Chiang Rai and Mae Sai, an unmade track branches off into the hills, hugging the contours for seven kilometres until it reaches a peaceful valley. At the head of the valley is a large village, Ban Huai Krai, inhabited by Haw traders and the families of soldiers serving with the Chinese irregulars. As we approached this village we saw a party of men loading heavy packages on to twenty or so mules. The operation was being supervised by soldiers in bush hats and olive-green uniforms. Dangling from their shoulders were M16s, the modern American combat rifle. A caravan was about to leave for Mae Salong, a day and a half's march across the mountains.

The man we had come to see was called Li Kwei Mei. He was a Lahu who had served with the K.M.T. and had then gone back to farming. His son Li Mi Kwa, aged 28, had until quite recently been working for the K.M.T. whose service he had left on buying some land. But he still carried out liaison duties between the Fifth Army's civil and military villages and it was he who was to be our guide on our expedition to Mae Salong. Li Mi Kwa spoke Chinese and Thai and had a reasonable command of English. We spent the night in his cool, spacious bamboo house before beginning our journey. On the wall hung a large portrait of Generalissimo Chiang Kai-shek, flanked by photographs of the Thai royal family and Sun Yat-sen, founder

10. The K.M.T. refuses to allow its competitors into Thailand if their caravans are beyond a certain size.
11. See Chapter 10.

of the Chinese Republic. Smoking a big Yunnanese bamboo pipe, Li Mi Kwa explained for our benefit how matters stood, every now and then turning to his father for confirmation.

'In the past, the K.M.T. was openly helped by Formosa. After large numbers of soldiers had been repatriated to Nationalist China, Generals Li Wen Huan and Tuan Shi Wen remustered two armies, the Third and the Fifth, and brought them up to strength by recruiting Lahus, Was and Shans. There is also a First, independent, Army which sends intelligence reports to the Thais, the Chinese in Formosa, the Americans and SEATO. Its missions take it across Burmese territory and may sometimes even involve sending agents into Yunnan. On the return journey it goes opium buying. Until recently it was the only army still engaging in political activity. The Third and Fifth did nothing but fetch opium from Burma and return with it to Thailand. Since 1969 increasing guerrilla activity in the north-east has led the Thais – at the instigation of their American advisers – to recruit Chinese irregulars from all these armies to fight the communist rebels.'

We asked him why he had decided to leave the K.M.T.

'The K.M.T. is an army of mercenaries,' [he replied]. 'At one time there were eight thousand of us. But a lot deserted because the pay was so bad. And that's why I left myself. They gave us rice, uniforms and twenty *baths* – a dollar – a month. Sometimes, after we'd been on the march for weeks escorting an opium caravan on its way back from Burma, they would hand out a kilo of opium to each man. Some kept it to smoke, others sold it. The rank and file are discontented. They often mutiny against their officers, or else desert. The generals and other officers are all very rich and they despise their men. It's they who pocket the takings from the opium traffic, while the troops get nothing or hardly anything. All the same, the K.M.T. never has any recruiting problems. If local tribesmen want to leave their villages where the life is very hard, they have no option but to enlist in the Chinese Nationalist armies. Soldiers of Chinese extraction can do nothing except stay in the K.M.T. For under Thai law the Chinese are not permitted to buy land. But the government sometimes makes an exception for men who have belonged to the K.M.T. So it's in their interest to put in a certain number of years' service if they aim at settling in Thailand for good.'

We asked him about the chances of visiting Fifth Army headquarters. 'You want to go to Mae Salong?' he asked. 'I'll do what I can to help you, but I very much doubt you'll get there. Mae Salong is one of the bases for the counter-guerrilla operations entrusted to the K.M.T. They don't let "Farangs"[12] in.'

He failed to mention another reason for the ban on foreigners. The village contains one of the more important refineries in the Golden Triangle. A confidential report issued by the C.I.A. in 1971 alleged that the largest refineries capable of producing heroin no. 4 were situated near Tachilek in Burma, at Ban Houei Sai and Nam Kheun in Laos, and at Mae Salong in Thailand. When interviewed in Washington in June 1972, an official of the B.N.D.D's Strategic Intelligence Office confirmed that a refinery had been in operation at Mae Salong. When we asked him why none of the laboratories mentioned in the C.I.A. report had been seized, he replied:

'As a counter-measure to the international law enforcement offensive launched in 1971, the refineries operating on Thai territory were moved to the interior of Burma. They are now grouped around Tachilek and are producing heroin, and also morphine for the Hong Kong market. Unfortunately we are powerless to act in Burma.'

This confirmed much of what Li Mi Kwa told us. 'Just now there are forty tons of opium stored in a godown I know near Tachilek,' he said. 'There are also three fortified camps belonging to the K.M.T. which are closed to everyone except officers. They are guarded all the time, and might possibly be refineries.' However he denied all knowledge of any such installations at Mae Salong. 'Anyway, you'll be able to see for yourselves – that is if they let you in,' he added with a knowing smile.

Paleu is a hamlet commanding the approach to Mae Salong. Getting there means a four-hour journey along a mountain road in the heavy truck which, twice a week, brings in provisions. Sacks of rice, chickens and pigs are piled in with the passengers – Chinese soldiers, Lahus and Meos. On steep gradients everybody has to get out. At Paleu the road is no

12. Term used in Thailand to designate whites or foreigners.

longer fit for motor vehicles. To get from there to Mae Salong takes four hours by mule or six on foot. Just outside Paleu there is a small military post manned by Thais. It was set up by the government in 1968 so that an eye could be kept on the doings of the K.M.T. The Thai soldiers, smoking and drinking Pepsi-Cola, showed no interest in our arrival.

The village, however, immediately sprang to life. Soldiers in motley uniforms hurried towards us to unload the truck. The sacks and bales were transferred to waiting mules which stood pawing the red earth. Since nothing is produced in Mae Salong itself, all provisions have to be brought in from Mae Sai or Chiang Rai to support the population of ten thousand, made up of some two thousand soldiers and their families and the few Haw traders who keep shop there. A kilo of rice bought for 30 *baths* (60p) in the plains is worth 45 (84p) by the time it arrives at Mae Salong.

Another post, this time manned by Chinese Nationalists, commands the entrance to the track leading to Mae Salong. We asked to see the commander of the garrison so as to obtain permission to proceed. Captain Tek Huehai, a man in his forties, clad in U.S. Army surplus trousers and a black shirt, was polite, but far from helpful. 'I can't let you through without authorization from my superiors,' he said. 'Those are my orders. Before I can allow foreigners into Mae Salong, I have to have letter from Yang Kho Kwang, the Chinese officer responsible for liaison between the K.M.T. and the Thai authorities at Mae Sai.' We asked him whether the Chinese were the responsible authority on this part of Thai territory. Smiling as ever, he replied: 'Yes, seeing that I am now stopping you from getting through.'

We returned to Mae Sai, a day's journey. Major Yang Kho Kwang, until 1965 in command of 150 Chinese irregulars in Burma, had grown rich on opium. In Mae Sai he owned a large, well-sited shop, the 'King Le' selling piece-goods. The establishment was run by his very beautiful Lahu wife. As we had anticipated, Major Yang Kho Kwang evaded our request by taking refuge behind his superiors. During our journey we had learnt that the major had a direct radio link with Mae Salong.

Taken aback by this display of inside knowledge, he agreed with bad grace to send a message on our behalf to General Tuan Shi Wen. Some hours later we were handed the expected reply. 'I will gladly authorize the *Farangs* to come to Mae Salong if they obtain prior authorization from the Thai authorities. They should address their request to the Governor of Chiang Rai.'

The intention was obvious. We were to be referred from one authority to the next without ever actually being presented with an out-and-out refusal. We knew now that we would not be allowed to visit Mae Salong. But we decided to go on trying in order to find out more about the relations between the K.M.T. and the Thai authorities.

The Governor of Chiang Rai received us amiably enough, but the smile vanished from his face when we told him the reason for our visit. With the Thais' inimitable gift for dodging awkward questions, he at once prevaricated. 'I don't know either this Major Yang Kho Kwang or this General Tuan you've been talking about,' he said, without batting an eyelid. 'Anyway, why do you want to go to Mae Salong? There's nothing to see there.'

'Then perhaps you would be so kind,' we said, 'as to issue us with a pass permitting us to go anywhere in your province so that, in case of arrest, we could invoke the liberal attitude of the Thai authorities towards freedom of movement in their country.'

The Governor looked more and more ill at ease. Finally he declared: 'Mae Salong is an area under military control. I am not empowered to authorize you to go there. You'll have to get a permit from the general commanding the Chiang Kong military district.'

1968 marked the beginning of the Thai government's large-scale operations against the Meo rebels, known in Thailand as the 'Red Meos'.

In September of that year the inhabitants of a Meo village made what was apparently an unprovoked attack on a Thai notable in the Pâ Wâi district; they also seized some land to

106

the north and south of the Phitsanulock–Lomsak road. In reprisal the Royal Thai Air Force dropped napalm on a number of villages. The terror-stricken Meos fled into the jungle, leaving in their wake innumerable bamboo traps of the kind used in the fifties by the Viet Minh against the French. They also poisoned wells and rivers. According to Air Marshal Dawee Chullasapya, Deputy Defence Minister, the Pathet Lao had been sending arms to the rebels by helicopter. Thereafter hardly a week went by without news of skirmishes in north Thailand.

In 1970 the Thai authorities began to make use of Chinese irregulars against the Red Meos. The K.M.T. units, which had given ample proof of their militant anti-communism, were well-versed in jungle operations, a form of warfare they had been practising for over twenty years. The same applied to the men recruited among the tribal minorities. Another advantage accruing to the Thais from the use of K.M.T. troops was the fact that it cost them nothing since the irregulars supported themselves by trafficking in opium. As for the Chinese Nationalists, they were only too pleased to be of service to the Thai government so long as they were permitted to remain in Thailand and continue their trading unmolested.

This relationship, however, underwent a change as the Thais came to rely to an ever increasing extent on the K.M.T. From 1971 onwards they supplied it with rice, arms and new uniforms, as we were able to see for ourselves at the Chinese base near Fang. Before long they also began to pay the irregulars. At the same time operations against the Meos have led to a considerable expansion of the K.M.T's sphere of influence. While its main bases are still at Fang, Tam Ngop and Mae Salong, strong detachments are stationed more or less permanently south-east of Chiang-Khong and Chiang Kham, a major trouble-spot. In that district, where clashes with the Red Meos are frequent, the irregulars are organized into flying columns, able to move instantly to the scene of action.

A glance at the disposition of the Chinese civilian villages and military camps in Thailand reveals that they are situated along the whole length of the frontier, from Burma in the west

107

to Laos in the east. But Chinese irregulars are also to be found on the Laotian side of the Golden Triangle, notably at Nam Kheun, a small village on the Mekong, where we lunched with two Chinese officers on the occasion of the Laotian New Year. They told us that they commanded a unit of two hundred men, permanently stationed in the vicinity of Nam Kheun. Their existence is, of course, denied by the Laotian authorities.

Curiously enough the constant extension of the zones under K.M.T. 'protection', far from containing the rebellion, has helped to spread it. This is because the Chinese Nationalists, at the same time as fighting the Red Meos, also pursue their own private ends. While ostensibly helping the government to prevent communist infiltration from Laos, they seek to occupy Meo territory. For when a Chinese soldier has grown too old to fight, his one ambition is to acquire a piece of land on which to farm. Since this is forbidden under Thai law, the usual procedure is to present the authorities with a *fait accompli.* Having forcibly evicted the Meos, the K.M.T. installs its ex-soldiers on the land as rice or opium cultivators.[13] The expropriated Meos become rebels, thus justifying both the K.M.T's action and its persecution of the 'Reds'. At the beginning of 1971, for instance, serious fighting broke out between the Chinese irregulars and the Meos in the Chiang Saen district, the disputed territory being the Doi Luang Hills. The Meos were driven out and today the land is cultivated by former soldiers of the K.M.T. As a rule the Thai authorities overlook such expropriations, if only because of the extent to which they rely on the services of the Chinese Nationalists for the conduct of military operations in the jungle regions of the north-north-east and for the protection of the frontier with Burma. An informant who had lived in the district for many years assured us that these 'annexations' were made with the tacit consent of the Thai authorities, the

13. In Thailand all land above the thousand metre level belongs to the king who places it at the disposal of the tribes. Hence the latter are not the actual owners of the land, nor would they wish to be since their nomadic habits are incompatible with private ownership. The Chinese circumvent Thai law, which forbids them to purchase land, by expelling the tribes and introducing a settled form of agriculture.

inference being that, if the K.M.T. wanted land so badly, it was up to them to evict the Meos.

From somewhat haphazard beginnings in 1969, collaboration between Thais and Chinese Nationalists had been placed on a more or less regular footing by the early months of 1972. Moreover these two parties were not the only ones involved; both Formosa and the ubiquitous C.I.A. also had a finger in the pie.

There has never been any real interruption of relations between Formosa and the Chinese irregulars, even though after 1961 shipments of arms and equipment were drastically reduced. The First Independent Army, with its base at Fang, continued to function on behalf of Formosa's intelligence services, while Nationalist China maintained an official representative at Chiang Mai to carry out consular duties. In recent years links between Formosa and the K.M.T. have become increasingly close. At Mae Salong there is a Chinese school staffed exclusively with teachers from Formosa. Among the thousand or more pupils are boys from places as far away as Bangkok and the Kengtung district of Burma. The K.M.T's new recruits include not only local tribesmen but also young Chinese. Since the latter speak Mandarin and not the Yunnanese dialect, they can only be assumed to have come from Formosa.

A high-ranking Thai officer who, for obvious reasons, wishes to remain anonymous, told us that in 1971 an airstrip for the reception of Caribou freight planes had been constructed in the mountains round Mae Salong. The cases brought in by these aircraft come from Formosa and contain Belgian rifles and standard NATO weapons. From the same source we learned that at the beginning of 1972, two American civilians had been present in the camp at Mae Salong. Yet at the United States Embassy in Bangkok, where they are highly evasive on the subject of the K.M.T., we were told by one of the advisers that American citizens were strictly prohibited from visiting districts under Chinese Nationalist control. Oddly enough, the presence of the two Americans at Mae Salong coincided with the arrival at Fifth Army headquarters of a delegation of Formosan secret service representatives accompanied by Air Marshal

Dawee Chullasapya, Deputy Defence Minister and prominent member of the National Executive Council, the military junta by which Thailand is ruled. The Air Marshal is also a distant cousin of Thanom Kittikachorn, the Thai army's Chief of Staff, and an intimate friend of General Praphas Charusathien, Minister of the Interior. Our military informant stated categorically that the purpose of the quadripartite discussions at Mae Salong had been to agree the nature of the part to be played by the K.M.T. leaders in future counter-guerrilla operations. Briefly, this was to be identical to the role played in Laos, under C.I.A. supervision, by General Vang Pao's secret Meo army.[14] The foregoing information would seem to be corroborated by, among other things, the amalgamation of the K.M.T. forces under the sole command of General Tuan Shi Wen, the support provided by Formosa in the shape of arms and reinforcements, the growing importance of the part played by the Chinese Nationalists in the repression of the Red Meos and, lastly, the deployment of the K.M.T. along the Burmese and Laotian borders.

There is every probability that opium was among the subjects discussed during the meetings at Mae Salong. Ever since the middle of 1971 Thailand has been repeatedly accused by American Congressmen of being an entrepôt for heroin destined for the United States. In a joint report submitted in May 1971 to the Congressional Foreign Affairs Committee,[15] Morgan M. Murphy (Democrat) and Robert H. Steele (Republican) wrote that from the American point of view Thailand is as important as Turkey to the control of the illicit drugs traffic. Even if all the opium of south-east Asia is not produced there, the greater part is brought out through Thailand. Murphy and Steele concluded that the United States can and should exert pressure on the governments of south-east Asia to obtain their cooperation in the battle against heroin. As they pointed out, the survival of Laos and South Vietnam depended on American economic and military aid, and Thailand's defence capacity would be seri-

14. See Chapter 8.
15. *The World Heroin Problem.* Report of special study mission by Morgan M. Murphy and Robert H. Steele. U.S Government Printing Office, Washington, 1971.

110

ously weakened with the withdrawal of U.S. military support.

In March 1972, Lester Wolff, a Democratic Representative, set the cat among the pigeons by announcing that he knew, 'not only the names of the twelve trawlers carrying opium and heroin from Bangkok to Hong Kong, but also those of leading personalities who were protecting the traffic'. He declared that he would not divulge them for fear of embarrassing the United States government, but was prepared to do so should the Thai authorities fail to take vigorous action. In June 1972 the three Congressmen persuaded the Foreign Affairs Committee to submit an amendment to the law on foreign aid, which would provide for a drastic reduction in the credits granted each year by the United States to Thailand, 'unless that country gives proof of having taken effective measures to put an end to the traffic in opium and heroin in its territory'.

This amendment, which had to be submitted to both Houses of Congress, had small chance of being voted before the presidential election in November 1972. Nevertheless it served as a sharp warning to Bangkok. But the Thais had already provided a token of their good faith. On 7 March 1972 twenty-six tons of opium, valued at over forty-seven million dollars on the American market, were publicly burned in north Thailand. According to the official handout, reproduced in the *Bangkok World*, this measure was part of an action programme aimed at discouraging the production and sale of opium in Thailand. The article went on to say that the opium had been bought from the tribes of the Chiang Mai and Chiang Rai districts in exchange for land, seed and livestock.

In fact it soon became generally known that this opium had been bought from the K.M.T. Mr Warner, chief of the B.N.D.D. Intelligence Office, told us during a conversation in Washington in June 1972:

'The Chinese irregulars clinched a first-class deal when they sold those twenty-six tons of opium to the Thais. In fact the speed at which the American combat troops were being repatriated from Vietnam had sent the price of heroin in south-east Asia plummeting. We believe that the K.M.T. has huge reserves of opium in the Tachilek region of Burma, perhaps as much as a thousand tons.

111

Quite obviously the Thai government would never buy that sort of quantity. But the show they put on in March enabled them to please the Americans at little cost to themselves.'

There is, of course, no question of the Thais being powerless to proceed against the Chinese Nationalists should they really want to put a stop to the traffic in narcotics in their country. But there are too many interests at stake. Nothing short of force would induce the K.M.T. to abandon a trade which brings in such immense profits. But the Thais cannot suppress the K.M.T. if they are to use it against the guerrillas, nor would they be anxious to do so in view of the fact that the Chinese officers are not alone in benefiting from the traffic. A number of highly placed Thais also have a hand in this lucrative business, as have their counterparts in Laos and Vietnam. A secret report prepared jointly by the C.I.A., the State Department and the Defense Department in February 1972 concluded that,

the gravest problem and one which unfortunately would appear to admit of no solution in the foreseeable future, is that of growing corruption within the governments of south-east Asia, particularly in Vietnam and Thailand, and of the indifference they display towards the traffic in drugs.

The same theme is echoed by the report laid before Congress by Murphy and Steele which alleged that Government and Army personnel were involved at all levels. At much the same time as General Praphas, Minister of the Interior, was being slated on American television, similar accusations made by a Thai journalist, Prasong Charasdamrong, went unchallenged, when he wrote:

The weak point in Thailand's plan of campaign against narcotics lies in the police themselves. In this country there are no police officers honest or conscientious enough to refuse a bribe or a sweetener. The agents of the Thai Bureau of Narcotics are usually better paid by the traffickers to keep their mouths shut than they are by the government to catch the traffickers.[16]

Thus the entire system is involved in the opium traffic and a major political upheaval would be needed to put an end to

16. *Bangkok World*, March 1972.

this state of affairs. Clearly such an eventuality must be discounted, as must any reduction in the military aid accorded to Bangkok. If Washington has to choose between two evils, the lesser will still be heroin. In June 1972 we were told by a disillusioned Lester Wolff: 'The United States government won't take the necessary steps against Thailand because of the strategic importance to us of this south-east Asian country.'

Since they are precluded for political reasons from grappling either with the producers of opium or with the actual organizers of the traffic in Thailand, the Americans have had to fall back on law enforcement measures whose main victim will be in effect the smaller middleman. The towns of Chiang Mai and Lampang, which straddle the routes leading from the production areas, have been selected as the principal centres for the operation. Check posts have also been set up at Fang and Mae Sai. In August 1971 an agreement was concluded between the Thai government and the United States aimed at improving collaboration between the police forces of the two countries. The Americans have provided the Thais with vehicles, two-way radios and modern weapons, while the B.N.D.D., which has ample funds at its disposal, has introduced a new scale of rewards for informers. By offering sums of ten thousand dollars or more in exchange for information, they hope to arouse sufficient cupidity in trafficking circles to disrupt at least the minor networks. Such a step can only be marginally effective, however. It is common knowledge that, even with a large and conscientious police force, there is little chance of keeping track of a consignment of opium once it has left the hands of the grower or crossed the frontier. But the Thai police force possesses only 420 officers with specialized training in narcotics. According to a B.N.D.D. agent working in Thailand, eight to ten thousand men would be needed to obtain worthwhile results. In addition steps would have to be taken to stamp out the widespread corruption prevailing in that country.

We were told by a diplomat that large consignments of opium are often intercepted as a result of collusion between police and traffickers. Acting as an 'informer', the trafficker tells his police accomplice when to expect his truck. The officer then seizes the opium and himself forwards it to the buyer in Bangkok, after

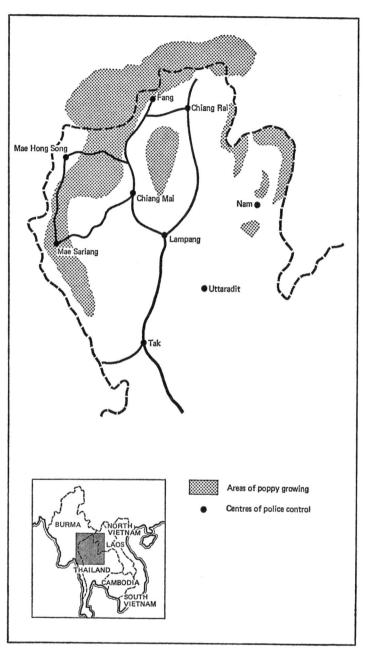

Police control and areas of poppy cultivation in Thailand

which the two accomplices share out the spoils, including the B.N.D.D's reward.

Opium and heroin trafficking will never be stamped out in Thailand simply by pouring money into an enterprise directed solely against the small trader. Most of the raw and refined opium shipped from Bangkok originates in Burma and its arrival in Thailand in such massive quantities depends wholly on the 'conveyor belt' operated by the K.M.T. which, as we have seen, is above the law. The situation is much the same in Laos which is becoming an increasingly important centre for the conversion and export of heroin, though its opium production continues to decline.

8   Laos: the Dwindling Kingdom

'Opium has never brought riches to the tribes who cultivate it in Laos,' we were told by Touby Ly Fong, chief of a large Meo tribe, as he sipped a glass of *nam châ*, the Laotian green tea.

'The poppy is a difficult crop. It only does well on very rich soil. Under favourable conditions and if all goes well, a family can harvest more than five or six kilos of opium a year. That will give them an annual income of two hundred to two hundred and fifty dollars.'

A rotund man with a jovial smile and a ready sense of humour, Ly Fong is extremely likeable. He excels at avoiding awkward questions and disconcerting logically-minded Europeans with his verbal acrobatics. He knows what he is talking about. As the head of a tribe of poppy-growers, he had worked for the French Opium Administration (Régie de l'opium, familiarly known as the RO), between 1939 and 1945.

'Before the war [he went on], 'the French government bought opium in Afghanistan and India, and warehoused it at Hanoi. During the war, when they could no longer import it, they encouraged local poppy-growing so that the Chinese, Vietnamese and French smokers in the colony could still get their supplies. The Laotians themselves have never smoked much. The crop was grown mainly by Meo tribes and the Yaos, and to some extent by the Lahus and Lissus. The chief growing areas were the provinces of Phong Saly, Sam Neua, Xieng Khouang, Luang Prabang and the Ban Houei Sai district. Opium from Xieng Khouang and Sam Neua was especially prized. It only had a seven per cent morphine content but according to those who smoked it the flavour was excellent.

'At that time we didn't have all the medicines we have today. Opium was the cure for stomach trouble, dysentery, lung complaints and toothache. Old men often used it to keep themselves going. Anyone over fifty who didn't smoke opium was racked with pain and riddled with disease.

116

'In each province the French set up buying offices where the opium was brought. But first they tried to deal direct with the producers, which didn't work out. They couldn't pay the producers until they knew the morphine content of their opium, and analyses took several weeks. The unfortunate growers were so poor they couldn't wait that long. So the French had to use middlemen, usually Chinese merchants who had some capital and were able to advance money. There were also Vietnamese, Laos and a few Meos who had grown rich. These "brokers" paid for the crop in cash, making sure that there was a handsome margin between the price they paid the peasants and the price they received from the French authorities. They paid the growers in silver bullion from the Bank of Indo-China or else with goods of various kinds, costed on the full price. So they made a double profit. Those were the people who grew rich on opium for, believe me, the Meos were well and truly exploited! Some of those merchants would deliver up to a ton and a half a time to the buying office, and they made a real packet.

'On average the French bought forty tons of opium a year. But now that our best poppy fields in the provinces of Phong Saly and Sam Neua are occupied by the Pathet Lao and the North Vietnamese, I'm pretty certain that not more than a ton a year is produced in Laos.'

If Touby Ly Fong is to be believed, this steep fall in production is not solely attributable to the fact that the communist-nationalist insurrection, represented by the Pathet Lao, extends over three quarters of Laotian territory and affects one third of the population. 'The traditional growers,' he explained, 'who live in the part of the country still controlled by the Royal Laotian Army, have come to see that opium is not a paying proposition.'

We heard the same story from General Vang Pao, the famous commander of the Meo mercenary army. The general's domain is the base at Long Cheng in the Plain of Jars, from which the C.I.A. runs the 'secret war' now being waged in Laos.

Vang Pao is a difficult man to get hold of. His headquarters, which he rarely leaves, is virtually barred to journalists. We were able to catch him at about six o'clock in the morning, just as he was leaving for Long Cheng, having spent the night at home with his family in Vientiane. After he had got over his

117

initial surprise he granted us a ten-minute interview. But once embarked on the subject of opium, in which he is more than a little interested, he became so animated that he went on talking for an hour and a half. A very short, robust man, his fingers laden with gold rings and wearing on his left wrist a gold chain weighing at least three hundred grammes, he bears little resemblance to the image of the powerful general conjured up by the Laotian press. Yet it was he who raised the only Laotian army corps on which the Americans could really count to stem the advance of the Pathet Lao. His jet-black hair is carefully brushed back, leaving forehead and temples exposed. His small, slanting eyes are keen and constantly on the move.

The General has no inhibitions about using earthy turns of speech, picked up, no doubt, during his early days in French barrack rooms.

'We're not afraid of opium, not like the Americans, who dread it like a dose of clap' [he told us by way of a preamble]. 'If their troops are poisoning themselves with heroin, the people to blame are the Saigon bar girls who want to relieve them of their money, not the opium growers here in this country. Anyway Laotians don't smoke much, except when they've caught the habit from visiting hippies.'

Having delivered himself of these definitive pronouncements on the mysteries of drug addiction, General Vang Pao went on to propound the view that the Meos had virtually ceased to produce opium in Laos:

'Opium is a difficult crop and needs a lot of work and attention — ten times as much as rice, for example.[1] It will only flourish at a certain altitude and in very hilly country covered with virgin forest. First the peasants have to burn a few hectares of forest, then grub out the stumps or else chop the trunks level with the ground. That means three months of hard work. Next they put in maize. Then the ground has to be weeded three times and finally turned with a mattock before the poppy can be sown. When it is so high' [here he indicated his knee], 'it has to be thinned so that the plants don't grow too close together. Harvesting is a very delicate operation. The

1. This is an exaggeration, but opium growing undoubtedly calls for cheap and abundant labour.

118

opium has to be gathered from each poppy-head – hour after hour. And all this just to produce two to six kilos per family. I speak from experience. My father was an opium grower. In 1942, when I was thirteen, I advised him to give it up. We were being swindled by the Chinese traders who used to charge us twelve thousand *kips* for pieces of cloth worth barely three thousand. We were twenty-two in our family – nothing out of the way by Meo standards – and my father couldn't earn enough from opium to feed us all. We were then living at Bag Ban near Long Het on Highway 7. The Vietnamese merchants were looking for livestock. We started to raise pigs and chickens and, later, cattle. In 1943 we managed to sell forty-five bullocks and that was the first time we ever had any money. We were happy. A new life seemed to lie ahead of us. Today most of the Meos have got the message. They grow rice and maize and raise cattle. But they don't want to live off opium any more. In fact they hardly ever grow it now.'

Needless to say neither Touby Ly Fong nor General Vang Pao should be taken too literally. Both have an interest in minimizing the amount of opium produced in Laos for they have been accused more than once, not only of involvement in the traffic, but of being its main beneficiaries. Moreover their tribal solidarity has been further strengthened by family ties since May Ko, Touby Ly Fong's daughter, is married to Vang Pao's eldest son, François. But the observations of these two Meo leaders reflect a state of affairs which too often goes unrecognized – namely that Laos is no longer a major producer of opium. For reasons attributable less to the Meos' economic insight than to the ravages of war, opium production has fallen dramatically since the mid-sixties.

No one knows exactly how much opium is being produced in Laos today, nor how many Meos, Yaos and other tribesmen are occupied in cultivating it. According to David Feingold, the American author of an essay on the subject,[2] opium production in Laos prior to the Second World War was somewhere between forty and a hundred tons a year. Most of it was bought by the French Opium Administration, the rest being sold on the

---

2. 'Opium and Politics in Laos', in *Laos: War and Revolution*, New York, Harper & Row, 1970.

side. Some five years after the end of the war, output was estimated at sixty-five tons a year and in 1964, according to United Nations figures, it was somewhere between eighty and a hundred and fifty tons. This tallies with the information we obtained locally, or were given by French, American and other experts, for the years preceding 1965. From the same sources we learnt that, while never as low as Touby Ly Fong would have us believe, subsequent production did not exceed thirty tons. According to the USAID[3] representative in Vientiane, current annual output would appear to be in the region of fifteen to seventeen tons.[4]

If we are to understand why Laotian opium production has dwindled by more than eighty per cent in the space of five years we must first of all consider in what ways the secret war in Laos has affected the poppy growers.

When the Americans began bombing North Vietnam in 1965, they had already spent the previous year systematically pounding those areas in Laos which might afford shelter to the Pathet Lao. These operations have remained unavowed, if not actually secret. Under the terms of the Geneva Agreements of 1962 the small kingdom of Laos is a neutral country in whose affairs no foreign army may intervene. Officially there is no war in Laos.

At that time the Government was in control of rather less than half the country, including the Vientiane Plain, the administrative capital, the Mekong Valley, the hill country in Xieng Khouang Province and the Long Tieng and Sam Tong districts. It also controlled the towns. By 1972 this area had dwindled considerably. In 1968, thanks to General Vang Pao's 'special forces', the Royal Laotian Army, with a stiffening of American military 'advisers', had managed to hold by the skin of its teeth the famous Long Cheng base and the area immediately surrounding it. By degrees the Pathet Lao and their North Vietnamese allies occupied the whole of the north and south-east until they controlled two-thirds of the country.

3. U.S. Agency for International Development.
4. He was citing a report prepared by the C.I.A., an organization known to have very close relations with USAID.

During this period life in Laos was completely disrupted by American strategy which demanded the depopulation of all territory evacuated by the Government forces so that the enemy should not, to quote Mao Tse-tung, be 'like fish in water'. In other words, the American intention was to deny the fish their water by compelling nearly everybody to leave the areas occupied by the nationalist-communist forces, thus making it difficult for the Pathet Lao to recruit porters, soldiers and administrative personnel. Moreover if there were no peasants there could be no opportunities for trade or barter. The creation of this void was one of the reasons for the escalation of the bombing attacks on the 'unsafe zones'.

In August 1971 J. W. Fulbright, Arkansas Senator and president of a Congressional commission of inquiry into the Laos situation, reported that American air force activity had grown less in 1970 and was now at a level lower than that of the first months of 1969. Then the Americans daily carried out approximately — raids on the north of Laos and — on the south – a total of four hundred raids a day. In 1970 the United States began to use B52 bombers in the north, apparently before the regular use of these aircraft. The Royal Laotian Air Force had more than doubled its operations in the previous year. Of the total approximately — were bombing raids with T28s and — with C47s. (Fulbright's figures were censored.)[5]

According to Senator Fulbright the American authorities stationed in Vientiane told him that these operations were aimed at the destruction of the enemy's infrastructure, particularly his lines of communication, and were confined exclusively to military targets. If the civilian population had been bombed this could only have been done in error – almost certainly by the Laotian Air Force which tended to be lax in its observance of the rules governing airborne missions. These assertions do not tally with the facts. In so far as the bombing in 1964 was intended to destroy the lines of communication, prevent concentrations of troops and provide tactical support for the Laotian ground

5. *Laos: April 1971*, a staff report prepared for use of the Subcommittee on Security Agreements and Commitments Abroad. U.S. Government Printing Office, Washington, 1971.

forces, it soon proved unprofitable. For since the communist forces move by night in small parties, along tracks concealed by thick jungle, they are as difficult to locate as they are to hit.

The Pentagon strategists then thought up a new way of dealing with the enemy, namely by isolating him and depriving him of the support of the local population. Thenceforward the object of the bombing was to terrorize and demoralize that population. Such inhabitants as did not flee from the territory captured by the Pathet Lao were at once suspected of being enemy sympathizers and bombs were rained on their villages. A Meo peasant to whom we talked in the Ban Xon military hospital in Government-controlled territory, told us:

'At the beginning of 1968 I was living in the part of Sam Neua Province occupied by the Pathet Lao. I and my family left our home in 1969. Life had become impossible. For two years running we had planted rice, maize and the poppy. But every time we wanted to harvest our crops the bombers arrived and we had to take refuge in trenches. We stayed there for weeks on end without being able to go into the fields. When at last we were able to come out there was nothing left, no fields, no rice, no poppies, no village. Everything had been flattened.'

There can be no doubt about the success of this strategy. To escape the bombing, hundreds upon thousands of Laotian peasants have made their way into Government-controlled territory which now contains two-thirds of the population. Among these refugees are thousands of former opium growers. By a strange paradox the war succeeded in drastically curtailing Laotian opium production well before Washington became concerned about the problem. The American policy of depopulating certain areas, combined with the conscription of minorities into General Vang Pao's secret army, has struck a mortal blow at the poppy and those who grow it.

According to figures supplied by the Vientiane authorities, six hundred thousand people have been evacuated to, or have otherwise entered, the Government-controlled zone since the bombing began in 1964. Fred Branfman, an American field worker who has made a close study of the question, believes that the number of persons 'displaced', whether voluntarily or otherwise, must amount to a million, or more than one-third of the population of this small country.[6] But refugee status is accorded only to those whose sole means of subsistence is American economic aid. That is why USAID estimates the number of refugees in Laos at no more than three hundred thousand.

Large numbers of these indirect victims of the war come from the hill country to the north and south of the Plain of Jars. They include a great many Meos, who represent roughly ten per cent of the Laotian population. Some sixty-five thousand of them are being assisted by USAID but the actual number of Meo refugees must amount to more than a hundred thousand.

New arrivals are relocated, or better said 'corralled', in the villages of the Government zone. Their customs are completely thrown out of gear, while the life they lead is precarious and often wretched. We were told by Mr McQueen, Deputy Director of USAID's refugee service, that,

'The problem with fixing up refugees is that there's not enough land to go round. To give you an example, more than eighty thousand people have had to be concentrated in the Ban Xon district where there's barely enough land to support twenty thousand. The Meos are used to living at altitudes of over three thousand feet. They can't grow the poppy below that altitude and at less than a thousand feet the heat is too much for them. But it's precisely on the hilltops where their villages used to be that the fighting is now taking place. Besides, there isn't much hill country in the Government-controlled zone. Now that they can't produce opium, the Meos are having to change their system. They raise pigs and grow a little rice if there's enough land. If not, we supply them with food.'

The standard monthly ration for one person consists of fifteen kilogrammes of rice, half a kilogramme of salt and ten tins of protein-enriched corned beef. If the ground lends itself to the construction of a rudimentary airstrip, these supplies are brought in by cargo aircraft. Otherwise they are delivered by parachute,

6. 'Presidential War in Laos: 1964–1970', in *Laos: War and Revolution*, Harper & Row, New York, 1970.

the drops being the responsibility of Air America and Continental Air Service, two charter companies on contract to the C.I.A. and the State Department. In this way 150 tons of rice are distributed daily throughout Laos. We were able to visit some of the refugee villages whose inhabitants have been compelled by the war to live on charity. It is heart-breaking to see these Meos, famed for their courage, endurance and love of the hills, still dressed in traditional costume, hanging about idly and virtually captive in villages where the ground is littered with old tins. Around them the war goes on. Often they have to move off at a few hours' notice in the face of a sudden communist advance. If they refuse to go, it is in the certain knowledge that, within a few days or a few weeks, they will see their village flattened by American bombers. 'In 1965 we still controlled much of Sam Neua Province,' McQueen continued. 'Suddenly, in 1968, we had to evacuate fifteen thousand people at very short notice. We did it in twelve days, with thirteen helicopters.' A number of communities were thus uprooted four or five times. Even if they had any land, the Meos would not cultivate it. They are waiting, passive and resigned, for the nightmare to end, so that they can 'go home', as one of them ingenuously told us.

The food distributed by the Americans does not provide for all the Meos' needs. In the early days many Meo heads of families enlisted in the army to earn money for such necessities as cloth or cooking utensils. It was the destitution of these homeless families which enabled General Vang Pao to raise his special forces, a *corps d'élite* with whose help he succeeded in holding the Plain of Jars. For a considerable time this mercenary army operated on a semi-clandestine basis.

The irregular forces' camps continued to be covered by the official secrets seal, as Senator Fulbright wrote in 1971 in his report on the Laos situation. This was particularly true of the most important of them, Long Tieng. No journalist was authorized to enter aircraft of Air America, Continental Air Service or the Laos Air Force going to or likely to land at Long Tieng, without a written authorization from General Vang Pao. The arguments given to Fulbright's commission in justification of such secrecy were the following: 1. General Vang Pao cannot allow the press to visit the base without risking his military security; 2. Journalists would emphasize the U.S. role in the base and underestimate the general's; 3. The C.I.A., which organized and financed Vang Pao's army, is a clandestine organization which is unaccustomed to work in the open and fears that its operations in other parts of the world would be compromised if its techniques and agents in Laos came to be known; 4. If American activities in Long Tieng were made public, the United States would be accused of violating the 1962 Geneva Agreements; 5. If the details of the Thai presence in the base were, . . . (censored).[7]

Vang Pao's secret army, first given the French designation *Bataillon Guerrier* (B.G.), but renamed S.G.U. (Special Guerrilla Units) by the Americans in 1970, is believed to consist of about thirty thousand mercenaries, most of whom are Meos. The force also includes Filipinos, Laos and Thais, the latter's presence in Laos being a flagrant contravention of the Geneva Agreements. The S.G.U. are undoubtedly more efficient than the Royal Laotian Army whose soldiers would be happy simply to stroll around with flowers in their rifles. They are also more accommodating *vis-à-vis* the Americans who have no direct hold over the Royal Army and are, moreover, exposed to the whims of the Laotian warlords commanding the five military regions.

Today Vang Pao's special forces act as a spearhead in the campaign against the Pathet Lao. In theory the Meos and other irregulars recruited by General Vang Pao's army used to be volunteers. They were better paid than the men of the Royal Army who receive the equivalent of five dollars a month, a pittance for which they are reluctant to risk their necks.

Stripped of their belongings, evicted from their homes and land, the Meos were invited to join the S.G.U. where they could earn what seemed to them the considerable sum of thirty to forty dollars a month, on top of which a bonus was payable for commando operations.

At first there was no shortage of recruits. In 1967 Vang Pao's

7. *Laos: April 1971*, a staff report prepared for use of the Subcommittee on Security Agreements and Commitments Abroad. U.S. Government Printing Office, Washington, 1971.

army numbered 38,000 men and by 1969 had risen to 40,000. Then it began to melt away. The special forces suffered heavy casualties in beating off the communist attacks on Long Cheng in 1969 and 1970, when thousands of Meos were killed or wounded. Desertions became frequent and recruiting fell off. The Meos had learnt from experience that it was wiser not to enlist. In 1972 they constituted less than twenty per cent of the S.G.U's strength as compared with fifty per cent in 1968. The remainder was made up of mercenaries from all parts of the Far East. It was now that the refugee villages saw the appearance of recruiting squads who were not above kidnapping the men they needed. A Laotian teacher told us angrily that at Sayaboury he had seen young Meos shut up in cages too small to allow them to stand upright. They were about to be forcibly taken to the front. In the neighbourhood of Ban Houei Sai we visited several Meo villages where the only people to be seen were women, children and old men. The younger men and youths had taken to the forests to escape the recruiting squads.

Thus the entire tribal population, even when far removed from the scene of fighting, has been hit by the war. The traditional opium producers – bombed, herded together, impressed into the army, pushed into the front line and killed in their thousands – were the first to suffer, thanks to the duplicity of tribal leaders like General Vang Pao who have turned their people into cannon-fodder. Under the circumstances it is hardly surprising that opium production should have fallen by more than eighty per cent within the space of five years, especially since the Phong Saly and Sam Neua Provinces, which contain the best poppy-growing districts, have been overrun by the Pathet Lao.

It is not known how much opium was produced in those two provinces during the sixties, or what the output is today. This lack of information obviously vitiates the statistics. All we know is that the Pathet Lao has not compelled the peasants in the districts under its control to abandon opium growing. On the contrary, this is encouraged. The aim is not to 'poison the youth of America', as alleged by credulous propagandists who bury their heads in the sand and, in complete disregard of the facts, seek

126

comfort in the thought that American youth is being poisoned, not by the allies of the United States government, but by its enemies. Like the North Vietnamese, the Pathet Lao requires large quantities of opium for the manufacture of pharmaceuticals used in the treatment of war victims, both military and civilian. There is no substance in the much canvassed suggestion that the forces of the Pathet Lao dispose of opium in the Government zone in return for goods of various kinds. In the first place there is nothing to prevent them from issuing forged currency – as, indeed, they would already appear to have done on occasion for the purchase of essentials. In the second place, their requirements of war material have long been met by China and other communist countries.

We discussed this matter with Soth Prasith, chairman of the Pathet Lao Permanent Delegation in Vientiane, who confirmed that the production of opium was permitted in zones under Pathet Lao control.

'You can easily imagine how much morphine and codeine we need. The peasants take their opium to the State store in their village. We convert some of it into morphine in Sam Neua Province where we have pharmaceutical factories. The remainder is exported to North Vietnam and other fraternal countries where it is used in the manufacture of more complicated preparations.'[8]

Wishing to learn from the producers themselves what was happening in those areas, we questioned a number of refugees from different parts of Laos, among them a group of Meo families who, eight months previously in August 1971, had left Sam Neua Province after two years of Pathet Lao rule. Before arriving in Ban Keo, a village six hours' march from Ban Xon base, they had moved house no less than eight times. To facilitate our visit, USAID had placed a helicopter and an interpreter at our disposal. For ten minutes we hovered above the tiny village nestling in the jungle, until the Meo sentries laid out two large letters made of white cloth indicating that it was safe to land. Having hastily set us down on the minute landing-

8. There is a shortage of morphine in communist countries, despite the large quantities produced in the U.S.S.R.

ground, the machine at once rose vertically so as to get beyond range of any Pathet Lao detachments that might be lurking in the vicinity. We had brought a radio transmitter with which to recall the aircraft when we had finished making our inquiries. In the absence of the village headman, we were received by his deputy.

'The Pathet Lao' [he told us] 'allowed us to grow rice and the poppy, and we also reared livestock. Their soldiers did the same when they weren't fighting. There were thirty small poppy fields for the whole village. At the People's Store we used to exchange opium for food, clothing and ready cash. We got 37,000 *kips* [about £25] for 24 *beers* [about one kilo]. We've heard that this year they're paying 48,000 *kips* [£28] because there's less opium about. In our village, the fields we worked last year have been completely destroyed by the bombing.'

At Ban Xon hospital another Meo refugee told us:

'With the Pathet Lao, opium can be sold or exchanged for food and, though less often, clothing. I've heard it said that this opium was sent to Russia and China to be made into medicine. At first the Pathet Lao allowed us to smoke. Five years later they told us we'd got to stop.'

Outside Luang Prabang, the royal capital, we talked to some refugees who, bombed out of their villages, had had to escape on foot. They confirmed what we had heard about the Pathet Lao's method of buying opium in the zones it had 'liberated'. These people had lived for a time in an area over which the Vientiane government had virtually lost control and where the Pathet Lao, though already predominant, had not yet set up an administrative system. In a sensitive region, such as this, where the population has still to be won over, the Pathet Lao's attitude towards the opium producers would appear to be less rigid. 'The Pathet Lao doesn't insist on the whole crop being handed over,' we were told by one of these Meo refugees. 'They allow in Vietnamese, Chinese and Laotian traders who merely have to pay the usual tax levied on all products in the communist zone.'

We spoke to one such trader, a Haw, in a village not far from Luang Prabang. He explained:

128

'I buy the opium and sell it to the smokers here, who are finding it more and more difficult to get supplies. The Pathet Lao lets us through if we're going to villages not too far from here. All we have to do is pay a small sum to the communist "customs". To be allowed into those parts you've got to be trusted by the Pathet Lao authorities. There's not many of us can say that. But opium has grown very expensive in the Pathet Lao zone because the two nearest producing areas of any size are in the middle of the fighting. These are Phatung, three hours' march north-eastwards from Luang Prabang, and Kucham, forty-five kilometres from the royal capital on Highway 13. That's where I go for my supplies. I believe they have about a ton of opium in reserve at Phatung, and rather less at Kucham.'

It is obviously impossible to say how much opium is now being produced in the zones under Pathet Lao control. But allowing for the intensity of the bombing and the drop in population, an annual output of not more than five tons would seem to be a realistic estimate.

Although the war has reduced opium production in Laos, it has given rise to the new and related problem of supplying habitual smokers. Like most of the tribes who grow the poppy, the Meos, Yaos, Lissus and Akhas have always smoked opium. However, it is only men too old to do their share of the communal work who are supposed to indulge in this pleasure. A young Meo who smokes is usually ostracized by his tribe. Such, at any rate, was the case before the war. But many of the young Meo recruits in the special forces have taken to smoking opium at the front, just as their western counterparts light up a 'fag' to allay boredom or calm their nerves.

A Laotian officer, deploring this manifestation among troops of such high quality, remarked:

'The fact that counter-guerrilla groups[9] are scattered about the country means that many of the men are stuck away on mountain

9. To prevent the Pathet Lao from infiltrating and from extending their territory, the Americans have set up a network of counter-guerrilla detachments or 'maquis'. Some thirty men, most of them hill-dwellers, together with a few American 'civilian' advisers, live in small camps on mountain peaks in the depths of the jungle, only a few of which are capable of receiving helicopters.

tops for weeks on end – no beer, no music, no amusements of any kind. Their only links with the outside world are the helicopters which come to drop rations, arms and ammunition. What else can they do except smoke opium?'

Thus, while new consumers have made their appearance, the erstwhile growers, forced to leave their poppy-fields, can no longer even meet their own needs.

In Laos the purchase of opium is permitted, but not its sale. This is the result of an anomalous piece of legislation dating back to November 1971. Until that time there had been no restrictions on the production, sale or consumption of opium. Today consumption alone is legal, although smokers must obtain a licence and patronize officially recognized opium dens. These establishments may not possess more than three pipes or stock more than one kilogramme of opium at any one time. None of those responsible for framing this law appear to have asked themselves where the proprietors were supposed to go for supplies, since trading in opium is forbidden. When we questioned some Vientiane proprietors on this point, their only answer was a knowing smile, as much as to say 'Where do you think?' No one in authority seems worried by these anomalies which, in the absence of a State opium administration on the French model, are shrugged off as inevitable. But setting up such an agency would mean legalizing production, something the American diplomats are determined at all costs to prevent. Moreover, State buying would demand an inspection system which, under wartime conditions, would be wholly impracticable.

Despite the existence of three hundred licensed opium dens in Laos, the authorities in Vientiane felt able to inform the International Narcotics Control Board in 1971 that the country's addicts amounted to no more than two. There are also a number of establishments which, though unlicensed, make little attempt at concealment. After nightfall the characteristic smell of burning opium comes wafting from at least one in every three of the fragile bamboo houses in the main street of Ban Houei Sai. In company with a young Laotian soldier, we visited four of them within a distance of half a mile. A knock and we entered, having first taken off our shoes. The mats were promptly unrolled and

130

trays set out bearing lamps, pipes and dippers. Out of politeness our guide smoked one or two pipes and engaged in desultory conversation with the family, after which we moved on to the next house. One proprietor, who had run out of opium, gave a small boy a 200 *kip* (12p) note with instructions to buy some more. Within five minutes the child was back, carrying a small bag containing twenty opium pellets.

Attempts to impose controls on smokers have had only one practical result – the appearance of heroin. The inhabitants of the low-lying regions of Laos smoke very little opium, whereas the Chinese and Vietnamese, of whom there are large numbers in the towns, smoke a great deal. If a man is a notable or a government official, he may object to registering as an opium smoker and turn instead to heroin which is less obtrusive in use. Here as in most parts of Asia heroin is smoked rather than injected. An ordinary cigarette is dipped in the white powder, up-ended and then inhaled. Before 1971 no one used heroin in Laos and even now there is little demand for it. But if Laotian opium remains in short supply, the number of heroin smokers may be expected to grow.

No one knows exactly how many opium smokers there are in Laos, but there can be no doubt that they number at least twenty thousand. On average a smoker uses a kilogramme and a half a year, which means that Laos requires a minimum of thirty-five to forty tons to meet her domestic requirements. In other words, the country is in deficit and must therefore import. Today many Laotians buy Burmese opium. As a Meo in the Ban Xon military hospital told us: 'Burmese opium can be bought in the market. It's very good, but also very expensive at 200 *kips* for five pipes.[10] I used to smoke at least fifteen a day, but now I've had to cut it down.'

Again, we were told by a Luang Prabang trafficker: 'When there's no Laotian opium to be had, I can get supplies from Burma.' And General Vang Pao himself admitted that 'the opium the soldiers smoke at Long Cheng is bought in Vientiane or Ban Xon. But it's Burmese opium.'

10. In Laos, one pipe equals three opium pellets.

The traffic in Laos, already flourishing before the sixties, has expanded rapidly in recent years. The war has created new outlets in the form of Laotian smokers and U.S. troops in Vietnam. Nor has the problem been solved by the withdrawal of the Americans. Habits have been formed, alliances concluded, and rings set up. The latter's tentacles extend into South Vietnam where the highest personages in the land have been explicitly and repeatedly castigated both by leading newspapers[11] and by American Congressmen. Among the names mentioned are those of Lieutenant-General Dzu, commanding the central region of the upland plateau, Nguyen Cao Ky, the former Vice-President, and even President Thieu himself. In a television programme, in July 1971, an N.B.C. commentator alleged that President Thieu was trafficking in opium to finance his campaign for re-election in October of that year. The same commentator also accused Lieutenant-General Dang Van Luang, one of Thieu's closest advisers, of being Vietnam's foremost trafficker. These and similar accusations did not deter the Nixon administration from doing everything in its power to prevent the removal of Thieu and his henchmen – this last being virtually the only condition for a cease-fire to be laid down by the N.L.F. in September 1972.

Even if the poppy were to be totally banished from Laos, the effect on world addiction would be negligible. And while Laos can no longer be described as the 'kingdom of opium', it is generally acknowledged to be a paradise for traffickers.

11. *Washington Post*, 19 April 1968, 9 and 18 September 1971. *New York Times*, 8 July 1971.

132

9   A Paradise for Traffickers

Every week there is a football match in Vientiane. On this particular Sunday, in August 1971, the show was free. Its organizers hoped to draw large crowds to witness the public burning of a hundred kilos of opium and six kilos of heroin. This solemn occasion was to usher in a new era: as from the following November, a ban was to be placed on the production, sale and purchase of opium in Laos. The event was not a resounding success, however. Not a single Laotian minister or official took the trouble to attend. The sole occupants of the platform were the U.S. Ambassador, Mr McMurtrie Godley, and a group of aides. In the higher reaches of Laotian officialdom it was rumoured with some amusement that the bonfire had given off, not the acrid smell of opium, but rather that of burning tar.

This insinuation was hotly denied by the American Embassy whose ceaseless efforts had been instrumental in persuading the authorities to promulgate a law against opium. The struggle had been a long one, for the Royal Laotian Government had been in no hurry to turn its attention to the opium problem, feeling that in a country torn by war there were more important things to attend to. Opium was, after all, part of the local way of life. Furthermore, it had enabled highly placed members of the regime to amass considerable fortunes.

While the opium traffic has assumed new proportions with American intervention in south-east Asia, it was already a thriving business under French rule. During the Second World War and the Second Indo-China War opium served as currency for successive armies; the Japanese, the French, the Chinese Nationalists and the Viet Minh have all, at one time or another, done battle to secure the crop.

It was not, however, until the French left Indo-China that the

133

traffic became organized along really professional lines. This period saw the emergence of specialist gangs who had no particular political or military axe to grind. At the beginning all kinds of people were involved – ex-soldiers, unemployed pilots and erstwhile members of the Expeditionary Corps who, having been bitten by the Asian bug, had no desire to return to France. The actual buying was left to the Chinese and Laotians who obtained the opium direct from the hill tribes, while the Europeans, most of whom were of Corsican origin, specialized mainly in its transportation.

Some of these old stagers are still to be found in certain bars in Vientiane. Most have retired from business and many have been chastened by a few years in gaol. They have now been ousted by Laotians who, taking advantage of the conditions arising out of the Vietnam war and the presence of U.S. troops, have gained control of the traffic. The expatriates are quite prepared to talk about their own experiences or those of 'a chum I'd rather not name'. As an example of their resourcefulness we were told the story of a driver, Jean-Pierre X, who did the trip regularly from Laos to Vietnam, carrying eight hundred kilos of opium hidden in great hollowed-out tree-trunks and the wheel-chocks of his vehicle. Or it might be tar barrels with false bottoms. He was killed, poor chap, run down by an unknown truck on a lonely road.

Aircraft were more commonly used. The big shots of the period were, it seems, 'Lerouzy and Tolesco, two Frenchmen. They used to hire Beechcrafts from a Corsican who had three of them. The opium was loaded in Vientiane and dropped in the Gulf of Siam, off the coast of Hong Kong or else on to a plantation in Vietnam. The pilot was Babal.' Babal, whose real name is René Anjebal, is one of Vientiane's characters. He first came to Indo-China with the French Expeditionary Corps and has remained there ever since. With more than thirty thousand flying hours to his credit, he is probably one of the world's most experienced pilots. Once he was intercepted by Thai fighters a few moments after he had dropped a cargo of opium in the Gulf of Siam. 'They were never able to prove that I'd been carrying "molasses",' he said, 'even though they knew very well I had. I got two weeks in gaol for entering Thai airspace without permission.' Seated at a table with some old comrades in arms and sipping a pastis, he told us that he had turned over a new leaf. Now he was flying special missions for the Americans, some of which involved parachuting weapons to Cambodian troops. He is also employed as a pilot by the Laotian national airline.

Small-time trafficking was not without its hazards, but as one ex-operator pointed out: 'At the time trading in opium wasn't regarded as an offence in Laos, but as a business like any other except that it called for rather more discretion.'

The Labanski affair provides a good illustration of the methods used by traffickers at that time. Labanski, a Frenchman born in Vietnam, was a trained pilot. In 1954 he bought three aircraft and, with three other partners, settled down to carrying opium between Laos and South Vietnam. He would buy opium from Chinese traders in Xieng Khouang and parachute it in parcels of two hundred kilogrammes off the coast of Vietnam. Each trip brought in about fifty million old francs. After a number of deliveries had been lost in the China Sea, the small gang decided to use makeshift landing-grounds in the large Vietnamese rubber plantations. Business continued to prosper until a competitor denounced them to the Vietnamese police. The four ringleaders and their Saigon associates, some twenty in all, were arrested while attending to a cargo, and put behind bars.

In its 'Corsican' days the traffic remained small and localized, being confined to opium and serving only those countries in south-east Asia which had banned the use of the drug. At that time more complex preparations such as base morphine and heroin were only to be found in Hong Kong where they were manufactured by the Chinese.

The build-up of the American presence in south-east Asia, the course of the Second Indo-China War from the sixties onwards and the arrival in Vietnam of American troops in 1965 – all these were to revolutionize the nature of the traffic, which now expanded at a dizzy rate. An epoch had come to an end, and with it the heyday of the Corsican adventurers. The importance of the role played by the Corsican Mafia had been due to the fact that, for ten years after the departure of the French, the latter's influence had still remained very strong within the administration and the armed forces of their former south-east Asian colonies. But the influence of the French gradually waned, to give way to that of the Americans.

A Corsican ex-trafficker, whose five years in a Saigon prison had given him ample time to meditate on his trade, told us:

'You can't buy, stock or transport drugs unless you have protection in political and administrative circles. The most useful sort is to be found half-way up the ladder, especially in the army, police and customs where the pay's bad and ambitions are unlimited. High-up officials have less need to help themselves along by breaking the law; but then, of course, a good few of them have got where they are because, at some stage or other of their career, they've made a packet out of corrupt deals. Best of all is the protection given by the hush-hush outfits who can save you no end of trouble. I've often flown their agents on secret missions of one kind or another. In return they'd wink at my other trips.'

But as the American presence gathered weight, the understanding, pro-French officials were gradually removed and replaced. In consequence the Corsicans found themselves deprived of the network of complicity on which their activities depended. The course taken by the war in Laos and Vietnam meant that they were no longer able to use private aircraft for the conveyance of 'molasses'. Frontiers were closely controlled, as were aircraft movements. Many of the plantations where they had maintained secret landing-grounds were now occupied by the N.L.F. The roads were becoming too dangerous and were frequently blocked. As their rings collapsed one by one the Corsicans found themselves being elbowed out of the traffic.

Once it had lost the monopoly of transport, the fate of the Franco-Corsican Mafia was finally sealed. Until 1965, the year in which the communists launched their first offensive in the Plain of Jars, the few aircraft Laos had possessed had been piloted by Frenchmen. But with increasing U.S. involvement in the war, the Americans felt impelled to build up the Laotian Air Force. Non-European pilots were trained, including Laotians,

Filipinos, and Chinese from Formosa. Now that they were masters in their own house and possessed of adequate transport facilities, the Chinese, Laotian and Vietnamese traffickers could dispense with French assistance and make their own private arrangements. French pilots found that they were unable to renew their licences. Those who failed to take the hint were subjected to rather more drastic treatment. For instance, a plastic bomb was planted in one of Labanski's machines in Vietnam.

By the beginning of 1967 the change-over was complete. The Chinese continued to buy from the growers as they had always done, while the Laotians provided the transport and political protection. Thus the traffic saw the rise of new luminaries such as General Ouane Rattikone, Commander-in-Chief of the Laotian Army from January 1965 to July 1971. Rattikone's activities have been fearlessly denounced by General Khamu, head of the Laotian Secret Service, who is in charge of the Special Narcotics Investigation Group set up in March 1972. In April of that year he granted us an interview with permission to print what he said:

'General Ouane Rattikone is the big boss of the traffic in opium and its derivatives in Laos. Here, as well as in Thailand and Vietnam, a number of high-up officials, both civilian and military, have amassed large fortunes by agreeing to turn a blind eye to activities of this kind. But the general, not content with taking bribes in return for protecting the traffic, actually organizes it. He controls an international ring with contacts in Bangkok, Saigon and Hong Kong, and uses military aircraft to carry the opium. He is also prepared to sell his services and is the owner of the 999 trademark under which he markets illicit morphine, renowned for its excellent quality. Any unauthorized person using this trademark without paying a royalty would soon be a dead man. In 1966 the general bought a C47 aircraft in his wife's name. Three years later the machine was shot down while flying over Vietnam without permission and was found to be carrying opium, heroin and gold. Again it was General Rattikone who, in 1967, sent in the Laotian Air Force so that he could lay his hands on an opium caravan which was being fought over by the K.M.T. and a gang from Burma. Among his many interests was the notorious Ban Houei refinery which was turning out a hundred kilos of heroin a month. Its manager had been a major

137

in the K.M.T. and now lives at Chiang Mai in Thailand. He was hand in glove with the general, who had provided a company of Laotian infantry to guard the installation. In January 1971 I sent a report to Prince Souvanna Phouma. General Ouane, duly summoned, denied all knowledge of the matter. As Commander-in-Chief of the Laotian forces he was then my superior officer. When I asked him for orders to carry out an inquiry on the spot, he instructed me to wait until June. No doubt he hoped to make use of this breathing-space to build up stocks and move the plant elsewhere. What really happened we shall never know, for in July he ordered army helicopters to bomb the installation and allowed no one to visit the site. Since the equipment in an efficient refinery is worth at least twenty million *kips* [about £12,000], it seems likely that he had simply shifted it elsewhere.'

A few weeks after the bombing of the refinery, General Ouane Rattikone retired from the army in which he had served for thirty years. In doing so he forfeited none of his power. The commanders of the Ban Houei Sai and Luang Prabang Military Regions are both devoted to him. Moreover he has the wherewithal to repay them generously for their loyalty and their services.

The general has never really made a secret of his activities. An interview he granted to an American journalist several years ago created something of a sensation. 'While others line their pockets by dipping into State funds,' he said in self-exoneration, 'I myself have never robbed anyone. On the contrary, I've helped to make a lot of people rich.'

We met the general in person at a big reception held in the royal palace to celebrate the Laotian New Year. Burly and self-assured, with a serene expression on his broad features, General Ouane betrayed neither surprise nor annoyance at our pointed questions.

'You mustn't forget' [he said] 'that until November 1971 trading in opium and even in heroin was not illegal in Laos, seeing there was nothing to forbid it. Before introducing the law of 1971 banning poppy cultivation and the sale of opium they ought to have remembered that this product was earning the country at least five million dollars a year.'

The general did not admit in our hearing that he was directly implicated in the heroin traffic, but neither did he deny it. Rather, he chose to confine his remarks to the difficulties facing the trade. 'The Chinese chemists in Laos are no good,' he said. 'They have to be brought in from Hong Kong. But the prices they ask are exorbitant – five hundred dollars for a kilo of heroin.'

Heroin was not manufactured in Laos until 1965, the year in which a new market was created by the arrival of American soldiers in Vietnam. At first only poor quality heroin no. 3 was manufactured, and production was mainly devoted to the famous 999 brand of morphine. It was some years before the traffickers succeeded in meeting the European and American demand for heroin no. 4, the fine, white variety. In this way Laos has gradually come to be a refining centre for Laotian and Burmese opium and an entrepôt for the countries of south-east Asia.

The situation was explained to us by the head of the Laotian Special Narcotics Investigation Group.

'Caravans from Burma reach Ban Houei Sai in the Golden Triangle by various routes. Laotian opium is also sent there. The people who buy the crop from the hill-dwellers are invariably Chinese. Cultivation is becoming increasingly concentrated in the area to the north of Luang Prabang. At Ban Houei Sai the opium is converted into base morphine or into heroin no. 3 or 4, according to the demands of the market. Though the refinery formerly under Ouane Rattikone's protection has been destroyed, we know that others exist and we are carrying out an active search for them. The finished product is taken to Vientiane, and sometimes to Luang Prabang. At Vientiane it is loaded aboard civil and military aircraft on international flights to Bangkok and the big American bases in Thailand and Vietnam. Accomplices are always on hand to collect the cargo. The traffickers are very well organized. They communicate by code and we've intercepted a number of their messages. Until the opium law was passed, Laos was an ideal distribution centre for the traffickers, not because controls were less rigid than elsewhere, but because they were non-existent. Hence it was easier to convert the opium in Laos and dispatch the morphine and heroin from Vientiane than to convey it through north Thailand. It was a shorter and more direct route to Vietnam since there were daily flights between the two countries. Moreover the road from Vientiane to Bangkok is less hilly than the one from Chiang Mai, and it carries far more traffic. A further advantage, at least until quite recently, was the total absence of customs checks on the Laotian borders.

However such checks can hardly hope to be effective. As a lackadaisical functionary at the Ministry of the Interior remarked, his arms upraised in a gesture of helplessness: 'If we're going to seal the frontier, we'll have to shorten the Mekong.'

At this point it might be pertinent to ask whether the American intelligence agencies responsible for conducting the secret war in Laos have simply closed their eyes to the traffic in opium and heroin (whose first victims were the G.I.s), or whether they have actually had a hand in it themselves. Despite its denials, there can be no doubt that the C.I.A. was mixed up in the traffic from the mid-sixties until 1968 if not later.[1]

A senior member of the United States Embassy in Vientiane admitted in our presence that 'certain agents of the American intelligence services may have dabbled in such matters in a private capacity, but certainly not on the orders of their superiors.'

His opinion is not shared by Mr Del Rosario, a former C.I.A. employee. After testifying publicly in San Francisco, Del Rosario told us:

'I enlisted in the Marines as a volunteer in 1961, and remained with them until 1966. I then joined the staff of Continental Air Service, a charter company working for the C.I.A. in Laos. At that time I was in complete agreement with the war we were fighting in Vietnam. At the end of 1968 I left Laos to do the same kind of job in Vietnam. I first began to have doubts about the validity of Ameri-

1. This accusation was made in an article which appeared in May 1971 in *Ramparts*, an American progressive periodical. It was repeated in *The Politics of Heroin in South-East Asia*, edited by an American academic, Alfred McCoy, and published in August 1972 by Harper & Row. The C.I.A. tried to prevent the publication of this book in which the State Department and the American Intelligence agencies are accused of having been implicated for years in the south-east Asian opium traffic. Since the C.I.A. was unable to provide adequate proof to the contrary, the book was allowed to appear.

can action in south-east Asia at the beginning of 1971. I spent my vacation in the States and that made me realize I'd been wrong. I then joined Vietnam Veterans Against the War. In 1971 I was an operations assistant with Continental Air Service. Since it was my job to deal with loading and flight plans, I knew the destinations and places of departure of all aircraft leaving or arriving in Laos.

'The company's cargo aircraft used to carry a great deal of rice. When the consignment note contained the entry "miscellaneous", I knew it stood for opium. As a rule the special operations telephone would ring and a voice say: "This is the customer", which was what we called the C.I.A. agents who recruited and paid us. "Watch out for flights arriving from Ban Houei Sai," the voice continued, "we're sending a cargo and somebody'll be coming to look after it. No one is to touch it in the meantime, and nothing is to be unloaded." These consignments always took priority and were handled by special personnel. They were known as "classified cargo".

'The largest delivery of this kind I ever saw arrived on board a DC3, and took up half the aircraft. It had come from Ban Houei Sai and was consigned to Vientiane. Sometimes the opium was unloaded at Vientiane and stored in the Air America sheds. At other times it was reloaded aboard other aircraft bound for Savannakhet and Pakse in Laos, the American bases at Udorn in Thailand or Danang in Vietnam, or else Bangkok. Most often these cargoes were routed Ban Houei Sai–Vientiane–Bangkok–Saigon. At Bangkok, aircraft in transit to Vietnam weren't subject to customs examination.'

When we asked him whether he was sure these consignments consisted solely of opium, he replied:

'What else? Mail? That's not sent by cargo aircraft, particularly if it's urgent or confidential. Most of it's carried in small high-speed planes. Not weapons either. No one ever sends weapons from Ban Houei Sai to Vientiane. It's always the other way round. In any case, people in Laos had stopped making a secret of gun-running long before 1967. At that time, my political opinions being what they were, no one had any cause to mistrust me. Several C.I.A. agents I mustn't name, who were directly concerned with the cargoes, actually told me it was opium. The aircraft also carried gold to the maquis in the hills, probably to pay the Meos for their opium.'

We then asked him whether he thought this traffic was the private concern of a few pilots, or was actually run by the C.I.A.

141

'It couldn't possibly be handled by a few pilots working on their own account' [he replied]. 'How could they carry and unload cargoes of this kind without their superiors finding out? Half a DC3 isn't something you can just slip into your pocket. You can't use American military equipment in this way unless you have orders from your superiors, or at least their consent. Bill Marshall, an ex-Green Beret from Detroit, testified that at an airport in Vietnam he had seen a military aircraft being loaded with opium in cases marked "Aero-engine spares".'

Upon being asked why he thought the C.I.A. might have been organizing the traffic, our informant replied:

'In my opinion it provided them with funds that didn't have to be accounted for to anyone in Washington. Buying and collecting the tribes' opium was another way of winning friends. Finally, I think they were rendering no small service to some other allies – the K.M.T. forces in Thailand – who couldn't send out their opium because they hadn't any aircraft.'

In 1968 or 1969 these disclosures might have created an uproar in the United States. But so much has been written on the subject in the meantime that the American authorities could not seriously contemplate disclaiming the role played by the C.I.A. in the opium traffic – as, indeed, the McCoy affair has shown.[2] Unable to refute McCoy's accusations, the State Department dismissed them as 'out of date', as did one of its senior officials when we interviewed him in Washington in June 1972. 'You can't change things from one day to the next,' he went on to tell us. 'It wasn't till June 1971, remember, that our President defined the battle against narcotics as having first priority in our national and international policy.'

Not long afterwards we also interviewed the head of the B.N.D.D's Intelligence Office. 'Since 1969 priorities have changed,' this man said. 'Admittedly before that date no one cared what the Meo chiefs did, provided they stayed on our side. The C.I.A. may have tacitly agreed to facilitate the transport of opium, but it certainly never took a hand in the traffic in order to provide itself with funds.'

2. Cf. note 1, p. 140.

On 22 July 1972 the *New York Times* quoted a member of the government as saying: 'Go back three or four years, and no one was concerned about this. It was not until our own troops started to get addicted, until 1968 or '69, that anyone was aware of the narcotics problem in south-east Asia.'

The C.I.A's unofficial activities were justified by the logic of the war. Although the communists occupied large stretches of territory, their advances were not always made on a wide front. The Government forces continued to control pockets of ground where they maintained 'maquis' of thirty to forty men whose task was to sow disorder in the enemy's rear. These 'maquis' were largely dependent on the cooperation of the local tribes which, for their part, had been cut off from the rest of the world by the war, their only means of communication being by plane or helicopter. The Americans sought to ensure their loyalty by flying out the opium they would normally have sold to the Chinese merchants, now precluded from visiting them by the turbulent state of the country.

Since the general intention of American strategy was to win over the tribal population in order to isolate the forces of the Pathet Lao, the policy of helping the tribes to market their opium crop was a shrewd one. Moreover the Americans needed the Meos to make up a military *corps d'élite* and hence were all the more anxious to conciliate them, and more especially their chiefs. If, therefore, General Vang Pao wanted to send opium from one place to another, why not oblige him? At the time there seemed to be no harm in it, so long as a blind eye was turned to the havoc being wrought by the drug among the American troops in Vietnam. And heroin had yet to attain third highest place in the preoccupations of the average American.

All this helps to explain the tolerant attitude adopted by the C.I.A. and the American military authorities towards those of their agents who traded in opium as a sideline. It is common knowledge that the three charter companies on contract to the C.I.A – Air America, Continental Air Service and Lao Development Air Service – recruited adventurers of all kinds as pilots. Not a few of the latter considered that the hazards involved in their special missions entitled them to certain privileges. Some

143

of those missions entailed flying over enemy occupied territory with fresh supplies of arms and ammunition for the counter-guerrilla 'maquis'. In so doing the pilots had to thread their way between mountain peaks before making an abrupt descent to drop their loads, or put down their heavy cargo aircraft on airstrips too short for the purpose.

As specialists in undercover operations, Air America and Continental Air Service were particularly well qualified for the task of transporting opium unobtrusively. Their machines, which do not display international registration letters, move freely between Laos, Thailand and Vietnam. In Laos they fly to the remotest parts of the country, carrying American military advisers and special detachments, evacuating the inhabitants of areas threatened by the Pathet Lao or distributing rice and weapons.[3]

What, then, was the final destination of the opium carried in these aircraft? Was the C.I.A. merely seeking to secure the support of some influential Laotian or Vietnamese personage, or had it taken over the role of the local traffickers, buying and selling opium on its own account for the purpose of profit? Nobody has yet been able to produce any evidence either way, but the first supposition would appear to be the more probable. Since the C.I.A. already has at its disposal vast sums whose exact distribution – much to the chagrin of Congress – remains a mystery, there would seem little reason to suppose that it would have needed to secure additional secret funds. Hence the likeliest explanation is that the C.I.A. made use of opium as a politico-military tool, allowing the more loyal of its allies to engage in the traffic and even providing them with facilities that enabled them to run it on a grand scale. By according them these advantages, the C.I.A. ensured their loyalty in exactly the same way as General Stroessner, the Paraguayan dictator, has secured the support of his generals by granting them 'smuggling rights'.

By all accounts the C.I.A. stretched its complaisance to considerable lengths. A number of reliable sources are agreed that

3. In 1972 it was believed that there were some three hundred jungle airstrips varying between 300 and 500 metres in length, and capable of receiving cargo aircraft.

the Long Cheng base harboured, amongst its other secret installations, a refinery for the manufacture of heroin.

Del Rosario described how

Every Thursday at dusk, a C130 without markings – only the U.S. Air Force uses C130s – used to land at Long Cheng. The engines were kept running while a special team unloaded wooden crates eight feet high by six feet wide and then put others on board. Only that particular team was allowed to see to the cargo which was stored in a building guarded day and night by Meo militia. Most likely this was the refinery. At all events that's what I was told by one of my friends who worked at Long Cheng. My duties brought me into direct contact with Udorn Base in Thailand and I learned by radio which machines were flying across Laos. The C130s from Long Cheng always used to make for that base.

When we questioned General Vang Pao on this point he not unnaturally refused to give us a straight answer. 'How could I possibly have been mixed up in that kind of traffic?' he said. 'It's a very long time since there's been any opium in Military Region 2, which is partly occupied by the Pathet Lao. As for the rest, the producing areas have been destroyed in the fighting.'

The argument is hardly convincing. With the means of transport at his disposal and his contacts in high places, both Laotian and American, General Vang Pao could easily have obtained all the opium he wanted from areas outside his own military region. Moreover, diplomats serving in Vientiane, who would prefer to remain anonymous, admit that Vang Pao is generally known to have been implicated in the opium traffic. However they believe that the commander of the Meo secret army abandoned these activities at the beginning of the seventies when the American Embassy's attitude to opium began to change.

It was a long time before public opinion in the United States became aware of the havoc being wrought by heroin in the ranks of the American forces in south-east Asia. The uproar was all the greater when, in July 1971 on their return from a fact-finding mission in Vietnam, Congressmen Murphy and Steele broke the news that between ten and fifteen per cent of the troops in that theatre were taking heroin. It was not till these revelations had been made that the High Command admitted what they already knew to be a fact. At the same time the growth of addiction at home was giving ever greater cause for anxiety. The Federal Government now began to concern itself seriously with the problem, and instructed its embassies abroad to investigate ways and means of putting a stop to the production and sale of opium. Steps were also taken to expand the B.N.D.D's overseas agencies.

The government's directives can hardly have been welcomed by the ambassadors serving in the war-torn countries of southeast Asia. But now that American public opinion had been alerted, some demonstration of good faith was called for. As we have already seen, repeated approaches on the part of the American Embassy eventually induced the Laotian government to promulgate a law against opium. The first draft expressly stipulated that the cultivation of the opium poppy be prohibited throughout the kingdom. This draft was modified at the insistence of deputies representing the interests of those who really wielded the power, namely the great Laotian families. A clause was added to the original text, to the effect that 'members of tribes whose villages are situated in hill and jungle country where the poppy has been cultivated for centuries, as well as all those who have been authorized so to do, may continue to produce opium and smoke what they themselves produce'. Needless to say, this materially restricted the scope of a law which, while it may not have conformed to the wishes of the United States Embassy, was nevertheless a step in the right direction.

At the time of its promulgation in 1971, a B.N.D.D. representative and four American customs officials were appointed to Vientiane on Washington's orders. The B.N.D.D. now has men posted at the nerve centres of the traffic, notably at Ban Houei Sai. It also pays informers and provides its Laotian counterpart, the Special Narcotics Investigation Group, with vehicles and radios. Positive steps have been taken to control the distribution of acetic acid, a chemical product essential to the manufacture of heroin.

The B.N.D.D. representative in Vientiane told us:

'The acetic acid used in Laos comes from Japan. For a long time it used to be sent to Bangkok and finally reached Houei

146

Sai by way of Burma. Now it goes there direct from Bangkok. At our request the Japanese police undertook to obtain lists of customers from all manufacturers of acetic acid, and one of our agents in Tokyo sends us details whenever a consignment is exported.'

Of all the steps taken in Laos to combat the traffic in narcotics, undoubtedly the most convincing is the appointment of General Khamu as head of the Special Narcotics Investigation Group. The General, who looks much younger than his forty years and wears his hair in a neat crew cut, enjoys a reputation for complete integrity – a rare phenomenon in Laos. He is fearless both in deed and word, as we discovered when we talked to him about General Ouane Rattikone. Moreover he is at once respected and feared, not to say detested, by his brother officers in the Laotian Army. Throughout his career he has served in the intelligence services, retaining his post after the French had left and the Americans arrived. Consequently he knows a number of things which others would rather have him forget. Since he enjoys the confidence of Prince Souvanna Phouma, he has considerable room for manœuvre and exercises a great deal of authority. 'He's the very man I myself would have chosen to take charge of the suppression of the traffic,' we were told by the American Ambassador, Mr McMurtrie Godley. Struck by the unintentional humour of such a remark in a country where the Americans are all-powerful and where he himself has been dubbed 'pro-consul' and 'viceroy', he hastened to add: 'Not that I had any say in the matter.'

General Khamu seems determined to obtain concrete results and in particular to discover the whereabouts of the refineries. Since the establishment of the Special Narcotics Investigation Group, he has confiscated nearly three thousand litres of acetic acid, sufficient to manufacture three tons of heroin no. 4. The various American intelligence services in Laos have received strict orders to pass on to General Khamu all available information on the subject of narcotics. This unprecedented step is proof of the confidence accorded the Laotian general by the American government's representatives in Vientiane.

To counteract the accusations levelled against them, the two charter companies, Air America and Continental Air Service, have overhauled their operating methods. The head of Air America, replying to Alfred McCoy's charge that his company had participated in the narcotics traffic, declared:

'Air America and USAID have collaborated closely in introducing a security programme designed to prevent the carriage of drugs on board our aircraft. Passengers, crew members, their baggage and the goods carried are examined by American inspectors . . . If passengers refuse to undergo this inspection, they are not permitted to board the aircraft. If they are found to be carrying contraband goods, their names are passed on to the Laotian authorities. Thanks to these measures, all attempts to transport opium aboard Air America aircraft have been detected and foiled.'

The tonnage of opium formerly carried by Air America could hardly have been accommodated in passengers' baggage. But the introduction of reasonably strict controls is evidence that both this company and Continental Air Service have had to call a halt to the more glaring of their illicit activities so as to silence the accusations of those opposed to the war in Vietnam.

Officially, the relationship between the Bureau of Narcotics, the intelligence services and the American Embassy in Laos is good and cooperation excellent. But it is a moot point whether the diplomats are in fact pleased to be allotted a watchdog in the person of a B.N.D.D. agent, whose task it is to remind them that, in the United States, the fight against drugs has been declared a number one priority.

'Our embassies assumed an air of bored nonchalance whenever we raised the problem of drugs,' was the indignant comment made by Congressman Steele after his return from his fact-finding tour of south-east Asia.

The fact is that the diplomats serving in Laos, Vietnam and Thailand, though showered with injunctions by their government, cannot fight two battles at once. If they are to be victorious in the new campaign against opium they will first have to remove from power the generals and highly placed officials on whom they have hitherto relied for support in their anti-communist crusade. A contradiction of this kind presupposes a choice between alternatives. That choice would appear to have been made, for who could envisage abandoning the aims in pursuit of which so costly a conflict has been waged for so many years? In April 1972 we interviewed Mr McMurtrie Godley, a diplomat known for his hawkish views who had been posted to Laos from the Congo. When asked what priority he would accord to the fight against the traffickers in Laos, he replied without a moment's hesitation: 'It's our second priority in this country. The first is the war against the communists and more precisely our determination to prevent North Vietnamese infiltration along the Ho Chi Minh Trail.'

It seems doubtful whether a few law enforcement measures will be enough to stamp out the traffic so long as the conditions which have favoured its growth remain unchanged. Once again American policy has fallen into its old error of grappling with the symptoms while ignoring the cause.

The political climate that obtains in Laos after ten years of unavailing conflict has bred corruption on an unprecedented scale. Those controlling the political machine know that their prosperity cannot last for ever and that sooner or later, when the Americans have left, the Pathet Lao will take over. In anticipation of that event they are busily amassing as much wealth as they can in the limited time still available. Now as before, one of the best ways of getting rich quick is to deal in narcotics. The political structure of Laos is favourable to the country's exploitation. Officially Laos has been a constitutional monarchy since 1946. In fact it might be likened to a confederation of local magnates, all more or less firmly established and controlling areas which, because of the war, cannot always be precisely defined. Such cohesion as it has may be attributed to the presence of the Americans and the anti-communism of the country's élite rather than to the prestige of a king who is virtually unknown save to those of his subjects living within a thirty-kilometre radius of the royal capital, Luang Prabang. In practice Laos is ruled and exploited by a handful of great families whose mutual relationships are characterized by a more or less benevolent neutrality. Alliances are made and unmade, and are frequently cemented by marriage. Military Region 1, which includes Luang Prabang and Ban Houei Sai, is held in fee by

General Ouane Rattikone. Although no longer Commander-in-Chief of the Army, he is still the political strong man in that part of Laos and may well be one of the most powerful people in the country. At the centre is Military Region 2 comprising the Plain of Jars. Here General Vang Pao reigns supreme over such parts of his territory as have not yet fallen to the communists. The south is in the hands of the powerful Na Champassak family headed by Prince Boun Oum. His lands extend from Pakse, where he has set up his headquarters, to Champassak where he has built himself a palace. He reigns like a feudal lord over the southern provinces, levying taxes on any enterprise he does not own, whether agricultural, commercial, banking or mining. The Vientiane region is under the sway of the Abhay family, one of whose members, General Kouprasith Abhay, is the military administrator of the Plain of Vientiane. The Abhays are allied to another very powerful clan, the Sananikones, known as the 'Rockefellers of Laos', who hold numerous posts in the government. Phoui Sananikone, the head of the family, is a former prime minister, and two of his kinsmen are deputies in the National Assembly.

The power of these families and their allies is founded on trafficking of various kinds. But they have been wise enough to share out the cake rather than fight over it. For instance General Ouane Rattikone, who has specialized in opium, owes his power, as a State Department official told us, 'largely to his good sense in allowing other highly placed personages to have an occasional share in the opium traffic while leaving them a free hand in areas such as gun-running.'

Prince Boun Oum is believed to have had an interest in the drug traffic in the days when Mme Nhu, the sister-in-law of President Diem of Vietnam, was Saigon's opium queen. Later he would seem to have found it more profitable to sell to the communists rice and weapons smuggled in from Thailand.

All these families have their men in the National Assembly and control a certain number of votes. At election time, they form alliances and combinations in accordance with their interests of the moment. But they are also represented in the government and the upper echelons of the army. Hence it is

150

they who are the mainstay of the Laotian political, administrative and military structure and who actively oppose the communist and nationalist forces. And it is they, and they alone, who can be counted on by the United States to give a Laotian veneer to the secret war being waged by Washington against the Pathet Lao and its North Vietnamese allies.

In these circumstances the suppression of the drug traffic is no longer merely a matter of law enforcement but has become an extremely complex political problem. Even when General Khamu's Special Narcotics Investigation Group has irrefutable evidence that a certain high-ranking personage is implicated, it is powerless to act for fear of seriously disturbing the relations of the political forces in Laos. To proceed against General Ouane Rattikone would mean jeopardizing the delicate equilibrium of Prince Souvanna Phouma's coalition government, while to annoy Prince Boun Oum might bring about the secession of the southern provinces. The extent of the deadlock is evident from the discouraging picture painted by General Khamu in April 1972. He told us that,

'At present, there are in Laos four big rings with international contacts; they are run by Overseas Chinese and Laotians. One is controlled by the proprietors of the Societé I.A.M., and another by Boon Khong Vong Phak Dy. Both trade in opium and heroin and both enjoy the protection of General Ouane Rattikone. Their refineries are probably located in the neighbourhood of Ban Houei Sai, but we haven't yet been able to pinpoint them. The third is headed by the wealthiest Chinaman in Laos, Mr Leng, who owns the "555" cigarette factory, one of the biggest concerns in the country. He regularly provides funds for the Ministry of the Interior which owes him large sums of money. The fourth ring is run by a Laotian soldier whose name I cannot divulge and who has the benefit of political protection in high places.'

These circumstances call to mind the notorious affair of Chao Sopsaisana. After he had been appointed ambassador in Paris, the French customs found among his many pieces of luggage a suitcase full of heroin. To avoid an incident he was recalled by Prince Souvanna Phouma, but suffered no further disgrace. In 1972 he was still Vice-President of the National Assembly

151

which includes among its deputies General Ouane Rattikone himself.

If the Americans are to persuade their more prominent collaborators to give up trafficking in opium they must dangle a new carrot under their noses. This they would appear to have done in the case of General Vang Pao, and they may well adopt the same tactics in that of Ouane Rattikone. As a diplomat serving in Vientiane put it:

'General Vang Pao has made his choice. He can earn more money waging war for the Americans than by continuing to traffic in narcotics. In any case, given the political climate now obtaining in the United States, it would be difficult for him to carry on both these activities at once.'

Again, we were told by a State Department official in Washington:

'General Ouane Rattikone has realized that, if he wants to go on with the traffic, he'll have to give up manufacturing heroin no. 4 and sending it to the United States. In any case this represents no more than about ten to fifteen per cent of his turnover, the rest of which comes from the sale in south-east Asia of opium and heroin no. 3. Our outlook in the United States is very egotistical. All we want is to stop heroin coming in. As for the rest,' [he added flippantly] 'we're not so mean as to want to prevent the poor old Chinese from smoking their three or four after-dinner pipes.'

Thus out of self-confessed egotism, the State Department is perfectly prepared to issue a licence to poison the whole of Asia with heroin no. 3, in return for the assurance that Americans will be spared.

In other words, the opium and heroin traffickers of Laos still have a rosy future before them, at least until there is a change of power. Meanwhile the Laotian upper crust are working indefatigably to provide against the day when, as the saying goes in Vientiane, they 'have to cross the Mekong'.

Part 3

Drugs and the Non-Aligned Nations

In countries such as Thailand, Laos and Turkey, which fall within the American sphere of influence, Washington can employ its full diplomatic, economic and political armoury as a means of persuading them to introduce controls on the production and sale of opium and its derivatives. Here the United States are inhibited only by the fear of prejudicing their interests in other fields which might, at some future date, take priority over the drug problem.

The situation is quite different in regions subject to the influence of other great powers. Thus America is unable to exert direct pressure on two countries, both of whose ever-increasing production finds its way on to the black market. These are Burma and Afghanistan, to which we must add Pakhtunistan, a territory lying between Pakistan and Afghanistan and disputed by both. The attainment of American aims is further impeded by the complexity of the political situation in these seriously underdeveloped countries where tribal questions play an extremely important role. If the American Bureau of Narcotics and the specialist agencies of the United Nations are to cut off at source the flood of opiates reaching Europe and the United States, they will have to tackle the problem of these major black spots.

10   Opium: the Burma Road

'In Burma, divided as she is, the tragedy now being played out may well go on indefinitely,' we were told by a western diplomat serving in Rangoon. 'Whoever hoped to make this country into a geographical whole must have been an amateur map-maker with a fertile imagination.' The 'fertile imagination' belonged, presumably, to the British who, in 1948, were compelled to grant independence to the peoples inhabiting what had been the easternmost portion of British India. Having practised for over a century their famous principle of 'divide and rule', they left behind them a motley federation of warring races without a common language[1] or creed.

The Union of Burma consists of a number of States. The Burmans themselves, a people of Mongol extraction, constitute no more than fifty per cent of the country's population. But ever since the civil war that followed independence they have held the reins of government virtually without interruption. It is a situation that has never been accepted by the Kachins, Shans, Karens and Mons who, throughout this period, have been in a state of rebellion. Nevertheless they have not succeeded in achieving the unity that would almost certainly have enabled them to overthrow the government in Rangoon. After a bitter struggle to consolidate their hold over the more utilizable part of the country – the Irrawaddy Valley where over four fifths of the population live – the Burmans are largely resigned to the fact of being unable to control more than forty per cent of the Union's territory. Nor does that forty per cent include the regions which have made Burma the world's largest producer of illicit opium. Hence it is easy to understand why the Burmese authorities, however genuinely anxious to respond to the appeals

1. Ten different languages are spoken in Burma.

of the international agencies, have not been able to control their production or even undertake to do so. Meanwhile the 'privileged' nations can only stand by in impotent despair as Burma sends opium pouring on to the black market.[2]

The main poppy-growing areas lie along the Chinese border in the Shan and Kachin States. Hardly any roads penetrate the thick jungle that covers the mountain slopes. Perched on summits between six and ten thousand feet high are groups of villages, each group being peculiar to a local tribe or people. In 1964, when members of a United Nations mission visited the Shan States, they were told that there were still head-hunters east of the Salween River. And Europeans are advised not to venture into the remote Akha villages of Burma and Thailand lest they be taken for evil spirits and put to death.

Nowhere is this area adequately administered, cut off as it is from the rest of the country by the absence of roads, no less than by the permanent state of rebellion that obtains there. The towns are held by the Burmese authorities, while guerrilla groups occupy the countryside.

The Kachin Independent Army was created in 1961 when the Premier, U Nu, declared Buddhism to be Burma's official religion. Most of the inhabitants of the Kachin State, especially north of Myitkyina, are Animists or Christians. The Kachin rebels are particularly strong in the so-called triangle formed by the two rivers which converge above that town to become the Irrawaddy. Under the leadership of two brothers, Zan Seng Zan and Tu Zan Dan, they have set up local administrations in the so-called liberated zones. But their life is far from easy. While supplies of rice are more or less adequate, there is a shortage of salt, medicaments and above all cloth.

As a force the Kachin Independent Army is more homogeneous than the Shan Liberation Armies, which are split up into a number of autonomous and often competing groups. Claiming that they belong to the Thai race, the Shans call themselves the *Dai Thai* or 'true Thais', although they are in fact more closely related to the Laos. As a colony Burma proper

2. According to the most optimistic estimates this amounts to between four hundred and seven hundred tons a year.

was under direct rule whereas the Shans were administered by their own chiefs, with the help of British advisers. After independence the Shans bitterly reproached the government in Rangoon for failing to implement the Federal Constitution. The Burmese authorities' natural inclination towards centralism became even more marked after General Ne Win's seizure of power in 1962. The Shans, who had been demanding greater freedom of action within the Union, now called for autonomy, and some of them are still fighting for the creation of an independent state.

Neither the Kachin Independent Army nor the Shan National Movement has any hope of winning the undeclared war they are waging against the government forces, who in turn have no prospect of prevailing in this mountainous terrain where they are surrounded by a hostile population. In rural areas they are quartered in small camps which they can only leave during the daytime. As a rule both sides tend to avoid each other.

The Burmese Army comprises àt most 130,000 men. This modest force cannot hope to patrol the three thousand kilometres of frontier separating Burma from China, India and Thailand, and at the same time effectively combat insurrection. For besides the Kachins and the Shans, several million Karens are also in a state of permanent rebellion. The latter, who are Roman Catholics, have formed themselves into the Karen National Defence Organization (K.N.D.O.) Not all of them live in their own State, for there are more than a million Karens in the Irrawaddy Delta. Under British rule they were strongly represented in the civil service and the army. During the civil war in 1948 they all but captured Rangoon and for the next ten years constituted a grave threat to the Central Government. Now they have joined the Mons rebels in a United National Liberation Front led by the former Prime Minister, U Nu, who was overthrown in 1962 by the present head of State, General Ne Win. This organization is active all along the Thai border in the Mon and Karen States and the south of the Shan State.

So far as Rangoon is concerned, however, the first priority is the struggle against the communists, most of whom belong to the pro-Chinese 'White Flag', or Communist Party of

Burma (C.P.B.), which controls a considerable area north of Lashio, between Nam Khan and Kunlong. The road from Burma to China runs through this region where part of the Shan State forms a wedge in Chinese territory. Another small group, the 'Red Flag', of Trotskyist persuasion, is of lesser importance. It operates in the Pegu Range, north of Rangoon, and also in the portion of Arakan bordering on Bangladesh. The old pro-Soviet Burmese Communist Party (B.C.P.) has all but disappeared. Some of its members have rallied to General Ne Win's 'Socialism in Neutrality', while others have joined the ranks of the White Flag.

The proximity of China and the existence of a very active if not numerically strong pro-Chinese communist organization with official Peking backing have inevitably created schisms within the independence movements by compelling them to adopt a position *vi-à-vis* the Chinese People's Republic. In the Shan, Kachin, Mon, and Karen communities there are communists and democrats, autonomists, and advocates of a complete break with Rangoon. The Kachin State, situated in the country's northern extremity, is particularly subject to the influence of Peking. The main point of contact between Burma and China has always been the region between Bhamo and Myitkyina, to the north of which the mountains rise to a height of over thirteen thousand feet. Before the completion of the Burma–China Road, Bhamo was the chief centre of trade with China whether licit or illicit.

In 1967 Peking is said to have suggested that the Kachin Independent Army should come under the control of the Communist Party of Burma. Although the K.I.A. refused, the two parties appear to have come to an arrangement in January 1968, enabling the C.P.B. to operate freely south-east of Myitkyina where there are relatively few Catholics. Since that time the Chinese would seem to have cut down their deliveries of war material to the insurgents, though still remaining their chief suppliers. In classic style the rebels make good the shortfall by exchanging opium for arms from Thailand.

Sometimes the rivalry between communists and non-communists degenerates into open conflict. One evening at twilight we visited a villa hidden away at the bottom of a neglected garden on the outskirts of the Thai town of Chiang Mai. On arrival we were received by a senior member of the Shan State Progress Party, one of the politico-military movements fighting for the independence of the Shan States. We sat on the ramshackle verandah in chairs rotted by the monsoon rains. Around us the floor was strewn with haversacks, weapons of the most diverse origin, and palliasses on which exhausted men were snatching a brief rest before moving on. Our host, a slight, sharp-featured man with a crew cut and eyes bright with intelligence and fatigue, was on the wanted list. 'Relations between the S.S.A. [Shan State Army] and the C.P.B. are neither good nor bad,' he told us.

'We're not communists. Our view is that, though communism may be all right for the Chinese, it isn't necessarily all right for us. The C.P.B. want to make the Shan State into a military base and don't give a damn for our nationalist aspirations. In fact in 1968, when they were being particularly aggressive, we became involved in no less than nine battles with their troops. Yet we're both fighting the same enemy – the Burmans – and we do our best not to hinder each other's efforts.'

Banditry thrives on the atmosphere of total insecurity created by the fighting between rival bands and between those bands and the Burmese Army. It is extremely inadvisable for a European or a Burman to venture into the Shan State by road. An escarpment rising some three thousand feet above the Plain of Mandalay marks the beginning of the Shan Plateau which is undoubtedly one of the most beautiful parts of Burma. The pine-clad hills, the streams that flow between them, and the cloudless skies recall the landscape of Haute Provence. The equable climate is in agreeable contrast to the intolerable heat and humidity of Rangoon, and it was here that the British liked to spend their furloughs. In the early sixties two representatives of international organizations were murdered in different parts of the district, a grim reminder that in the Shan States they kill you first and check your credentials afterwards. Anyone who cannot speak the regional language is as good as dead. If a Burman, he is an enemy, if a European, an agent of the C.I.A. His assailants may belong to a political group or may simply be a gang of highway robbers taking advantage of the general confusion. It is by no means unusual to see a whole busload, including the driver, arrive stark naked at their destination after an ambush. Aware of this hazard, everyone travels as light as possible. If there happens to be a notable among the passengers he will be held up for ransom. As for the peasants, they are bled white by imposts surrendered more or less willingly to the forces of the Shan Liberation Movement, and reluctantly, if not under compulsion, to the Burmese Army or to gangs of bandits. Finally both the Shans and the Kachins have to endure the hostility of the hill tribes. The Kachin States consist of sixty-two tribes, all speaking different dialects. In the Shan States only one third of the population is Shan.[3] Their alliances with the other two thirds – Was, Akhas, Lissus and Lahus, many of them extremely primitive – are made and unmade according to the vagaries of local politics. But all are united in their hatred of the Burmans.

These same tribes of Sino-Tibetan origin are also found, but in far greater numbers, in the province of Yunnan on the Chinese side of the frontier – a frontier which, to them, is largely fictitious. The poppy is cultivated not only by the Akhas and Lahus, but also by the Shans. In the Shan States, where opium has been cultivated for two centuries or more, the main growing areas lie east of the Salween River; in north-east Kunlong ninety per cent of the population is dependent on the crop. Opium is also the main source of income for the inhabitants of the Bhamo region in the south-east of the Kachin State, where local observers report a sharp increase in production in recent years. A certain amount of opium is also grown west of the Salween River – in the uplands round the town of Loikaw, in the southern part of the Shan States and in the Chin Hills. But since there is a law forbidding the cultivation of the poppy on Burmese territory, the crops in these more accessible districts are frequently destroyed by the authorities.

In Burma, as in neighbouring countries, the opium producers

---

3. Out of a population of five and a half millions, one third is made up of Akhas and one third of Lahus and other tribal minorities.

are extremely poor. They live on difficult terrain where no other crop can be grown, at least at the present time. 'Opium production is a matter of life and death for a lot of our hill-dwellers,' we were told by one of the leaders of the Shan rebellion.

'A third, maybe even half, of the inhabitants of the Shan States who live east of the Salween River have no other source of income, Most of them live in villages that are completely isolated, and have never known the sound of a car or radio. For centuries they've been totally deprived. Even if we were politically strong enough to suppress poppy cultivation – assuming we were in power – we would still lack the resources to do so. Any other kind of produce would be impossible to market because the villages are so inaccessible.'

The price of opium remains stable despite the depreciation of the Burmese currency whose black market value is three times less than the official rate.[4] Indeed, local tribesmen refuse to accept the Burmese kyat and insist on being paid in solid silver Indian rupees, issued in the days of British rule.

As in Thailand the peasants deforest stretches of mountainside during the summer and burn the tree stumps at the end of the rainy season. They sow the poppy in September and October and harvest it over a three week period in January and February. At most a family will collect eight to sixteen kilos of opium a year, which fetches the equivalent of twenty dollars a kilo as a standing crop and forty dollars harvested.[5] Theoretically this represents an annual income of between three hundred and six hundred dollars per family. But for the greater part of the time the cultivators never see a penny of it. For the 'law pans', the Chinese merchants who buy the crop, pay for it in ordinary household goods such as salt, matches, pots and pans, and cloth, for which they charge exorbitant prices. Not content with that, they then proceed to lend cash to their opium suppliers at interest rates ranging from ten to twenty per cent a month. This means that the peasant becomes the slave of his crop and seeks to grow as much as he can in order to pay his debts.

4. In 1972 a dollar was worth 5 kyats at the official rate and 14 kyats on the black market.
5. A viss (= 1·6 kg.) fetches 50 Indian silver rupees (about 500 kyats) as a standing crop, and twice as much when harvested.

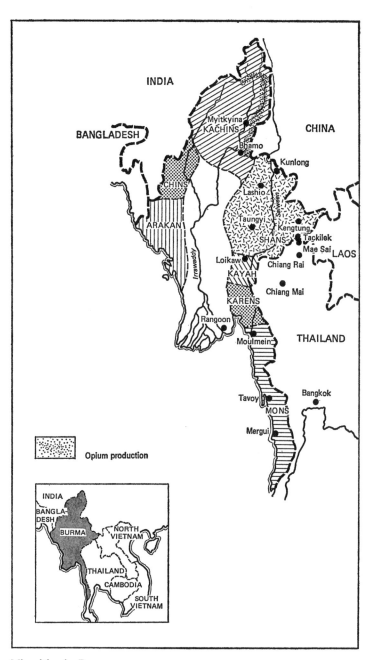

Minorities in Burma

Opium enables the peasants to buy the necessities of life, and helps the liberation movements to procure arms, ammunition, uniforms and medical supplies. For the middlemen, however, it is simply a means of lining their pockets. Having traded weapons and other contraband goods for opium, they then transport it to Thailand. But the crop, once harvested, often becomes a matter for dispute. The right to buy opium from the producers is shared out among the various armed bands operating in the Shan States, more or less in accordance with the territory they happen to control. But it is not unusual for one opium chieftain to encroach on the territory of another, thus sparking off a small localized war.

The Shan guerrilla groups, which comprise traditional war lords as well as politically orientated nationalist groups, buy their opium in the heartland of the Shan States between Kengtung and Kunlong. Their chief rivals are the mercenary 'self-defence forces', more often known as the K.K.Y., which have undertaken to support the government troops in their campaign against communists, Shan rebels and 'foreign invaders' of all kinds. The K.K.Y. is divided into three units commanded by Lo Hsing Han, Yang Shi Li and Hsu Chia Chu. The first consists of 'White' (as opposed to Red) Chinese, most of them ex-K.M.T. men. Its area of operations is in the north-east, on the Sino-Laotian border. The second is made up mainly of Lahus and is based in the hills south-west of Tachilek, while the third, composed of pro-government Shans, is located in the plain west of Kengtung. However, part of this latter unit has now gone over to the enemy and has been incorporated into ex-Premier U Nu's shock troops. Its commander, Jimmy Yang, was formerly one of the Shan feudal princelings, or 'Sawbwas' entrusted by the British with responsibility for local administration. These men also enjoyed the hereditary right of levying a tax on opium, a privilege that was withdrawn on General Ne Win's accession to power. Jimmy Yang supports the United National Liberation Front and has set up his headquarters west of the Salween, on the border of the Kayah and the Shan States. The K.K.Y. receives no aid whatever, either financial or technical, from the Central Government. In drawing its revenue almost exclusively

163

from opium and the black market it has the unofficial blessing of Rangoon. For the rest it lives off the country.

The area north of Tachilek is controlled by those K.M.T. elements which, in 1954 and 1961, refused either to return to Formosa or to move to Thailand. Their number is estimated at around three thousand. According to several reliable sources, whose accounts are consistent if not readily verifiable, they have set up three fortified camps north of Tachilek, close to the Laotian border. These are said to contain refineries manufacturing heroin no. 3 and no. 4. We were told by a former member of the K.M.T. that the bases are out of bounds to all save senior officers. If attacked by the Burmese Army, the K.M.T. break camp.

Here we might ask whether the pro-Chinese communists also traffic in opium. On the face of it they would seem to have little incentive to do so since the militants of the Communist Party of Burma are not compelled to sell the drug as a means of procuring arms, these being easily obtainable from the People's Republic. But as we have already seen, the Kunlong district where they have their headquarters is one in which the peasants depend almost entirely on opium to meet their daily needs, and it would seem that, like the Pathet Lao in the region north of Luang Prabang, the C.P.B. allows merchants to come and buy the crop.

'Logic just doesn't apply hereabouts' [we were told by a European diplomat serving in Rangoon] 'as you will see from the following story. During the civil war that followed independence, the Karens and Burmese were fighting a battle in a small town about a hundred kilometres from here. Finding themselves short of ammunition, the Karens sent a delegation across to the Burmese to ask if they could buy some. The government troops agreed and that evening staged a mock battle, firing into the air south of the town, while the deal was being clinched to the north of it. Both sides retired satisfied. Next day the Burmese sent an urgent signal to Rangoon: "Karen unit routed. Require more ammunition."

'There's no such thing as Manichaeism here' [he went on]. 'Communists and non-communists don't hate each other's guts. There are almost certainly private agreements between the various bands operating in the Shan States. After all, the whole lot of them are of Chinese extraction, whether Sino-Tibetan or Sino-Thai. It's more than probable that some groups act as intermediaries in the opium trade between pro-Chinese communists and Chinese Nationalists.'

Our informant cited the case of Chang Chi Foo, the notorious opium chieftain who sparked off a minor war in 1967 when he tried to take an opium caravan across K.M.T. territory without paying a levy.[6] Chang Chi Foo, part-Chinese and part-Shan, had pledged himself to the Central Government by joining the K.K.Y. But he grew too powerful and independent for the peace of mind of the authorities who accordingly instructed the Burmese Army to attack him. In doing so they lost an ally and gained a relentless adversary with an armed band of his own. Though he was eventually arrested towards the end of the sixties, his lieutenants continued to trade in opium.

'Chang Chi Foo' [our diplomat friend went on] 'was ideally qualified to go opium buying in the communist controlled zones north of Lashio. For one thing he was trusted by the communists because he had rebelled against the Government and had, moreover, fallen out with the Chinese Nationalists of the K.M.T. who had beaten him in 1967. This defeat had forced him to sell his opium to the K.M.T. or at least to pay it a large levy whenever he wished to cross the territory under its control.'

According to a member of the B.N.D.D's Intelligence Office, another independent rebel by the name of Peng Chia Chiang is at present in contact with the Burmese communists who allow him to buy opium in their zone.

It is not improbable that bands of hill-dwellers enter China proper in search of opium. There is a great deal of overlapping between the tribes in Yunnan and those in the Shan States. At first sight it is impossible to say whether an Akha or a Wa lives on this or that side of the border. They all dress alike and speak the same language. Moreover it is by no means unusual for whole communities to move away from the hillsides they have devastated by their methods of cultivation and set off in search of new land. The Chinese take advantage of these migrations to introduce

6. See Chapter 7.

communist-indoctrinated communities into Burma – a particularly sore point with the Shan nationalists. No doubt a good deal of smuggling goes on between China and Burma, most probably with the tacit consent of the Chinese who can thus obtain certain goods such as medicaments. Already in the days of the British, this mountainous region on the Sino-Burmese border was a no man's land which local traders were able to cross without hindrance.

In the market-place at Taung-gyi – but it could equally well have been at Kengtung – we saw bags, electric fans, military uniforms and felt and velvet footwear, all manufactured in communist China. While opium probably accompanies this merchandise, the quantity is impossible to estimate without knowing how efficiently the Chinese Army patrols the Yunnan border. For in this region the jungle tracks wind upwards towards mountain peaks between nine and thirteen thousand feet high. Nevertheless it is difficult to believe that a caravan of two hundred mules could cross the frontier without the knowledge of the Chinese authorities. In so far as the traffic exists, therefore, it is unlikely to be very considerable. At all events, whenever we questioned American officials on this point, whether in Asia or in Washington, we were invariably given the same stock answer:

'The poppy is, of course, grown in Yunnan, but that's hardly surprising, if you think of the needs of a pharmaceutical industry with seven hundred million Chinese to supply. We have no proof whatever that massive quantities of opium are being exported from Communist China.'

Since independence, the production and use of opium have been officially banned throughout the Union, an exception being made for the Shan States, and for the Kachin State where consumption was allowed but not production. These privileges were abolished in 1966. At the same time the authorities introduced a plan to suppress all poppy cultivation within the space of four years. Just how it fared we have already seen. Indeed six years later the International Narcotics Control Board at Geneva cited Burma as being in the forefront of those countries which help to supply the black market and do nothing to remedy this state of affairs. Officially the Burmese government refuses to admit that it has no control over a large part of its territory, a fact which explains its resolutely passive attitude towards the international organizations. Innumerable letters, proposals for fact-finding missions and even offers of financial aid emanating from the United Nations Commission on Narcotic Drugs have remained unanswered.

Burma has not always been so uncooperative. In 1964, at her own request, a United Nations mission made an extensive tour of the country, even penetrating as far as the Shan States. Despite reservations dictated by the political situation, their conclusions were relatively optimistic, mainly because of the goodwill shown by Rangoon. At the time Burma hoped that she would be included among the countries authorized to supply opium to the world pharmaceutical industry. By setting up a State-controlled agency for the purchase of opium, the government would then be able to divert into its own exchequer the immense profits that would otherwise be pocketed by the traffickers of all breeds operating within the Union.

The United Nations were unable to endorse this proposal. To do so would have meant encouraging opium production in a country which, because of the permanent state of turmoil in its poppy-growing areas, was wholly incapable of controlling the growers. The mission therefore advised the Burmese to stamp out the cultivation of the poppy, but failed to offer adequate financial compensation. Since that time contact has never been properly re-established. While Burma agreed to send an observer to the international conference at Geneva in 1971, she refused to take part in the Canberra Conference nine months later when thirteen Asian countries, from Pakistan to Indonesia, undertook to support the campaign against drug addiction.

Both the United Nations and the American Bureau of Narcotics are deeply concerned about Burma. An official U.S. envoy, Mr Groove, was sent to south-east Asia by President Nixon to investigate the drug traffic. His account of a discreet visit paid to Rangoon in August 1971 was not reassuring. The Burmese authorities had been as understanding as they could be in the

167

circumstances. However, they had inferred that, since they must give absolute priority to the problem of insurrection, they could not afford to ban a crop so profitable to the peoples whose collaboration they hoped to gain in the fight against the insurgents. They went on to point out that the suppression of opium production in Burma was not just a matter of law enforcement, but a wider problem of underdevelopment which could only be resolved in the long term after the investment of large sums of money. Finally they declared that drug addiction was confined to the hill tribes in the producing regions and did not affect the Burmans themselves who consumed relatively little opium. Consequently the problem was purely a western one and it was up to the west to put its own house in order instead of blaming its troubles on Burma.

The unwillingness of the Burmese to cooperate with the western powers is a cause for concern to the international organizations who fear that Burma will rapidly become a traffickers' paradise. All the prerequisites are to hand – large-scale production, a virtual state of anarchy in the producing regions, apparent indifference on the part of the Central Government and, most important, a disastrous economic situation conducive to corruption of every sort.

Between 1948 and 1958 Burma was ruled by Premier U Nu who came to power after the assassination of General Aung San, the champion of Burmese independence.

In 1958, faced with a rising tide of political, economic and, above all, racial troubles, U Nu called on General Ne Win to form a provisional government. A former post office clerk, this officer had, like U Nu, been one of the 'Thirty Comrades' who had fought at the side of Aung San, the father of the country. For fourteen years he had combated the rebels, both communist and non-communist. Though his real name is Uu Shu Maung, he continues to use the pseudonym Ne Win (Sun of Glory)[7] by which he was known during the war of independence.

U Nu, having been triumphantly re-elected in 1960, reformed the Anti-Fascist People's Freedom League (A.F.P.F.L.) which is

7. Claude Moisy, *La Birmanie*, Éd. Rencontre, 'Atlas des Voyages' series.

affiliated to the Socialist International. He also opened negotiations with the country's ethnic minorities and coopted a Karen, a Shan and a Muslim into his government.

On 2 March 1962 Ne Win seized power after arresting U Nu and his cabinet. At the same time he denounced corruption within the administration, the growth of the black market and the alleged intention of the minorities to overthrow the Central Government with the help of the imperialist powers. His next move was to introduce the 'Burmese way to socialism', or 'socialism within and neutralism without'. In the event Ne Win's socialism proved to be of the nationalist-authoritarian variety. Everything was nationalized, from banks to pedlars, while the army was put in charge of commerce and industry. One of the General's reasons for embarking on such a vast nationalization programme was to rid himself of the millions of Indians and countless thousands of Chinese who controlled trade and industry and owned a quarter of the fertile land in the Irrawaddy Valley. They were gradually elbowed out, leaving the country seriously short of qualified men. Parliament and the constitution were abolished and all power vested in the thirteen members of the Revolutionary Council presided over by General Ne Win. According to the statutes of the new regime the army must restore power to the civilians at the end of ten years. That is why *Bogyoke*[8] Ne Win, together with the whole of his entourage, resigned from the army in March 1972 to form a civil government. Today he is known simply as U (or Mr) Ne Win.

But during those ten years the economic state of the country, potentially one of the richest in Asia, deteriorated appreciably. Burma used to be entirely dependent on rice exports which in 1940 amounted to three million tons. Commercial disruption inside the country brought about a fall in production[9] and by 1971 exports had dropped to less than a million tons. In an attempt to maintain its reserves of foreign currency, the government introduced rice rationing. But this measure was can-

8. An affectionate and familiar form of address for a general.
9. In 1940 Burma produced 7·5 million tons of rice. In 1972 production had fallen to 6·5 million, against a population growth of 2·2 per cent per annum.

169

celled out by falling prices on the world market. By April 1972, Burma's monetary reserves were practically exhausted.

The population are supposed to buy their supplies from State shops whose chief characteristic is a scarcity of goods. Customers draw lots for the little that is available. Corruption is so widespread, communications so poor and the roads so unsafe that, outside the larger towns, the State shops rarely receive supplies. The black market has become virtually an institution, tolerated by the authorities because it acts as a safety valve. In Rangoon its operators occupy an area of several acres in the city centre where all basic necessities can be bought. But the prices are exorbitant. From time to time the police swoop down, seize everything within reach and pile it into trucks, doubtless with the intention of supplying another market and pocketing the proceeds themselves. For this reason the salesmen have taken to displaying their wares in half-open sacks which can be whisked away when the law appears on the scene. However, as often as not, the police are content to exact a percentage of the vendors' profits.

Foodstuffs are strictly rationed and very expensive even at the official price. Condensed milk, oil and sugar can only be obtained on the black market. No one is entitled to more than two and a half kilos of rice a month; also a small quantity of *ngapi*, a seasoning made of fish paste which the Burmese find indispensable. The salt ration is 1·6 kilos every six months, while a *longyi* – the traditional Burmese garment, a kind of skirt made of a single piece of material in a small check design – has to last a whole year.

The average wage is some 100 kyats a month (£2.80) in the towns and 40 kyats (£1.12) in the country, and this for families of seven to eight children. One person's monthly rice ration costs 28p in a State shop and 42p on the black market in Rangoon. Other examples are 22p for one and a half litres of oil, at least 42p for rent, and 8p for a kilo of fish paste. A family's monthly expenditure on tea is 20p. Duck costs 22p a kilo and fish anything from 12p to 24p. Thus after the basic necessities have been bought, nothing remains for clothing or household goods. Chicken and fruit are luxuries.

Housing conditions are, for the most part, appalling. Property can no longer be handed down, and Rangoon has become a shabby as well as an over-populated city. Buses are both infrequent and unpunctual and take an interminable time to cross the vast, sprawling capital built by the British round two large lakes. Rather than wait for hours most of the inhabitants still prefer to walk, sheltering from the sun under big black umbrellas. Life is difficult for everyone save the military who enjoy numerous privileges. As Claude Moisy put it: 'It is not so much socialism in neutrality as stagnation in isolation'.[10] In Burma today a single piece of cloth will buy any number of accomplices.

In such conditions Rangoon and Moulmein, the country's second city, could well become entrepôts for the international traffic in opium. Hitherto the bulk of the opium produced in the Kachin and Shan States has been exported through Thailand but according to a trafficker we spoke to in Rangoon, an appreciable quantity is already passing through the Burmese capital. This was confirmed by a Burmese living in Kengtung. Opium, like all other contraband goods arriving at Tachilek from Thailand, is conveyed by car or truck along the only road linking Kengtung and Rangoon. A bribe of a thousand kyats (£28) has to be paid at each check-point, the total disbursements for the round trip being ten thousand kyats or £280.

From Rangoon the opium may be transported by fishing boat to Penang Island west of the Malay Peninsula. There it is loaded on board the vessels of the Ocean Shipping Line, a company owned by Hong Kong Chinese. Sometimes the goods are conveyed by the *Aung Zeya* of the Five Stars Line, the Burmese national company, which carries passengers from Moulmein to Kantang in Thailand, calling at Tavoy and Mergui. The opium may be unloaded at either of these ports, where accomplices are easy to come by, after which it is taken by mule through the jungle to Thailand and Bangkok. The boat's outward journey takes a week, and from Kengtung to Mergui is no more than three and a half days' journey by truck. Hence this route is a good deal quicker than the one that crosses the mountains of

10. Claude Moisy, *La Birmanie*, Éd. Rencontre, 'Atlas des Voyages' series.

171

the Golden Triangle. It might also prove easier should American pressure lead to the introduction of stricter controls in north Thailand.

In Burma as elsewhere in Asia the traffic is in the hands of the Chinese who have contacts in Hong Kong and Bangkok.[11] A seaman belonging to the Five Stars Line, who operates as a middleman between Rangoon and Hong Kong, told us about his experiences:

'In Rangoon I buy parcels of raw opium from the Chinese in Twenty-first Street. The stuff is shaped into bricks and wrapped in paper stamped with the trademark, a handprint. It's a first class brand, dark green in colour. On each trip I take sixteen kilos which cost me 15,000 kyats [£420]. I also have to slip the police or the customs 500 kyats [£14]. But often they prefer me to bring back something from Hong Kong – a camera, say, or a tape-recorder or a radio. Once there I sell the opium for £108 a kilo, which means a profit of something over a thousand pounds a trip.

In Hong Kong it costs me the equivalent of 60p to have a junk come alongside and fetch the opium. The parcel isn't all that bulky, so I drop it down to them over the rail. Then I go to Black Pier in Hong Kong Island and wait for it in a taxi. From there I get the driver to take me to Wanchai, where I go to a discotheque facing Hennessy Road and the naval dockyard, deliver the goods and get my money. Then I book in at the Hilton and send for some girls.'

'Trafficking in Burma,' our informant went on, 'is easy enough. When you've got money you can do what you like, since everyone needs it so badly.' And he told us the story of a Sino-Burmese by the name of Lamba who, before leaving Burma in 1964 to settle in Hong Kong, used to make shipments of 160 kilogrammes at a time. 'He had so much money,' the sailor said, 'that he could buy literally anyone. Incidentally, if a trafficker, whether Chinese or Burmese, happens to be picked up, the worst he can expect is a fine of ten thousand kyats [£200].'

11. There are still three to six hundred thousand Chinese in Burma, despite the fact that large numbers were expelled or failed to get their passports renewed after 1962. Many of the Chinese have become naturalized and have married Burmese women.

No one in Rangoon has any illusions about the extent of corruption within the police and the administration, at least in the middle grades. To obtain even so much as a packet of nails means filling in an almost incredible number of forms and then bribing the official responsible for allocations. Whenever we asked if corruption was equally rife in government circles, we always received the same, typically oriental, answer: 'The leaders of the Revolutionary Council are incorruptible. The same cannot always be said of their wives.'

Thus the concern of the western governments is understandable. If Burma were to adopt a less restrictive attitude towards foreigners,[12] a *rapprochement* might eventually take place between the international Mafiosi and the Chinese who control the local opium market. Indeed the Chinese might even serve as intermediaries should the gangs seek to safeguard their opium supplies by giving financial aid to the rebel movements in northern and eastern Burma.

However, the west has no hold whatever on a country which, first, has practised isolationism for over a decade and, secondly, occupies a key strategic position in south-east Asia. Between Burma and China there are thousands of miles of ill-defined and indefensible frontier, and almost as much again between Burma and India where Soviet influence has been increasing steadily since the end of the sixties. Longest of all is the frontier with Thailand, a country which has close links with the United States. Thus, since Burma adjoins the spheres of influence of three great powers, her government acted wisely in basing its foreign policy on neutralism.

At all events this was what Peking wanted and the Burmese have always been very attentive to the opinions of their close neighbour, the more so since the Chinese have built four roads giving access to the Burmese frontier – 101, 202, 203 and 404 – one of which passes through the narrow wedge of Chinese territory at the junction of the Kachin and Shan States.

Burma was the first non-communist country to recognize Mao Tse-tung's government in 1949. For more than twenty

12. Between 1962 and 1970 it was virtually impossible for a foreigner to obtain a visa valid for longer than forty-eight hours.

years relations between the two countries remained excellent.[13] After Burmese independence U Nu paid several visits to Peking and Chou En-lai was received in Rangoon. On his accession to power, Ne Win was hailed as a friend by the government of the People's Republic. Indeed Burma was now generally regarded in the west as a kind of Chinese satellite.

A drastic change came about in 1967 as a result of the Cultural Revolution then taking place in China. The entire staff of the Chinese Embassy in Rangoon were recalled and their place taken by Red Guards. Violent anti-Chinese rioting broke out in June following a series of incidents which began with Chinese pupils in Rangoon schools being ordered to remove their red and gold Mao Tse-tung badges. The boys came out on the streets and, after a certain amount of brawling, burnt the Burmese national flag and a portrait of Aung San, 'the father of the country'. The Rangoon mob then broke into Chinese-owned shops[14] and went on looting for days. An official of the People's Republic, caught up in a violent demonstration outside the Chinese Embassy, subsequently died of his injuries. Peking made this a pretext for breaking off diplomatic relations between the two countries. From that time on Ne Win was always described in the Chinese Press as a 'bloodthirsty fascist' or 'Burma's Chiang Kai-shek'. No longer was there any talk of Burmese 'socialism', but only of 'General Ne Win's military government'.

Sino-Burmese relations returned to normal in 1970. In November of that year the Burmese Embassy re-opened in Peking, the Chinese following suit in Rangoon six months later. However China has maintained pressure on the northern frontier through her chosen instrument, the Communist Party of Burma. For example, shortly after Ne Win's goodwill visit to Peking in 1971, White Flag militants invested the town of Kunlong as a

13. For Sino-Burmese relations, see Frank Nitrager, *Burma from Kingdom to Republic*, Praeger, New York, 1966.

14. These riots, by interfering with the normal functioning of the black market, caused food prices to rise by 300 per cent, a fact which underlines the extent to which commerce is still dominated by the Chinese, despite nationalization.

warning both to the Americans and the Russians. The Chinese have no expansionist designs on Burma, but neither will they tolerate the presence of another great power in a region which they wish to remain neutral. For the stabilization of the southern frontier would enable Peking to concentrate wholly on its northern confines where China and the U.S.S.R. have as yet to resolve their differences. There can be no doubt that any further growth of Russian influence in India would at once be reflected in a renewal of pro-Chinese guerrilla activity in north-east Burma, as happened at the time of the war in Bangladesh.

Thus the United States, in any case far from popular in Burma since Ne Win's accession to power, can bring no influence to bear on the government in Rangoon. They cannot, as in Thailand and Laos, threaten to reduce their economic aid as a means of inducing the Burmese authorities to take the opium problem seriously. Moreover the complexity of the political situation inside Burma compels Washington to tread delicately. 'For a long time the Americans hoped that Ne Win would fall,' we were told by a leader of the Shan Liberation Army.

'Hence they didn't object to the presence in north-east Burma of a focal point of anti-government insurrection. But at the same time they don't want that focal point to spark off an international conflagration, and for this reason they aren't sympathetic to our demands for independence. All the same, the Americans ought to realize that, if they were moved by certain political considerations such as the opium problem to make friends with Ne Win, they would inevitably drive us into the arms of the communists since we'd have no other alternative.'

When Ne Win seized power in order to impose his doctrine of 'socialism in neutrality', the State Department taxed him with communism while extolling the virtues of U Nu throughout the whole of Asia. Ten years later, having finally realized that they could not so easily rid themselves of Ne Win, the Americans adopted a more subtle approach in the hope of gradually improving their position in the country. In April 1972 we discussed this matter with an American diplomat serving in Rangoon.

'Our presence here' [he told us] 'could be described as low profile. Today our position is better than it was in the past. In 1962 the Burmese expelled the personnel of the American oil companies. This year the Gulf Oil Company has concluded an agreement with the Burmese to help them prospect for offshore oil. In a general way the Burmese government is more receptive than it used to be to offers of international and bilateral foreign aid. Moreover they have recently had some very considerable loans from the Japanese and West Germans.'[15]

Undoubtedly Burma's economic difficulties have tempered Rangoon's attitude towards other countries. The duration of a visa has now been extended to eight days and there seems every probability that this period will be increased in the interests of the tourist trade. Police regulations are no longer so stringent and it is now slightly less difficult for a westerner to make contact with a Burmese at official level. Finally, in 1972 the government signed four major contracts with American corporations – in its way an epoch-making event.

But despite this incipient thaw the Americans do not, it seems, see any immediate prospect of bringing the present Burmese authorities to the conference table to discuss the opium question.

As we were told by the same American diplomat:

'Even if the Burmese have accepted the principle of American aid to enable them to finance certain projects, they seem in no way inclined to invest the money in the rebel zones. The greater part of the subventions made to Burma under the Colombo Plan[16] are being voted to the Irrawaddy Plain. In any case, even if fabulous sums were invested in the opium producing regions, the result would be nil, in view of the geographical conditions and, more particularly, the political climate that obtains there. There's no solution for Burma outside of a national reconciliation movement round U Nu.'

15. The Japanese have granted a twenty-year loan of eighty million dollars. Thus their aid has now reached the same level as that of Peking.

16. A plan for the development of south-east Asia devised by the British Commonwealth Foreign Ministers in the course of two conferences at Colombo in 1950 and 1951.

11   The Future of the Traffic: Pakhtunistan and Afghanistan

Afghanistan and northern Pakistan represent a source of opium as yet virtually untapped by European traffickers whose supplies came from Turkey until poppy cultivation was banned there in 1972. Situated at the junction of the Middle East and southeast Asia, the two territories are not as far from Marseilles or Munich as are Burma and Laos. The political conditions in their opium producing areas make these places an ideal refuge where racketeers from Europe could go about their business untroubled by the international law enforcement agencies. This applies particularly to the frontier region known as Pakhtunistan which enjoys not only extraterritorial status guaranteed by Pakistan's Constitution but also independent status conferred by the Afghans.

The North-West Frontier Province, one of the four which go to make up Pakistan, contains the Tribal, or Free, Agencies. These are autonomous zones in which Pakistani jurisdiction is confined to the road leading to the Afghan border. If someone is kidnapped or murdered at a distance of more than fifteen feet from the roadside, the authorities are powerless to intervene. There are six Tribal Agencies, Khyber, Mohmand, Kurram, North Waziristan, South Waziristan, and Malakand, having a total population of seven millions, all belonging to Pathan tribes.[1] This probably unique situation, in which a State has voluntarily renounced all authority over a vast part of its territory is, needless to say, one of the legacies of the British Raj.

On the pretext of the threat – real or imaginary -- presented

---

1. The tribes are generally described as 'Pathan' and their language as 'Pushtu'. Perhaps we should point out that, while the name Pakhtunistan is commonly used, it is associated in official circles with secession.

by Afghanistan's immediate neighbour, tsarist Russia, to their possessions south of the Indus, the British compelled the Afghans to sign the Treaty of Gandamak in 1878. The most important clause of this treaty gave the British jurisdiction over the whole of the area south of the line formed by the Suliman Hills where the population comprised some of the most powerful Pathan tribes, among them the Afridis, Mohmands, Mahsoodis and Waziris. This arbitrary line of demarcation, known as the Durand Line,[2] meant that the provinces of Baluchistan and Pakhtunistan were split in two, and with them a number of villages and tribal lands.

More than half the inhabitants of the Afghan kingdom are Pathans,[3] the king himself being a member of the Durrani tribe. The Afghans were never able to reconcile themselves to the partition imposed upon them, nor did they abandon hope of recovering the territory of which they had been dispossessed. But since they could not achieve their purpose by force of arms, they had to content themselves with fomenting unrest south of the demarcation line.

The British, for their part, were unable to subdue the Pathans who proved to have exceptional fighting qualities. Punitive expeditions sent out against them resulted in heavy losses on the British side, as is evident from the numerous soldiers' graves to be seen in the Khyber Pass. Rather than fritter away its forces on profitless operations, the government decided to create the Tribal Agencies, thereby giving special status to the Pathans. From then on, the tribes enjoyed almost complete independence, the Government of India being represented only by political officers who negotiated with the Pathan chiefs. To keep the latter quiet they were accorded subsidies amounting to £7,500,000, which also provided a means of bringing pressure to bear in case of rebellion. If, however, the tribesmen continued to prove recalcitrant, their villages were bombarded. When these territories became part of Pakistan, the

2. After Sir Mortimer Durand, Foreign Affairs Secretary to the Government of India.
3. According to official estimates, the most recent of which are ten years old.

government of that country undertook to maintain the *status quo* there.

Before leaving India in 1947, the British held a referendum on the basis of which they partitioned the country between Muslims and Hindus to form the sovereign States of Pakistan and India. On that occasion the Afghans demanded that the Pathans, who had been forcibly detached from Afghanistan, be given a further alternative, namely, the choice between reunion with Afghanistan and the formation of an independent Pathan State. The British, anxious to counter possible future hostility on the part of India by building up the strength of Pakistan, did not even deign to reply. For they knew that, as Muslims, the Pathans would certainly opt for Pakistan rather than India.

After the creation of Pakistan, Afghanistan began campaigning for the formation of Pakhtunistan, an independent state that would comprise the Pathans of the Tribal Agencies, North-West Frontier Province and Baluchistan. Pakistan's riposte was to increase her subsidies to the Agencies.

Repeated clashes brought about the rupture of diplomatic relations between the two countries in September 1961.[4] As a result Afghanistan found herself deprived of her most direct access to the sea and hence of all the imports, including oil, that had formerly reached her through Pakistani ports. Relations were resumed in 1963 but the question of Pakhtunistan has remained unresolved. The only people to have benefited from this dispute are the Pathans of the Tribal Agencies who, while enjoying complete freedom on the Pakistani side, can look on Afghanistan as their home. Indeed they deliberately disregard the frontier between the two countries, crossing it at will when seeking new pastures for their flocks or, more frequently, when carrying contraband.

Being beholden to no constitutional authority, the Tribal Agencies are veritable states within the State of Pakistan. But they are states without an administration, without a police

---

4. cf. *Afghanistan, Highway of Conquest,* Arnold Fletcher, Cornell University Press, New York, 1966.

force, and with only one law, that of retaliation. The tribes settle accounts among themselves and owe obedience only to their local chiefs who have power of life and death over their subjects and themselves see that justice is done. All in all, the Tribal Agencies are a smuggler's paradise.

Pathans become smugglers as others become tailors or grocers. It is an extremely lucrative trade since goods are imported duty-free into Afghanistan,[5] unlike Pakistan where duties are very high. A handsome profit can be earned by purchasing in Afghanistan goods of all kinds – beauty products, refrigerators, radios, electric fans, etc – and selling them in Pakistan at prices slightly below those of legitimate, and hence dutiable, imports. From there the people of the Tribal Agencies have branched out, first into commerce and then into the manufacture of various types of prohibited merchandise such as arms, ammunition and, of course, drugs.

Unfortunately for the west but fortunately for the Pathans, the largest poppy-growing areas in the district are situated in Pakhtunistan, on either side of the Afghan-Pakistan frontier. And since the Pakistani government has no control over the Tribal Agencies it can obviously do nothing about opium production, all of which finds its way on to the black market. Nor are the Pakistanis particularly anxious to arouse the belligerent instincts of the Pathans or to drive them into the arms of the Afghans by attempting to put a stop to their smuggling activities. Hence the somewhat paradoxical situation which arose in 1952, when the Pakistanis were obliged to start growing opium in parts of the country other than the Tribal Agencies so as to supply their pharmaceutical industry.[6] Even so they are having difficulty in meeting competition from the traffickers since a large part of the official crop is diverted on to the black market where the price is more attractive. This is the more galling in that Pakistan's pharmaceutical industry is still short

5. Only thirty per cent of the luxury goods imported into Afghanistan remain in that country.

6. The opium grown in the plains, having an eight to ten per cent morphine content, is greatly inferior to hill-grown opium which contains fourteen per cent – almost as much as Turkish opium.

of opium. One factory is already in production at Lahore and another in course of construction at Peshawar. Seventeen tons of opium a year would be needed to keep both supplied. But in a good year all that the Excise Department[7] can manage to collect is eight tons. According to the B.N.D.D's Intelligence Office, between 175 and 200 tons of opium elude government control.

In late April 1972 we found ourselves at Toppi in North-West Frontier Province at the time when the Excise Department was buying in the opium crop.

'To keep an eye on the eighteen thousand peasants in the district where opium is grown under licence [one of the Department's officials remarked] we have forty-eight agents and one solitary jeep. The Tribal Agencies, needless to say, are pretty well barred to us. With a staff of this size there can obviously be no question of keeping tabs on the producers at harvest-time. They bring the opium to buying centres, like this one here at Toppi. To go by the acreage put down to the poppy, we ought to collect nearly eleven tons, but all we get is eight, if that. By a curious coincidence the peasants always seem to have been the victims of some meteorological disaster. Not only that, but they give extra bulk to what they bring us by adding leaves, soil and the like. The black market competition's too much for us. If our price for a *sir* [900 grammes] of medium quality opium is 140 rupees, the traffickers will offer 300.[8] If we raise the price, the traffickers do likewise. We've tried increasing the acreage so as to step up supplies to our pharmaceutical industry but the amount the peasants bring us never varies. The extra goes on to the black market. There's always a demand there because American and European consumption keeps going up and up. In fact we control no more than a fraction of the opium produced in Pakistan.'

Our journey to the tribal zone was made in the company of a Pathan guide. Ten kilometres out of Peshawar we passed through a sort of customs barrier where the officials have long since given up any thought of catching smugglers red-handed. The trucks and camel caravans carrying contraband goods into

7. In Pakistan this department also deals with drug control.
8. i.e. £12 instead of £5.60. On the black market a rupee is worth 4p.

Pakistan do not use the road but go by mountain tracks where the customs men would not dream of venturing. A few kilometres further on we arrived at Barra Bazaar. This market, a collection of very new-looking booths and stalls standing in the middle of the desert, was graciously bestowed on the tribes by the Pakistani government. Displayed there we saw all kinds of Japanese electrical and photographic apparatus selling at Hong Kong prices, as well as fire-arms and watches. Our guide had come to buy a tape-recorder. Having chosen one and paid for it, he left the booth empty-handed. 'You never take away what you've bought here', he said by way of explanation, 'since none of these things are supposed to be imported into Pakistan. You'll see; my tape-recorder will be in Peshawar by this evening. All these goods are smuggled across the mountains. You don't have to give the matter another thought, even if you buy a refrigerator.'

'But,' we objected, 'you weren't even given a receipt. Aren't you afraid of being cheated?'

'The Pathans are the most honest traders in the world,' he replied. 'Their wealth is founded on confidence. They'll never do you down. It's known as the trust system. And then you mustn't forget that among the Pathans theft is punishable with death.'

Next we came to stalls where fire-arms, opium and hashish were on open display. Our guide introduced us as potential buyers to one of the traders, a Pathan of impressive physique. Like most of the other men in the market he wore a pair of bandoliers which, passing over shoulders and chest, crossed at the stomach. Not a cartridge was missing. On his head he wore the Persian lamb cap traditional among the Pathans. His fierce features, adorned with enormous, well-waxed moustachios, broke into a broad smile as soon as we entered his shop where we were treated to a demonstration of the Pathans' remarkable commercial gifts. He seemed in no way irritated by our flood of questions. Indeed all spoke freely here, for no one was conscious of being engaged in a reprehensible activity; it was simply business, no more. While we were chatting, our friend laid out on his counter parcels of newly harvested opium the size of a man's palm. Not as yet hardened, it was still a soft, brown paste and was wrapped in large, green leaves similar to those of a vine. He showed us various qualities of hashish, known locally as *charras*. A small amount of *cannabis sativa*[9] is grown in the Tribal Agencies, but most of it comes from Afghanistan, being sold in large slabs measuring forty by twenty centimetres. Some, made of pure compressed pollen, were pale yellow in colour and extremely friable. Others, darker, smoother and more compact, were produced from the sap in the leaves and stalks of the cannabis plant.

'Just now,' our trader told us, 'I'm selling opium at 600 rupees [£24] a kilo. It's never worth less than 400 rupees [£16]. *Charras* costs 200 rupees [£8] a kilo. It's first-rate stuff. The same quality in Karachi would cost you at least six to eight hundred rupees.'

He followed up his persuasive patter by slipping a quarter slab into one of our pockets 'so that you can try it before making up your mind'. In France his 'small sample' would have fetched 1,000 francs (£80) if not more.

When we asked him how much opium he could deliver, our friend, with a majestic sweep of the hand, indicated his shelves where fire-arms of every description kept company with large square bales wrapped in jute. 'I've got a ton here in my shop which I can deliver immediately if you wish,' he said. 'If you want more I shall need a day or two to get it together. But I could let you have five to eight tons fairly quickly.' Having offered us enough to supply the American market for a month, the Pathan continued: 'You can trust me, you know. I have other customers from abroad. I've known them buy three or four million rupees' worth [£120,000–£160,000][10] within the space of a few months.'

'Would you be able to deliver to Europe?'

'Yes. I've done it before,' came the unequivocal answer. 'How is it arranged?'

'We take the goods to Afghanistan. We've got an agent there

9. Plant from which hashish and marijuana are obtained.
10. Roughly the equivalent of six tons.

who sends them on to Europe. We've got another in Karachi who knows some diplomats.'

He had obviously told us all he knew about the conveyance of opium to distant parts. He was a wholesaler and his interest went no further.

We visited another booth where the merchant asked slightly less for his opium, the difference being about fifty rupees a kilogramme. The other had been trying to swindle us; in these parts one must always haggle. Again we were assured that delivery could be made in Europe. The second merchant, it seemed, also had contacts of his own. 'The goods will pass through Karachi,' he told us. 'But I can only undertake to have them shipped to Europe if you agree to their being dropped fifteen miles off the French coast. Otherwise it's too risky. You'll be responsible for the freight charges.'

Darra, another village, situated in the Kohat Pass some twenty kilometres from Peshawar, has a very specialized industry, the making by hand of copies of any and every type of weapon. Here you can buy a Beretta, a Colt, a Mauser 98, an M16 (a very up-to-date model), a Czech sub-machine-gun, a mortar, even a pom-pom. All you have to do is say what you want and put down your money; within an hour you'll be supplied. Also on sale are little pistols made to look like fountain-pens; they hold a single round and the clip acts as a trigger. If the model you want does not happen to be in stock, it will be made to order. The choice of craftsmen is wide since every shop in Darra's single street sells fire-arms.

The man we had come to see was a leading gun-runner and opium smuggler. He belonged to the same tribe and came from the same village as our guide, an official in the Pakistani department responsible for controlling opium production outside the Tribal Agencies. For the occasion he had abandoned his Excise officer's uniform in favour of the traditional Pathan garb consisting of baggy trousers gathered in at the waist and ankles, and a soft, white, knee-length shirt. Over his chest he wore the inevitable crossed bandoliers while an outsize pistol dangled at his left hip.

Smiling, our host greeted us at the entrance to his shop. Like all the inhabitants of this village, he wore a woollen cap with a wide turned-up edge strikingly like those worn at the French court in Louis XI's day.

Before getting down to business he served us with tea and showed us round his workshop. A few months previously he had replaced his manually operated lathe with a new machine powered by an electric generator. Most of the components for the weapons he made were still hand-forged. We were shown a copy of a Beretta which was indistinguishable from the original save for the double legend 'Made in Italy – Made in Pakistan' engraved on its butt by some over-zealous craftsman.

While we were talking, the peace of the small village was suddenly shattered by the sound of ragged volleys. The noise came from some Pathans who were trying out fire-arms and ammunition before finally deciding on a purchase.

Our host raised no objection when questioned about the ins and outs of the opium traffic in the tribal zones. In accordance with the tradition of hospitality sacrosanct among the Pathans,[11] he treated us as friends because friends had introduced us to him.

In the tribal zone' [he said] 'most of the opium is grown in the Tirah district, very wild country about sixty kilometres from here. A family may sell sixteen to eighteen kilos a year for the equivalent of six hundred dollars. But as often as not they barter the whole or part of the crop for cloth, salt, flour and weapons. Darra's the biggest opium market, bigger even than Barra which specializes more in opium. We exchange fire-arms for opium which we then sell. The weapons we make travel a long way. I know for a fact that in Thailand they're using so-called Chinese rifles made in this village.

'Most of the opium goes to Afghanistan. We cross the border at night, with small caravans of camels, horses or donkeys, protected by armed guards. An average cargo weighs two and a half tons. Once the opium has reached Kabul my job is finished. The cargo is taken

11. Those who seek hospitality among the Pathans are never refused. Thus large numbers of Pakistanis, wanted for theft or some other crime, have sought refuge in the Tribal Agencies. But they have to obey the local rules. If they commit any crimes on Pathan territory they are summarily executed.

185

over by an Afghan trader who sees to its onward dispatch. Most of it usually goes to Iran for local consumption. There are a lot of smokers in Iran and practically none in Afghanistan. But some passes straight through to one of the small ports on the Persian Gulf or the Gulf of Oman from where an Iranian merchant ships it to the Emirate of Dubai. Once there it fetches eight hundred rupees [£32] a kilo. But opium bound for Dubai is more often smuggled through Karachi, which is also the port of shipment for Hong Kong and Singapore. We have to pay 4,000 rupees [£160] to get across Pakistan to Karachi by truck. Or else we may simply take the opium to Quetta, another big market in the tribal zone. From there it's conveyed to one of the small, remote ports such as Pasni or Gwader in Pakistani Baluchistan, where it's put aboard fishing boats and taken across the Persian Gulf to Dubai.'

'But why Dubai?' we asked him.

'It's a distribution centre. Dubai specializes in the export of contraband gold to India. The people who trade in opium are often the same as those who trade in gold. One commodity passes down the pipeline and the other goes up. Gold is worth three times as much in India as in Europe and its importation is prohibited. Dubai's a free port and a place of call for big ships from all over the world, especially tankers. You meet people of all nationalities there – Iranians, Europeans and Chinese. And then it's an excellent staging-post on the route to Egypt where a great deal of opium is consumed. Only one country has to be crossed and that is Saudi Arabia where no one's going to bother about searching a caravan in mid-desert. Big weights of opium also go from Dubai to Denmark.'

When we asked if any heroin was manufactured in Dubai our guide-cum-Excise officer, who was acting as interpreter, looked at us in bewilderment. He had never heard the word heroin, nor had his friends. We tried to explain it to them, surprised that men so conversant with the drug's supply routes should know nothing about the existence and use of this white powder. Faced with their total incomprehension, we did not insist. They would find out soon enough. Indeed some of their compatriots had found out already.

Landi Kotal is another hotbed of contraband. To reach this large village you have to cross the impressive Khyber Pass, that defile, flanked by craggy mountains, through which Alexander the Great and all other invaders of India have taken their armies. Today the traveller is still liable to be attacked by brigands. A large sign at the entrance to the pass advises motorists not to enter it after four in the afternoon and to remain within fifteen feet of the road. The narrow defile gradually widens out to become a plateau. Here and there on the mountain slopes are fortress-like structures without any apparent apertures. These are the fortified depots used for the storage of contraband merchandise before it is distributed to the markets in the tribal zone.

Landi Kotal lies at a bend of the road that crosses the pass, and it was there that we were to meet Mahmoud and his brothers. The three Pathans, girt about with bandoliers, were armed to the teeth. One had his rifle nonchalantly slung from his shoulder, as did many of his fellows strolling about the alleyways. While perfectly willing to tell us what we wanted, they expected to be given information in return. Baring his yellow teeth in a broad grin, one of them broke the ice by telling us, in halting but tolerably correct English, that he had just completed a three months' gaol sentence in a European capital. He had been carrying fifty kilogrammes of hashish in his car. Since he was patently a smuggler born and bred, we could only wonder how he had managed to get so far without being stopped. All three brothers were extremely rich and owned a highly prosperous contraband store in the bazaar at Peshawar. They belonged to one of the most warlike Pathan tribes, the Afridis, who are the traditional guardians of the Khyber Pass.

'Mahmoud has been to Europe,' the eldest brother explained. 'He saw that there was a lot of money to be made out of manufacturing heroin. We'd like to produce it ourselves. How do we go about it? And where can we find someone to help us set up a factory? Where can we get hold of an expert? We'd pay him very well, and he'd be quite safe in our village. It's tucked away in the hills, three days' march on foot from here. All the villagers belong to our family. The factory could be guarded by eighty soldiers. We're very well armed and even have mortars. A Pakistani soldier or policeman would never venture so far and there'd be no difficulty about raw material since a lot of opium is already produced in our district and even more could be grown if wanted.'

There can be no doubt that these questions will soon be answered in concrete form, and that refining will become a flourishing industry in Pakhtunistan.

No one knows how much opium is produced in Afghanistan. According to the B.N.D.D's Intelligence Office, the country supplies the black market with at least a hundred tons a year. But the Afghans have little taste for statistics. The exact size of the population is unknown to them, as are the income per capita and the growth rate of the country's gross national product. Hence experts on international affairs have to do the best they can to obtain an approximate idea of the economic situation.

The country has not yet fully emerged from feudalism. It was formed in 1747 out of the union of several Pathan tribes which had hitherto enjoyed independence within the somewhat lax framework of the Persian Empire. Afghanistan still remains a kind of federation of ethnic groups in which chief, clan and tribe are of greater importance than the national idea.[12] The Central Government exercises no more than a notional authority over the provinces whose governors are omnipotent. Power is in the hands of the Pathans. But the other tribes, the Uzbeks, the Hazars, the Kirghiz (of Turko-Mongolian origin), the Tadjiks, the Brahuis, the Nuristanis and the Kashite nomads, who constitute more than half the country's twelve to fourteen million inhabitants, are becoming increasingly intolerant of Pathan domination.

Afghanistan has not yet become industrialized. Over eighty per cent of its population is dependent on agriculture, and one fifth is nomadic. Only thirteen per cent has abandoned the barter system in favour of coinage. According to figures produced by international organizations, income per capita does not exceed sixty dollars a year. Religion still has a strong hold over

12. Until the 1964 Constitution, all ministers were members of the royal family.

the people and in consequence women can play no part in the production process. They still wear the *pardah*, a voluminous cotton or silk veil which leaves no part of the body uncovered. A kind of embroidered grille at eye-level allows them to see without being seen. All this means that the government has other priorities and other cares besides the fight against opium.

As an immediate neighbour of the U.S.S.R., from which she has received massive economic aid, Afghanistan has made neutralism the overriding principle of her foreign policy. The Afghan authorities, long exposed to the opposing influences of Russia and Britain, have grown skilful at playing off one great power against another. For this reason America's field of diplomatic action is almost as circumscribed here as in Burma, and the U.S. Embassy in Kabul has still to convince the Afghans of the need to solve the opium problem.

At the end of the sixties Kabul, like Nepal, became a focal point for hippies of all nations. In the alleyways of the old bazaar and in the vast, modern, Soviet-style avenues of the new city, we saw hundreds of Americans, French, English, Germans, Swedes and Danes who were 'making the trip'. With a few dollars in their pockets they had set out from Europe to southeast Asia on a journey of perhaps several months or years. Hotels providing dormitory accommodation for the equivalent of 12p or 16p have mushroomed in the new Sharinao district and in the bazaar. The same amount will buy a reasonable meal.

Afghanistan makes a good halting place. Not only is the country very beautiful, but those in search of, as it were, an artificial paradise can find one with little or no difficulty. Hashish and opium are sold almost openly in the bazaar. Opium costs forty-five dollars a kilo and good quality hashish twenty dollars, while six dollars will buy a kilogramme of hashish of slightly inferior quality. A slab of LSD costs a dollar and morphine is available at some chemists' shops at two and a half dollars a tablet.[13] Although heroin and cocaine are rather more expensive, the price of a fix is much lower in Kabul than in New York.

13. Usually of German origin. They can be bought virtually without restriction in certain Kabul chemists' shops and are then smuggled back into Europe.

A few hundred out of the fifty thousand Europeans and Americans who stayed in Kabul in 1971 paid for their drugs and travelling expenses by becoming traffickers themselves. An outlay of about ten thousand dollars is enough to secure fifty kilogrammes of hashish, the connivance of a customs official and an airline ticket to the United States. The cargo will find a ready sale in Montreal or New York, where it will fetch ninety thousand dollars – a profit, that is, of eighty thousand dollars. So great is the temptation that many become ensnared. For as often as not the amateur is subsequently contacted by members of the international underworld who secure his collaboration by threatening to denounce him to the police. Thus he becomes a professional smuggler who, if caught, may very well rot for several years, chained to the wall of some unspeakable prison in Iran, Libya or Pakistan.[14] For the producer countries are only too happy to apprehend a foreigner and thus demonstrate that it is not they who are responsible for the addiction prevalent in the western world.

What the B.N.D.D. chiefly fears is to see the network of semi-professional hashish traffickers turn their attention to opium and its derivatives as soon as the big racketeers, both French and American, set out to find replacements for their Turkish suppliers. This fear is well-founded, the more so since there are already at least two refineries transforming opium into morphine in Afghanistan, one at Herat and another at Kandahar. Both are said to belong to highly placed Afghans.

However the Bureau of Narcotics realizes that it can bring little influence to bear on Afghanistan, whose government shows small inclination to cooperate. True, there is a law prohibiting the cultivation and consumption of opium, but no penalties for these offences have ever been laid down. Hence the law is inoperative. The Afghan authorities' lack of enthusiasm is explicable since they do not feel that they are involved in the drug problem. There are no opium addicts in Afghanistan and the

14. At present some 700 American citizens are serving sentences of imprisonment in various countries for drug trafficking. Despite strenuous efforts, their consulates have not been able to secure either their release or their extradition to the United States.

government's view has been neatly summed up by a western diplomat: 'Since it's your own nationals who are addicted, it's your own problem.'

Even if it wished to do so, the Afghan government would not have sufficient resources to ban poppy cultivation within its territory. The producing areas are situated in districts where intervention is impossible for reasons at once geographical, political and economic. The poppy is grown in Afghan Pakhtunistan along the whole length of the Pakistani border from Jalalabad in the north to the important southern town of Kandahar; also in the Nuristan Hills, north of Jalalabad, and in the province of Badakshan on the Russian border.

To forbid opium growing in Afghan Pakhtunistan would be to play into the hands of the Pakistanis by arousing anti-Afghan sentiment among the Pathan tribes. Nuristan is inhabited by Kafirs, Badakshan by Tadjiks, these being the two largest ethnic groups after the Pathans. The Tadjiks alone constitute a third of Afghanistan's population. Both tribes are ready to seize on the first available pretext to free themselves from the Pathans whose authority they already regard as an intolerable burden. Kabul is extremely anxious to avoid precipitating rebellion, thereby jeopardizing the country's unity for the sake of a problem that does not directly concern it. In addition, the producing regions are almost inaccessible. Although a few secondary roads lead to the Pakistani border, the only means of travel in Nuristan and Badakshan is on horseback. The highway to Faydabad in the north bypasses Nuristan. Moreover these two regions are completely cut off from the Kabul plateau by the Hindu Kush massif. This huge barrier, whose peaks rise to twenty-four thousand feet and more, divides Afghanistan in two.

In these remote regions, snowbound for more than half the year, the peasants have no means of livelihood other than the cultivation of the poppy. 'It's all very well worrying about human beings smoking and injecting themselves with the stuff,' was the bitter comment of a senior Afghan official, 'but that doesn't mean you've got to allow the people who actually grow the opium to starve to death. They're human beings as well. And if

191

you take away their means of subsistence, how are they going to live?'

The Afghan authorities, like their counterparts in all the other producer countries we passed through, are exasperated by the censorious attitude adopted towards them by the western nations.

'They ask us to stamp out opium-growing,' remarked Colonel Katawazi, the Afghan police chief. 'And we for our part ask why the consumer countries don't stamp out their gangs of racketeers. It's they who harbour the racketeers, not we.'

A fine-looking man with flashing eyes in a tanned face, a hooked nose and a wolfish smile, the colonel wore a close-fitting, impeccably cut uniform. He was typically Afghan – at once very proud and very courteous. With complete frankness he explained his point of view, which appeared to be shared by official circles generally.

'Until the middle of the sixties, the drug problem didn't exist so far as we were concerned. Since then we've had a flood of European tourists, some of whom come here to smoke opium and hashish. And now the accusing finger is being pointed at us Afghans! Ours is a poor country. It's impossible for us to control the crops with the few police we have at our disposal. After all, I can't send men on a march of several days into some desolate region to destroy pocket-handkerchief-sized fields scattered over several hundreds of acres. The peasants often grow opium in their gardens, but these are barred to us under Koranic Law.[15] Nor are we equipped to combat the traffic. We don't have the money to pay informers. When we seize other kinds of contraband we sell it in the bazaar and pay fifteen per cent of the receipts to the person who tipped us off. Obviously we can't do the same with opium and hashish. And so far as our frontier with Persia is concerned, all we have is a squad of

---

15. Strangers have no right to enter places frequented by the women of the house. We ourselves witnessed how seriously this matter is taken by Muslims. Near Peshawar we watched a minor riot after some villagers had stopped a bus carrying passengers on its roof. Their lofty position had enabled them to see the women in the inner courtyards. After a violent clash all the passengers were bundled into the interior of the bus which was then allowed to proceed.

ten unmounted gendarmes for every forty kilometres. They have neither jeeps, telephones nor radios.'

Despite increasingly stringent controls, small quantities of morphine continue to find their way through Kabul's international airport. Up till 1970 the Afghan capital was an ideal dispatch point, since couriers could fly direct to Paris, London or Frankfurt by *Ariana*, the national airline, without stopping off in Iran where traffickers are liable to the death penalty. The excellent relations between Afghanistan and the U.S.S.R. provided opportunities for new supply routes. For instance, one of the many young Afghan students visiting the U.S.S.R. each year might go to Leningrad or Moscow and thence to Prague or Warsaw, taking with him a suitcaseful of morphine. There he would meet another Afghan, who had travelled from western Europe, posing as a tourist. The latter would take over the merchandise and return to the west, as often as not without being searched, since a person arriving from behind the Iron Curtain would be unlikely to arouse the suspicions of the officials responsible for narcotics control.

The bulk of the traffic, however, is directed towards Iran where there are countless opium addicts. The merchants who specialize in buying and selling the drug live for the most part in Kabul and Kandahar. They provide the producers with money for seed and may also make an advance payment for part of the crop. For many years the opium was taken to Herat by truck, concealed in sacks of corn or other merchandise. It was then smuggled into Iran through the rugged and inhospitable mountains that lie between Herat and Meshed on the Persian side of the border. The tightening up of legislation in Iran has already brought more than one trafficker to the gallows and induced smugglers to cross the border further south, in Seistan. The new route not only obviates the need to take the opium all the way to Herat but facilitates the diversion of part of the cargo, once safely in Iran, to the Persian Gulf and Dubai.

But the principle remains the same. The nomads who contract to smuggle the opium must leave their wives and children as hostages to the bosses in Kandahar. The smugglers know that,

193

if they are caught or have to abandon their cargo when pursued by Iranian gendarmes, the lives of their families will be forfeit. Hence they will fight to the death to preserve their precious loads. If, having lost the battle, they succeed in escaping, they frequently hold the inhabitants of Iranian villages to ransom in the hope of raising enough money to take back to their masters.

For the Afghans, the control of the traffic is not simply a matter of law enforcement. In a society where salaries are extremely low, bribery has become an institution. Although a minister cannot earn more than 10,000 afghanis (£56), he will run a chauffeur-driven car. A departmental head in a ministry receives 2,500 afghanis (£12), a university teacher 2,500 afghanis (£11) and a police officer 1,800 afghanis (£10). The chef in a foreign embassy earns more than the head of a ministry. In such circumstances, which also obtain in Pakistan and a number of other countries, almost anybody will render a small service in order to supplement his income. This is not regarded as in any way reprehensible, but simply as one of the local customs. In 1971, for instance, two American nationals were apprehended for having bought drugs. They had paid two hundred dollars for twenty litres of alcohol and fifteen kilogrammes of hashish, hoping to sell the latter in liquid form in the United States at the going price of six million dollars. The court had fixed their bail at 3,000 afghanis (£17). But finding it simpler to pay this sum direct to their gaolers, the paid walked out of prison and much to the chagrin of the American Embassy, left Afghanistan without further ado.

The kid-glove treatment meted out to foreigners by the Afghans is also extended to their own nationals, despite requests from western governments that more energetic measures be taken. Here we may discern another legacy of British colonialism. An Afghan policeman who collaborated with an American or European to catch an Afghan trafficker would be regarded as a traitor to his race, tribe and family. Consequently the American Bureau of Narcotics is able to elicit little or no response from the local police.

With undisguised irritation Colonel Katawazi told us:

'We're not members of Interpol and we don't work with the B.N.D.D. We collaborate with the Bureau if they ask us, as happens almost every day. For our part, we never approach them since we don't need their information. In any case, we're the only people empowered to act in Afghanistan. They can, of course, warn us of the arrival of notorious traffickers, but under no circumstances are they authorized to arrest them.'

The United States have no means of bringing pressure to bear on the Afghan government. Despite the constant efforts of the American Embassy in Kabul, little headway has been made in this respect. Indeed, the influence of the U.S.S.R. is very much more in evidence, a legacy of the cold war between these two great powers.

In the years following the Second World War the United States regarded Afghanistan as a country of secondary importance and treated her as such. Between 1947 and 1953 the ambassadors posted there were men approaching the end of their careers. Diplomats tended to look on Kabul as a punishment station.[16]

But the Afghans found even greater cause for resentment in the persistent refusal of the Americans to help them modernize their army. Even in the late fifties the Afghan infantry was still equipped with nineteenth century rifles and was, moreover, short of ammunition. The Air Force comprised no more than twelve aircraft of First World War vintage. Furthermore, the country's unity was jeopardized by the fact that several of the Pathan tribes were better equipped than the Royal Army.

During this period the Americans had not stinted their subsidies to Iran, Iraq and Pakistan, particularly after 1953 when General Eisenhower and John Foster Dulles held sway in Washington. According to Arnold Fletcher, author of *Afghanistan, Highway of Conquest*, no other non-communist country abutting on the Sino-Soviet sphere of influence was as neglected as Afghanistan.

The American attitude was due to the fear that, were Afghanistan to possess a modern army, she would immediately turn it

16. *Afghanistan, Highway of Conquest*, Arnold Fletcher, Cornell University Press, New York, 1966.

against Pakistan in an attempt to recover Pakhtunistan. Indeed, to judge by the technical aid given to Iran and Pakistan (over 100 million dollars each) and that granted to Afghanistan (6 million dollars), America was obviously counting on the first two countries to safeguard her position in Asia.

Hence the Afghans had ceased to expect anything further of the United States when Nikita Khruschev visited Kabul in November 1956. To the dismay of the American diplomats the Russian leader announced that the Soviet Union intended to grant Afghanistan development aid amounting to a hundred million dollars. That aid was renewed several times and, by the end of 1971, totalled five hundred million dollars. The Americans, despite their desire to make good what had been an obvious error, have lagged far behind, with loans currently totalling two hundred million dollars.

The Russians have, of course, met the wishes of the Afghans in replacing their military equipment, nearly all of which comes from the U.S.S.R. Afghanistan now possesses jet bombers and fighters. Moreover nearly all the country's motor transport, whether civil or military, is of Soviet origin. The interruption of diplomatic relations between Afghanistan and Pakistan from 1961 to 1963 gave the Russians an even greater hold over the Afghan economy. The road system was so poor that the import and export trade, which normally passed through Karachi, could not be re-routed through Iran. Thus the U.S.S.R. became Afghanistan's only link with the outside world, its dominance being further reinforced by the fact that imports of American durable goods, precluded from passing through Russian territory, were cut off for the space of two years. In addition the Soviet authorities organized an air-lift consisting of fifteen cargo aircraft, and also helped the Afghans to speed up the construction of a road leading to Kushka on the Russian border.

The extent of the Soviet presence does not mean that Afghanistan is a satellite of the U.S.S.R. Coveted since her earliest days by the British as well as by the Russians, who would only have needed to cross the Amu Darya to seize the great northern plains, Afghanistan has been colonized by neither. Though the British won a few battles they were never able to establish them-

196

selves in the country. One rebellion followed another, each attended by a massacre of British citizens.

Afghanistan is well-versed in the art of dealing with the great powers, and of playing off one against the other to safeguard her own interests. Where opium is concerned, the nature of her strategy is becoming clearly discernible. If at some future date she is compelled to yield to international pressure, she does not intend to bear the cost herself, and her cooperation will be proportionate to the aid received.

'The opium problem can only be resolved at production level,' [Colonel Katawazi told us]. 'But that presupposes a considerably enlarged police force and, still more important, the provision of alternative means of subsistence for the poppy-growers. We can't possibly shoulder the burden ourselves. A programme of this nature involving development schemes would call for international aid on a massive scale. Up till now, however, all the United Nations have done is to send us *experts*. But that doesn't solve the peasants' problems. After all, they can't very well eat an expert.'

Nevertheless, the Afghans have prudentially formed two ministerial committees, one responsible to the Ministry of the Interior and the other to the Ministry of Agriculture, their task being to work out concrete proposals, accompanied by the relevant figures, for submission to the international organizations should the latter become too importunate. But the government is sceptical. As early as 1965 the United Nations had made promises which were never kept. And without tangible support the Afghans are not prepared to embark on an enterprise as hazardous as that of banning the production of opium.

Since the beginning of the seventies the Afghan economy has been passing through a very difficult phase. Two consecutive droughts have seriously affected agriculture and more especially stock farming. Thousands of sheep have been lost and peasants have come flocking into the towns. The extent of these difficulties can be gauged from the growing numbers of ragged beggars in the streets of Kabul. There would seem to be little or no hope of finding a solution to these problems. Afghanistan is not yet sufficiently industrialized to cope with the influx from the rural areas which now seems unavoidable. Moreover, she

197

must make provision, on a budget of a billion dollars, for the repayment of her external debt amounting to thirty million dollars a year.

The problem of suppressing opium in Afghanistan can be reduced to a simple question: Who is going to pay? The Americans are not prepared, as in Turkey, to spend considerable sums on a country where they have no control over the political, economic and administrative machinery. They would far rather delegate this role to the U.N. or some other international organization to which they would, of course, make a fair contribution on condition that other countries did the same. They have also been responsible for organizing several meetings between the ambassadors in Kabul to decide upon a common stance *vis-à-vis* the Afghan authorities, the better to bring pressure to bear on them. But the minutes of these discussions reveal that France, for example, with relatively important cultural and economic interests at stake, is reluctant to interfere in Afghanistan's internal affairs merely to help solve a problem that is specifically American.

While waiting to see what effect, if any, these measures will have, the United States are applying to Afghanistan, as they have already done to Burma, the principle of the *cordon sanitaire*. The Bureau of Narcotics, while intensifying its own efforts in Thailand and Laos, is largely counting on Iran to stop the flow of Pakistani and Afghan opium from reaching Europe and its ultimate destination, the United States. 'Our immediate intention,' we were told by a B.N.D.D. agent serving in the Near East, 'is to set up a police cordon round Afghanistan that would act like a barbed wire entanglement. That is what we are now engaged in doing.'

Part 4

Opium: the Political and Economic Aspects

By exerting the utmost pressure on the authorities in Ankara the United States have finally succeeded in persuading them to ban the cultivation of the poppy as from 1972. But this hard-won victory seems unlikely to endure, such is the frustration prevalent in Turkey where the financial compensation proposed is generally regarded as in no way commensurate with the sacrifices made.

Even supposing the Turkish government never goes back on its decision to ban the production of opium, this measure is unlikely to have far-reaching effects in view of the difficulty of coordinating production policies at international level. Iran is a case in point: having banned production for thirteen years, she resumed the cultivation of the poppy in 1969 because her addicts were obtaining opium illicitly from Afghanistan and Pakistan. If Iran succeeds in growing enough to meet her own needs, the hundreds of tons of opium produced by the first two countries will become available to fill the gap left by Turkey.

The impossibility of achieving satisfactory international coordination in this field derives from the existence of national economic interests so powerful that they obtrude upon the world community, regardless of humanitarian considerations. This is why the diplomatic offensives being conducted through the United Nations have little prospect of success. Neither that organization nor its numerous specialist agencies are invested with the supranational powers that would enable them to adjudicate between the conflicting interests of member countries. The extent of their impotence may be gauged from the fact that, despite the proliferation of international treaties governing the production and sale of narcotics, the availability of illicit opium has in no way diminished.

Nor can the international Fund for Drug Control, set up in 1971, be regarded with anything but scepticism. If that organization is to play a significant role in extirpating illicit production and sales, the more prosperous countries – supposedly responsible for financing the scheme – must drastically change their attitude towards the distribution of the world's wealth. And this they show no signs of doing.

12   Turkish Diplomacy and the Poppy

At one time Turkey was able to produce, without let or hindrance, opium of excellent quality much valued for its high morphine content, which might be as much as fifteen per cent.[1] She was one of the few privileged countries authorized under the international conventions to export opium to the world's pharmaceutical industry, thereby earning appreciable amounts of foreign currency. True, part of her production found its way on to the black market to be converted into heroin and sold by international traffickers operating in the Middle East, Europe and the United States. But to the authorities in Ankara this was no more than a minor problem if not a time-honoured tradition. Moreover their own country had been free of addiction since the fifties.

In 1966 Turkey suddenly found herself in the pillory. On the other side of the Atlantic the spectre of heroin addiction had grown ever more menacing, and with increasing frequency Turkey was singled out as being the main source of the raw material used in the manufacture of the drug. It was now that John Cusacks, head of the American Bureau of Narcotics, decided to sound the alarm. 'Eighty per cent of the heroin consumed in the United States,' he declared, 'comes from France and originates in the Turkish poppy-fields.' This remark caused a sensation, although there was little or nothing to substantiate it. The ensuing hubbub marked the beginning of America's major offensive against Turkish opium. From then on the United States waged a war of attrition aimed at suppressing poppy cultivation in Turkey. In this way they hoped to cut the supply-line along which the base morphine was conveyed to Marseilles for conversion into heroin. Since it had proved

1. In most other producer countries the morphine content does not exceed nine or ten per cent.

impossible to eliminate the Marseilles laboratories, Washington argued, the problem must be tackled at source, in other words at production level.

The poppy has been cultivated in Turkey from time immemorial. In the museum at Pergamum near Izmir the flower may be seen in Greek bas-reliefs dating back two thousand years. It formed an integral part of the daily life of tens of thousands of Turkish peasants. Up till 1972 nearly ninety thousand farming families were dependent on this crop from which their income mainly derived. Part of their production was sold to the State through the Office of Agricultural Produce,[2] while the rest, often as much as half the crop, was carefully concealed from the government inspectors and sold on the black market to brokers acting for international racketeers. But opium had many other uses. When crushed the seeds yielded a vegetable oil much valued not only in Turkish kitchens but also abroad. The oil-cakes were used for cattle-feed and, according to the peasants of Afyon Province, helped to produce the best yoghurt in Turkey. Dried poppy-seeds were also used in making traditional pastries, those sweet and exquisitely crunchy confections known as *Silgin Boereghi* and *Hashash Coereghi*. Again, the poppy-heads could be infused to make a sedative drink. Sometimes, too, they were exported as 'poppy-straw' to Holland and to various eastern countries where morphine sulphate was extracted by a series of somewhat complex processes.

For centuries opium has been an essential part of the local pharmacopoeia. In country districts parents would slip an opium pellet under the pillow of an over-excited child to make it sleep better.

Opium has another advantage – it is non-perishable, and hence represents an ideal form of saving. In Turkey there are known to be stocks of opium which have been kept for a hundred years without deteriorating. In fact, after the birth of a male child, a Turkish peasant family would set aside a small

2. The weights of opium sold to the Office of Agricultural Produce were as follows: 1967, 119 tons; 1968, 125 tons; 1969, 128 tons; 1970, 63 tons; 1971, 149 tons.

quantity each year, so that when he came to marry he had the wherewithal to pay the traditional bride-price which was often very high. Hoarding opium was also a form of health insurance. Turkish doctors were often surprised to see peasants pay cash down for their very expensive hospital treatment and here again it was the opium 'nest-egg' that provided the funds. The drug never depreciates in value, at least on the black market. Prices may rise and money lose its value, but the happy owner of an opium hoard has no need to worry. All monetary fluctuations, whether at home or abroad, are immediately compensated by the traffickers.

Under the Ottoman Empire – that is, until Kemal Atatürk's accession to power and the advent of a republican government in 1923 – opium could be exported from Turkey virtually without restriction. A number of substantial fortunes were founded on this trade which explains why, before the 1914 war, there should have been a branch of the great Anglo-French Ottoman Bank in a remote little town near Afyon Province. After coming to power, Atatürk put a stop to the free trade in opium and introduced a system of compulsory State purchase. But production remained unrestricted and largely uncontrolled.

As an important member of the 'free world' and wishing no doubt to conform, Turkey sent a delegation to New York in 1961 to take part in the international narcotics conference which marked the beginning of the world campaign aimed at tackling the problem at production level. American public opinion had not as yet been alerted to the dangers of drug addiction and discussion of the subject was largely confined to a small circle of experts and to the corridors of the United Nations. Turkey did not even trouble to ratify the 1961 Convention, although she expressly undertook to implement some of its articles. In order to facilitate the control of opium production, poppy cultivation was confined to smaller areas well removed from the frontiers. In 1964 only sixteen provinces were permitted to grow the crop, but two years later, in response to pressure from the peasants, this number was increased to twenty-one. The only effect of the reduction in acreage was a corresponding reduction in the amount of opium sold to the government. On the other hand the quantities reaching the black market remained stable – as did supplies to the illicit laboratories, if what the American authorities say is true.

In 1965 the United States began to exert discreet economic pressure on Ankara with a view to 'marginalizing' Turkey as a producer and exporter of licit opium. Thereafter U.S. purchases of Turkish opium for the pharmaceutical industry declined steadily. From 118 tons in 1965, deliveries had fallen to 31·6 tons in 1969, although American opiate requirements had not diminished. At the same time the United States, together with certain of their NATO allies, stepped up their purchases from India.

From 1969 onwards, Senators and Representatives in Washington vied with each other in laying before Congress bills aimed at reducing economic aid to Turkey, 'should that country fail to take definite and effective steps to stem the tide of illicit opium that is flooding the United States'.

This was no empty threat. Since the Second World War, the Turkish economy had been dependent upon external aid, both European and American. After a phase of rapid expansion during the early fifties – the boom period of the Korean War – Turkey began to run into difficulties which manifested themselves in an adverse balance of payments, sometimes of catastrophic proportions. Some ten years later she asked her NATO allies for increased economic aid and for a reduction of the military commitments she had incurred as a member of the North Atlantic Alliance. While according a favourable reply to the second request, they referred the first to the Organization for European Economic Cooperation (now the O.E.C.D.). The latter set up an international consortium consisting of Canada, the United States and twelve European countries to help Turkey finance her external trade and her industrial investment projects. These arrangements are still in force today. Further assistance takes the form of bilateral aid, mainly supplied by the United States and the German Federal Republic. In the circumstances the Turkish government cannot lightly dismiss any question connected with help from abroad.

204

Indeed, after its victory in 1965, Mr Süleyman's Justice Party had embarked on a 'goodwill' policy in regard to opium. This involved the progressive reduction of the number of provinces authorized to grow opium; from eighteen in 1967, these had dwindled to seven in 1970.[3] On 27 December 1966 the Turkish Assembly approved the Single Convention on Narcotic Drugs, drawn up in Geneva five years previously. The Convention provided among other things for the issue of licences to growers on the basis of which estimates could be made of the yield to be expected from the acreage under cultivation. In Turkey this provision was not fully implemented until 1971.

Towards the middle of 1970 the Americans began to increase their pressure. In effect the Turks were presented with two alternatives: either they controlled production and thus stopped leakages on to the black market, or they banned the poppy altogether.

William Handley, the U.S. Ambassador in Ankara, undoubtedly hoped that the Turks would adopt the latter course, for he had little faith in their ability to curb the traffic, despite the 'technical contribution' made by his government.

There can be no doubt that Turkey was a smuggler's paradise. She produced some of the best opium in the world. A hundred kilos of Turkish opium yielded thirteen or fourteen kilos of heroin as compared with the ten kilos or less obtained from the east Asian crops. Only Yugoslavia and Afghanistan produced opium of comparable quality.

It was easy enough to tax the Turkish government with negligence. In fact, adequate supervision of production would have called for a system as complex as it was expensive. Until the very day of the harvest, it was virtually impossible to tell what the yield would be. In Turkey a hectare might produce anything from four to eleven kilos of opium. But a spring frost or, worse still, a heavy downpour the night after the poppy-heads had been tapped, would mean the loss of the crop. In the circumstances the peasants could easily divert part of their

3. The number of provinces authorized to cultivate the poppy were: 1961, 35; 1962, 25; 1964, 16, 1965, 19; 1966, 21; 1967, 18; 1968, 11; 1969, 9; 1970, 7; 1971, 4; 1972, 0.

205

produce on to the black market. All they had to do, if the deliveries made to the Office of Agricultural Produce were suspiciously small, was to blame the weather, for the officials concerned had no means of checking their statements. Leakages could only have been prevented by on-the-spot inspection at the very moment the crop was harvested. But this presupposed an enormous staff, since the area involved was 50,000 hectares comprising at least 90,000 holdings, all of which would have to be inspected within a harvest period of at most three weeks. Various countries, including Iran, have decided to introduce controls of this nature, but the enormous expense of such an undertaking increases the cost of opium to such an extent that it is priced out of the licit market. It follows that a country which adopts this policy – unless, like India, it has a plentiful supply of cheap labour – inevitably loses its exports, thus voluntarily forfeiting part of its revenue. And so paradoxical is the situation that, were all the producer countries to introduce rigid controls to prevent leakages on to the black market, the only real sufferer would be the pharmaceutical industry because of the inevitable rise in price.

Turkey's resources would not have enabled her to post an Excise man alongside every peasant. Moreover the strained relations between the peasantry and the central government would have made the introduction of such a system doubly difficult. Thus, from the forties onwards little was done in the way of control. The peasants had to declare the acreage they had sown and forecast the yield, their statements being checked shortly before the harvest by a handful of 'experts' who then provided their own production estimates. But the information, whether it came from peasants or experts, was equally unreliable. There was nothing to prevent the producer, who had harvested five kilogrammes of opium, from declaring and surrendering four, more especially since there was usually an interval of over a month between the day the crop was gathered and the time of its delivery to the Office of Agricultural Produce. The grower could take advantage of this delay to adulterate his opium, as a wine-grower waters his wine. Having abstracted some of the harvest he would make up the weight with various additives such as resin or egg yolks. As for the 'inspectors', often drawn from the very villages whose crops they inspected, and as likely as not related to most of the inhabitants, they tended greatly to underestimate the probable yields, a tendency almost certainly reinforced by the rewards they received for doing so. But apart from this, the sheer solidarity of the village communities is enough to explain the ineffectiveness of the controls.

Since the racketeers paid better prices than the State, it might seem otiose to ask why the peasants should have preferred to sell the major part of their crop on the black market. The problem, however, is not as simple as it looks at first sight.

Turkish peasants are poor, often to the point of penury and, contrary to general belief, the opium growers were no exception. They were tempted not only by the lure of higher profits but also by the fact that, unlike the government, the trafficker paid cash on delivery. In the ordinary course of things a peasant often needed ready money, either for food, seed or implements. He would then pledge a few kilogrammes of his future crop to obtain a cash advance from one of the local black market buyers. Over the years this gave rise to a stable if illicit credit system. Thus the government's failure to pay on the nail was exploited by the traffickers' local agents to ensure a regular supply of opium. Many of these men had been government buyers in Atatürk's day and had long been associated with the peasants. The ties between them were further reinforced by the vagaries of the official purchasing system which, on occasion, actually drove the growers into the arms of the black marketeers. In 1962 and 1963, for instance, the government reduced its purchases of opium because of low prices on the world market, thereby compelling the peasants to sell their produce illicitly.

After coming to power in 1966, the Demirel government did its best to respond to increasing U.S. pressure without unduly compromising Turkish interests. The number of provinces authorized to grow opium were progressively reduced. By 1970 they had fallen to seven and by 1971 numbered no more than four. However this did not deceive the Americans who realized that these measures had done little or nothing to change the situation, and that those four provinces, namely Afyon, Kütahya,

Isparta and Burdur, were in fact yielding as much opium as had been formerly produced in all the provinces now subject to the ban. In private – and not perhaps without good reason – the Americans further pointed out that the choice of these four had not been fortuitous but dictated rather by political demagogy. Demirel represented the province of Isparta where he enjoyed great popularity. He was the peasants' spokesman and, as a boy, had often helped harvest the opium in his father's poppy fields. Mesur Erez, his Finance Minister[4] and member for Kütahya, was no less averse to offending his electorate. The province of Burdur produced the best, and also the most expensive, opium in the world. Known locally as 'brown gold', its morphine content was as high as fourteen or fifteen per cent. Finally, the province of Afyon Karahisar – literally 'black citadel of opium' – had to be handled tactfully for electoral reasons since it contained fifty thousand peasant families, two thirds of whose income derived from opium.

Another of the Demirel government's measures, and one not altogether devoid of machiavellianism, was to have unexpected and disastrous results. By August 1970 the Exchequer was empty and the Turkish lira in a precarious state. This called for strong medicine and the currency was devalued by sixty-six per cent. As is usual in such cases, the export price of agricultural produce was simultaneously raised so as to safeguard the already marginal standard of living of the peasantry. However it was decided not to touch the price of opium, the intention being to bring about an artificial fall so as to induce the peasants to switch over to other crops promising better remuneration. In this way the government hoped to avoid having recourse to legislative measures.[5] As anticipated, production dropped steeply in 1970, totalling no more than sixty-three tons as against 125 tons in 1968. But these figures only related to the quantity sold to the State. Far larger amounts than in previous years were sold to the traffickers who had raised their prices – already

4. From 1969 to 1971.
5. The licit price of opium was then 100 Turkish liras (about 11 dollars) for 1 kilo of opium having a morphine content of over thirteen per cent.

much higher than the official rate – by keeping in step with the devaluation of the lira. Opium has been aptly described as a form of 'hard currency'[6] since it is insulated from market fluctuations. A Turkish government inquiry revealed that in 1970 ninety tons of opium had been illicitly sold to traffickers, a quantity considerably in excess of licit sales. When, however, the official price was raised in 1971, deliveries to the Office of Agricultural Produce rose to the more normal level of 149 tons.

After pressure from the Army had brought about the fall of Mr Demirel on 12 March 1971, Professor Erim formed a new government more in keeping with the wishes of the military. This was at the height of America's campaign against 'Turkey, the chief source of the opium which is poisoning the youth of America'. More than seventy bills aimed at reducing aid to Turkey had been laid before Congress. And on 21 June John Mitchell, the Attorney-General, informed the Senate that, unless Turkey took steps to halt the production of opium, the United States might decide to impose economic sanctions.

A few weeks after his accession to power, Professor Erim was called on by William Handley, the United States Ambassador, who informed him of his government's views on the opium question. The following week, on 5 April, the Turkish Prime Minister declared:

'My government believes that human values are at stake. I shall devote a great deal of attention to the problems raised by the opium traffic which is wreaking such terrible havoc among the youth of the entire world. We shall re-orientate our country's opium producers towards a new mode of life.'

Although there had been no mention of specific measures or dates, this statement of policy seemed to indicate that the government intended to ban the poppy and substitute other crops.

Each year, on 29 June, a list of provinces authorized to grow the poppy was published by the authorities. In 1971 this list proved a disagreeable shock for the opium farmers. Not only

6. *Opium monnaie forte*, Jacques Armand Prevost, *L'ordre du joir* series, La Table ronde, 1962.

209

did the government restrict its authorization to four provinces; it also announced that the 1972 harvest was to be the last. The unexpected haste with which this decision was taken can be attributed to the quite exceptional pressure exerted by the American Embassy. A few days previously the Ambassador had received a personal cable from President Nixon which, though its text has never been made public, is known to have called for immediate and tangible results in the matter of Turkish opium. On 17 June, in a long televised speech, the President had promised the Americans spectacular progress in the fight against drugs. It was rumoured in Washington that success in Turkey had become for him a matter of personal prestige. His insistence is all the more comprehensible in that the limelight was thereby deflected from south-east Asia where leading political figures, upon whom Washington counted for support, had become the target both of journalists and of Senate investigation committees.

On the day following the announcement of the definitive ban on poppy cultivation, the press and a number of Turkish members of Parliament gave vent to their indignation. They were outraged by the fact that the decision had been made before the United States had given any formal undertaking to offset the inevitable social and economic consequences of such a step. In August 1971 twenty-one Turkish senators laid before the Assembly a bill aimed at repealing the ban. Anti-American sentiment, always latent in Turkey, again reared its head. Mr Suphi Gursoytrak, who had been made a life Senator for the part he had played in overthrowing Menderes in 1960, declared bitterly: 'Basically what this decree means is that we are abandoning our opium growers to American charity.' Speaking before the Assembly in February 1972, at a session devoted to the opium problem, the Independent Senator for Malatya declared:

'Thanks to the exploitation of humanitarian sentiment, the opium-growers have been sacrificed to the whims of American magnates. It seems ironical that we should have to ban the production of opium while the United States expands the manufacture of synthetic drugs. A large proportion of those drugs, and particularly LSD, is being introduced into Turkey without any attempt on the part of the United States to stop the traffic, despite repeated requests from the Turkish government.'

But viewed objectively the best-founded argument would seem to be that put forward by Ahmet Kabakli in the newspaper *Tercuman*:[7]

The poppy is Turkey's oil. We could and should have developed an alkaloid industry based on the poppy, after placing opium production entirely under the control of a State monopoly. Had we done so, the world pharmaceutical industry would have needed us for our high-quality opium, and we should have earned tens of millions of dollars.

Finally, Ismail Cem, a popular columnist on Turkey's biggest independent newspaper, *Milliyet*, declared that his country had been made a scapegoat for the shortcomings of the French and American police. 'It is easier for the United States to put a stop to production in Turkey than to lay their hands on the Marseilles laboratories,' he wrote, and went on to blame the Prime Minister, not only for having yielded to U.S. persuasion without prior guarantees, but for failing to bargain with the Americans before the decision had been reached. 'In Turkey,' he commented, not without humour, 'you generally bargain first and clinch the deal afterwards.'

The decision to suppress opium production could not be implemented until ways and means had been found for redeploying the growers, some hundred thousand all told. If this operation was to be carried out successfully, it was essential to have financial assistance from the United States. The two parties now entered upon a series of negotiations which seemed likely to be protracted. To give added weight to its arguments, the Erim government had raised the price of opium by sixty-five per cent. In as much as it offset the effects of the 1970 devaluation, the increase provided a more favourable basis on which to negotiate the indemnities to be paid by the United

7. Ahmet Kabakli, 'The Poppy is Turkey's Oil', *Tercuman*, 16 November 1971.

States – a last-minute strategem which, however, did not prevent the discussions from turning to Turkey's disadvantage. Nor is this surprising, for the decision to ban opium had already been ratified, promulgated and published in the official gazette. Hence there was little left to negotiate. The Turkish authorities, who had estimated that the ban on opium production would cost the country 432 million dollars, had finally to content themselves with compensation amounting to 35 million dollars.

At the beginning of June 1971 important and confidential discussions had taken place between the United States Embassy and the Erim government. Both parties had advanced their views as to how the opium problem should be settled. From the outset Washington refused to envisage the possibility of merely controlling production, for this had already proved unworkable. What they wanted was an outright ban. But the Turkish negotiators had to concede yet another point. The object of these discussions was not to calculate the amount of compensation due to Turkey for services rendered; rather the Americans took the view that, though Turkey had signed the 1912 Hague Convention and endorsed each successive international agreement on narcotics, including the 1961 Convention, she had never enforced them, except in a manner so desultory as to be totally ineffective. Hence, far from asking a favour of Turkey, the Americans were simply demanding that she respect her international obligations. Once this principle had been accepted, their argument ran, the government of the United States, in concert with international organizations such as the United Nations and the World Bank, would be prepared to help Turkey overcome the economic and social difficulties resulting from the total ban on opium production.

By pointing out to the Turks that no compensation of any kind attached to the fulfilment of international obligations freely incurred, the Americans were able to dismiss Turkish pretensions and place themselves in a position of strength. Nevertheless, they undertook to provide sufficient aid not only to alleviate immediate hardship among the growers but also, by means of medium and long-term investment, to facilitate

212

diversification in the affected areas. But the actual extent of that aid was to be determined by the United States alone.

A Turkish team drawn from various Departments and led by the Minister of Agriculture had prepared a White Paper upon which the government had hoped the discussions might be based. This document set out the probable loss of earnings to the Turkish economy generally and the peasants in particular that would result from the ban on poppy cultivation. The production of licit opium for the world pharmaceutical industry had provided a means of livelihood for close on a hundred thousand farming families, or some six hundred thousand persons in all. If account were also taken of workers in other occupations associated with opium production (oil mills, sack making, confectionery, transport, the Office of Agricultural Produce etc.), the number of persons affected would rise to a million and a half.

The Turkish negotiators had estimated the annual loss of income resulting from the disappearance of these various activities at 22·5 million dollars. They also believed that it would take six years to provide alternative means of livelihood for the workers who had hitherto depended on opium. Moreover this undertaking implied a very large investment. Thus they felt justified in asking the United States not only for an initial sum of 106·9 million dollars with which to indemnify the affected workers during the four years of their redeployment, but also for a second slice of 324 million dollars payable over six years to finance the remainder of the operation. In all, therefore, their bill amounted to half a billion dollars.

The American diplomats in Ankara rejected these calculations out of hand, believing that the figures in the White Paper had purely and simply been cooked. According to Mr Kaufmann, USAID's deputy director in Turkey, the total indemnification should not exceed thirty-six million dollars, or less than one tenth of the sum demanded by the Turks.

It cannot be denied that a careful study of the White Paper reveals methodological mistakes, omissions, faulty calculations and exaggerated estimates. But in fact these apparent errors reflect a deep cleavage of opinion within the Turkish team.

213

Unlike the Prime Minister, several of his colleagues held that, in order to form a realistic assessment of the damage suffered by Turkey, account must be taken both of the licit and the illicit sale of opium, since each contributed to the peasants' income. Similarly, at the level of the national economy, sales of opium on the black market represented a valuable source of dollars, these being imported by the traffickers, changed into liras by Turkish banks, and used to pay the growers, agents and accomplices of various kinds in the villages. To some extent, therefore, the illegal traffic helped to buttress the nation's currency. Obviously this could not be put to the Americans since to do so would be tantamount to admitting that the Turkish government was an accessory to the fact. Nor could the United States very well be asked to help finance the Turkish economy by taking over the role of the international rings. On the other hand, if the revenue generated by the illegal traffic were not taken into account, the Turks would be faced with a very considerable loss.

The amount involved cannot be exactly computed since available figures are necessarily inaccurate, but an approximate estimate can be made. The average annual income from sales of Turkish opium to the world pharmaceutical industry was somewhere in the neighbourhood of 12·2 million dollars.[8] Generally speaking, the going price on the domestic black market was at least double the official price, and leakages amounted to roughly half as much as was sold to the government. On the lowest estimate, therefore, the income from illicit sales of opium prior to 1972 amounted to some 12.2 million dollars, making a grand total of 24·4 million dollars a year. To this, of course, must also be added the monies collected by other agents engaged in the traffic, both in town and country.

In fact the astonishing disparity between the American and Turkish estimates was due to a basic misunderstanding. An eminent Turkish technocrat who took part in the negotiations (and who wishes to remain anonymous) analysed the reasons

8. *Estimating the Value of the Poppy Crop*, USAID confidential report from Ankara.

for this failure in communication. A man in his late forties and a nationalist and liberal in the Atatürk tradition, our informant made no attempt to conceal his indignation, as he talked to us.

'The highest Turkish authorities and the American negotiators issued a joint report in which they specifically stated that it was not merely a question of making good the income lost by the Turkish peasants and the country's economy but, as Professor Erim himself put it, of creating better rural living conditions. The title of that report was "Improving the Standard of Living of Farmers in the Poppy-growing Regions".

'In the circumstances it seemed natural enough for us to look beyond mere monetary indemnification and seek to develop the areas affected by the ban on poppy cultivation so as to open up new sources of revenue. We therefore suggested various projects. For example, we demonstrated that, by substituting suger-beet for the poppy, the farmers' standard of living could be raised appreciably. But besides substantial investment such a scheme would demand an assured outlet, in other words an undertaking from the U.S. Congress that Turkey would be granted a small fraction of the quotas allocated to America's normal sugar suppliers – mainly the Latin-American countries. This the Americans refused, at the same time accusing us not only of trying to take advantage of the negotiations over the poppy by broaching economic topics largely outside their terms of reference, but also of using the opium problem as a form of blackmail to improve our commercial position. In fact our American opposite numbers were afraid of "politicizing" the issue by bringing it out into the open, that is, placing it before Congress which alone is empowered to take decisions of this nature. They had no wish to make generally known the immensity of the sacrifice involved in combating the drug at production level. So matters reached a deadlock. The same thing happened with wheat. Unlike most other plants, the poppy will thrive in very dry conditions, but to grow wheat we would have to embark on large-scale irrigation works which, of course, would cost a great deal of money. Here again the Americans accused us of cashing in on their difficulties by trying to underwrite our agricultural development as a whole instead of concentrating on the opium problem.

'I'll give you another example—which shows exactly what they mean by aid on the other side of the Atlantic. A few years ago – in 1965, to be precise – there were some business talks between Pan

American and the Turkish Red Crescent, proprietor of Afyon Mineral Waters, the best in Turkey. The affair came to nothing because we didn't manufacture the cans which would have enabled Pan Am to serve the water to their passengers. We raised this matter again during the recent negotiations over the suppression of the poppy, and asked for a cannery to be set up in the Afyon district so that we could export our mineral water. But the American team included representatives of private interests who had no desire to see the emergence of Turkish competition in this field. Indeed all our discussions have been largely dominated by the presence of American private interests. If you were to take a look at the professional background of the individual members of their team, you'd be surprised.

'But what really shocked us was the insertion into the joint report of an American-inspired clause aimed at modifying the legislation governing foreign investment in Turkey, at present prohibited in the agricultural sector. This clause emphasizes the fact that foreign investment in the agro-industrial sector (canneries etc.) would speed up Turkey's economic development. I quote: "In order to attract foreign, and stimulate local, investment, the Turkish government should simplify the regulations governing investment so that these are not susceptible to different interpretations. This set of regulations should be recognized by the different political parties in Turkey, thereby ensuring that it remains unaltered, irrespective of the party that happens to be in power." You can't help asking yourself' [our informant remarked bitterly] 'whether their purpose is to help Turkey resolve the problems posed by the ban on opium production, or whether they're trying to take advantage of the occasion to facilitate the entry of American capital whose role in this country is already considerable.'

How lightly the Turkish arguments weighed in Washington may be gauged from the fact that the compensation finally granted to Turkey by the United States in return for banning the poppy corresponds exactly to the estimate made by USAID's deputy director, Mr Kaufman,[9] namely 35·7 million dollars. Fifteen million dollars are to be used to indemnify the peasants over a four year period. They will be paid 525 Turkish

9. The dissenting Turkish negotiators, including our informant, resigned six months later and were replaced by men apparently more amenable.

liras (about 35 dollars) per kilogramme of opium, based on the number of kilos delivered to the office of Agricultural Produce in 1971.[10] Twenty million dollars are to be earmarked for long-term investment projects. In accordance with the best traditions of American aid the funds will be largely devoted to the purchase of United States goods, and exporters on the other side of the Atlantic are doubtless already licking their lips. A further three hundred thousand dollars have been released for the purpose of reinforcing the inspectorate in the poppy fields during the 1971–2 harvest, whereby it is hoped to reduce to a minimum the final rush of traffickers.

So far as the United States are concerned, their 'poppy diplomacy' in Turkey can be said to be successful, at least in the short term. It has also scored a political point for President Nixon who can count on a wide popular consensus in the matter of drugs. The gains registered in Turkey have masked the reverses suffered in south-east Asia. Economically the operation is proving far from ruinous, having cost comparatively little, at least until now. To a certain extent it may also prove beneficial to such sectors of American industry as participate in the redevelopment programme in the former opium producing regions. But the success of the Turkish operation is less in evidence when seen from the perspective of reducing addiction in the world as a whole and in the United States in particular.

The elimination of Turkey as a source of narcotics will, no doubt, ultimately help to break the traditional bonds between the Turkish traffickers and the Marseilles refiners, for the latter will perforce have to obtain their supplies elsewhere. But it would be a mistake to suppose that the measures taken in Turkey will yield rapid results. The country contains large secret stocks of opium, hoarded by the peasants. Both Turkish and American observers are agreed that in 1973 these stocks will still be somewhere in the region of a hundred or two hundred tons, in other words enough to satisfy American heroin requirements for up to two years.

10. This was meant to induce the peasants to deliver a much larger proportion of the 1971 and 1972 crops, and thus prevent them from accumulating illicit stocks.

Nor can the possibility of illicit production be excluded. In Mexico today illegal poppy cultivation is being organized and financed by American racketeers who, having bought land under assumed names, advance money to the peasants for seed and take the whole of their crop. They also have accomplices in the army and local police, who are paid to turn a blind eye to the poppy fields in the districts under their control. There would seem to be nothing to stop the same kind of thing happening in Turkey, where laxity is no less prevalent among government officials and local police. Moreover such an undertaking would be favoured by the country's geographical conditions which in many ways resemble those of Mexico. While the Americans do not completely dismiss this eventuality, they choose to discount it, the more so since the amounts of illicit opium thus obtainable would be infinitesimal compared with the leakages prior to 1972.

The satisfaction felt by the Americans is in no way shared by the Turks. A number of leading Turkish officials have privately confessed that they regard the proposed compensation as wholly incommensurate with the losses sustained by the peasants and the economy, let alone with the promise to improve rural living conditions. A better offer 'is absolutely vital', they maintain.

While the difficulties may be temporarily obscured by the fifteen million dollars earmarked as direct indemnification for the peasants, the real issue has merely been postponed. In 1976 the problem will arise as to what further provision can be made for the former growers since it may be assumed that the investment programmes will not by then have made sufficient progress to provide jobs and incomes comparable to those offered by opium cultivation.

There can be no doubt that, once their payments are stopped, the peasants will bitterly regret their traditional occupation. Time will indubitably show that the decision to promulgate the decree of 29 June 1971 was a questionable one and that the Turks were ill-advised to place the whole emphasis on the amount of indemnity to be paid. At a time when every underdeveloped country was looking for industries that would make use of local raw material, the Turkish negotiators spent months haggling over the compensation they were to be paid for forfeiting that very possibility. Turkey produced some of the best opium in the world, while the demand from the world's pharmaceutical industry kept rising year by year. Moreover, on several occasions she had been offered economic and technical aid to help her set up a pharmaceutical industry based on opium. In 1968, for instance, Hungary proposed a loan for the construction of a morphine production plant. For reasons that still remain obscure, that offer was turned down.

By the end of 1972 the more farsighted members of the Assembly realized that the government had been regrettably precipitate in giving way to the Americans. They shrewdly observed that there was no real reason to fear America's threat to cut down economic aid. For though the Turks might need U.S. assistance for economic reasons, the reverse held true where military strategy was concerned. Indeed it is difficult to imagine the United States applying sanctions to a pillar of NATO situated on the Asian marches of the communist world. Political observers are generally agreed that if, as seems likely, Mr Demirel or his party are returned to power in the next elections (scheduled to take place in October 1973) the opium question will undoubtedly be reviewed.

The optimism of the American authorities, however, would appear to be unshakable. Mr Mann, special adviser to the American Ambassador in Turkey, told us in May 1972 that 'a Turkish government which took such a decision would probably have to pay the price in terms of the inevitable political repercussions it would unfailingly evoke'. But he refused to say anything more specific. In any case he believed that a resumption of opium production in the immediate future was highly improbable and that no one was contemplating such an eventuality.

The facts do not bear him out. When Senator Urguplu was called on to form a new government in May 1972, his ministerial team was rejected by the President of the Republic (an event unique in Turkish parliamentary history) on the grounds that 'its composition is incompatible both with the Military Command's memorandum of 12 March 1971 and with the demands of the present situation in Turkey'. Ever since 1970, Urguplu had been strongly opposed to the suppression of opium production and could be expected to renew his onslaught on Professor Erim's policy. Though the President's apprehensions on this score were not the main reason for his decision, they undoubtedly played some part in his refusal to endorse the Senator's proposed team before its investiture by the Assembly. For while Urguplu, would have been unlikely to revoke the edict banning poppy cultivation, he would unquestionably have reopened negotiations with the United States on the matter of indemnification.

In commenting on this incident and denying that 'the American Embassy was in any way implicated', Mr Mann failed to mention another which had taken place a few months previously. By February 1972 the ban had begun to make itself felt in those provinces not permitted to participate in what was to be the final opium harvest. Delegations of farmers and small oil-millers, accompanied by their parliamentary representatives, had called on the Prime Minister to complain of the difficulties they would have to face in the future. In his reply Professor Erim said:

'On humanitarian grounds we have collaborated with the United States which, since the end of the Second World War, have provided us with economic aid amounting to millions and millions of dollars. In deciding to prohibit all production of opium after 1972, the Turkish government did not, however, enter into any definite bilateral agreements. If our economy, our farmers, cannot overcome the difficulties created by this measure, there is nothing to prevent us from resuming poppy cultivation.'

Again, on 14 August 1972 two hundred Representatives belonging to Demirel's Justice Party signed the draft of a bill aimed at repealing the decree banning opium production.

It would, of course, have been out of the question for Washington to pay the astronomical sums demanded by Turkey. Congress might conceivably have been persuaded, though not without considerable difficulty, to vote the necessary credits, but politically such a precedent would have been unthinkable. The United States are conducting a world-wide campaign against narcotics, and Turkey is only one of the pawns in that struggle. Had they accepted Ankara's figure, other countries such as Iran, Thailand, Pakistan and even, perhaps, Burma and Afghanistan would certainly have offered to renew their efforts to ban the poppy, always on the understanding that they would receive adequate compensation. Thus the fight against the illicit production and sale of narcotics would have involved the disbursement of billions of dollars.

No one, of course, contemplates such a thing. Turkey's case will probably remain unique because largely factitious, having been created to serve as one of Mr Nixon's mainstays during the political manœuvring that preceded the presidential elections in November 1972.

13   Iran: a Retrograde Step

When in 1955 Teheran announced its decision to ban poppy cultivation throughout Iran, the move was vociferously applauded by the member states of the United Nations, not excluding those opium producing countries which had no intention of following suit. All evinced an equal dismay when, thirteen years later, Iran declared that she intended 'provisionally' to resume opium cultivation.

At a meeting of the Commission on Narcotic Drugs held at the Palais des Nations at Geneva in 1971 John Ingersoll, head of the American Bureau of Narcotics, expressed his 'consternation and alarm' at a measure which he could only regard as the most retrograde step to have been taken in the fight against narcotics since the end of the Second World War.

On the same occasion Dr Azarakhch, the Iranian delegate, pointed out that,

'the total ban on poppy cultivation has had grave social and economic repercussions in Iran. It has not only deprived the country of a source of revenue in the form of opium sales to the world pharmaceutical industry, but has been responsible for a heavy drain on our holdings of foreign currency as a result of illegal purchases of opiates in neighbouring countries. It was a situation we could no longer tolerate.'

Iran, an important producer of opium, is first and foremost a consumer. In 1955 she had no less than two million addicts who, between them, consumed a minimum of two tons of opium a day. This may seem surprising in view of the fact that Turkey, her next-door neighbour, has no addiction problem. The explanation lies in history.

In the nineteenth century the Iranians needed foreign exchange in order to import goods of European manufacture, and opium was then the sole means of obtaining it. The proximity of British

India, for which two opium wars had opened up the Chinese market, enabled Iran to find a ready outlet for her production. Hence an ever greater acreage was put down to poppy cultivation. Further, medicine in Iran was extremely backward; no medical school was built there until 1850, and opium was used to treat any and every kind of ailment. Indeed the drug is commonly known as *teriac* (antidote or cure-all) rather than *afyon* (the Persian word for opium). And when the government opened official smoking shops in 1931 these were known as 'treatment houses'. In this way addiction, having become part of everyday life, spread throughout the country. Supplies of the drug were freely available, especially in the tea-houses. In some of the localities in Gorgan and Khorassan ninety per cent of the population smoked opium, and as many as sixteen smoking shops might be found in a village of no more than six hundred inhabitants.

Two years after the ban had come into force, the official number of addicts had fallen to three hundred thousand, that is, one per cent of the population against 7·5 per cent during the fifties. This hard core, which was certainly a good deal larger than the authorities were prepared to admit, now turned to the black market for its supplies. Turkish, Afghan and Pakistani traffickers were quick to climb on to the band-waggon and meet the demands of Iranian addicts. Since they insisted on payment in gold, Iran's bullion reserves began to melt away. Moreover the country was losing foreign currency at the rate of ten if not fifteen million dollars a year. These losses were compounded by the stoppage of licit opium exports to Europe and the United States which, until 1955, had been running at about a hundred tons and represented annual earnings of forty million dollars.

The spread of heroin addiction was another scourge which induced the Iranians to lift the ban on opium. The law of 1955 allowed opium addicts six months in which to rid themselves of the habit. If, at the end of that period, they persisted in using the drug, they were liable to a term of imprisonment ranging from one month to three years. For selling opium the penalty was anything from three months to five years' imprisonment

223

and for growing it, six months to three years. Anyone who opened a smoking-shop could be jailed for up to ten years.

In 1969 over 13,000 people were detained for having contravened this law, and seventy per cent of the prison population had been sentenced for the same reason. To keep out of the clutches of the police, addicts gave up opium in favour of heroin which is less obtrusive in use. In Iran heroin is either snuffed, or else smoked, Hong Kong fashion, to 'chase the dragon'. Injection is rare, since the drug is of such poor quality that, if taken in this way, it may prove fatal.

In 1972 heroin addicts were officially estimated at ten thousand and opium addicts at three hundred thousand. However, several Teheran doctors told us that these figures could safely be multiplied by ten.

Heroin is widely used in the cities, more especially in Teheran. Consumers are mostly to be found among the young, few of whom are addicted to opium. In 1970 the most select girls' school in Tabriz was closed as a result of a heroin scandal, while in May 1972 one of Teheran's more popular foreign schools experienced a similar incident.

Disturbed by this unexpected turn of events the authorities, after thirteen years of prohibition, went back on their decision. They had come to the conclusion that the problem of addiction did not admit of so simple a solution as an outright ban which had already proved as ineffective as it was costly. The blame for the failure of their 'courageous' policy was laid at the door of their immediate neighbours, Turkey, Afghanistan and Pakistan. Not only had these countries carefully refrained from following Iran's example but they had benefited financially from Teheran's measures by allowing contraband opium to cross their borders. Finally, the pharmaceutical industry's three main suppliers, the U.S.S.R., India and Turkey, had filled the gap left by Iran on the licit world market.

Provoked beyond endurance, the Iranian government decided to resume the cultivation of the poppy. In the words of Dr Azarakhch, 'The resumption of opium production will enable us provisionally to meet the domestic demand, pending a total ban on poppy cultivation throughout the entire zone.'

At the end of May 1969 a discussion took place between a representative of the Secretary-General of the U.N. Commission on Narcótic Drugs and the Prime Minister and Foreign Affairs Minister of Iran. The Iranians complained that they were tired of hearing others sing the praises of the ban they had imposed in 1955, a decision which had not only called for great financial sacrifice, but had been taken in defiance of public opinion. Drastic changes had finally brought all opium production to a halt. 'We had achieved the impossible,' the Prime Minister exclaimed,

'but our measures called for corresponding action on the part of our neighbours. No such action was taken. An ever-rising tide of illicit opium flowed into Iran, while gold left our coffers to swell the invisibles in the balance of payments of adjacent countries. Could Iran be expected to go on suffering these losses caused by her neighbours' refusal to change their policy in regard to opium? My government is determined to stamp out opium production – which it has recently decided to resume – as soon as it receives an assurance that its neighbours will do the same.'

The law of June 1969 authorized a resumption of production in circumscribed areas under rigid government control. Opium may now be consumed by addicts over sixty years of age and also by those who, for medical reasons, do not respond to disintoxication.

These people are issued with a special card bearing their photograph which enables them to obtain opium legally from chemist's shops – five grammes a week if smoked, two if taken orally. The opium comes in the form of a pale yellow stick about two centimetres in diameter and the length of four razor blades. And in fact a razor blade is used as a measure when dividing the twenty gramme stick into four sections, or *tiqs*, of five grammes each.

Smokers must produce the ashes of their previous ration before they can obtain the next one, and permits have to be renewed every six months. These restrictions, combined with the opprobrium attaching to the card-holding addict, deter many from registering, a fact which accounts for the relatively low number of card-holders – a hundred thousand all told.

225

Moreover, the opium sold by chemists is comparatively expensive at 17 rials, or 9p, per gramme. This means that, in a country where the average annual income is approximately £140, the smoker has to pay 45p for his daily dose. Hence many of them prefer to obtain their supplies on the black market where a gramme of opium costs only 12 rials, or about 6p. If they cannot afford even this amount they buy *shireh*, or opium ash, from other addicts.

The law provides for extremely severe sentences in the case of traffickers. Any person found in possession of more than two kilos of opium or ten grammes of heroin is liable to the death penalty. This is no empty threat. By the end of 1971 280 persons had been executed for trafficking in opiates. Even though some opponents of the Shah's regime may have been equated with traffickers out of political expediency, the determination of the Iranian authorities to stop illegal imports of opium is not in doubt. At every frontier post large notices with red lettering on a white ground warn the foreigner in three languages. The message runs,

In pursuance of the law, any person buying, selling, importing, exporting or possessing illicit narcotics including hashish (cannabis) will be liable, as the case may be, to a fine of from 5 to 42 dollars for every gramme and to a term of 5–15 years' imprisonment. More specifically, where morphine, heroin, cocaine, and opium are concerned, the law provides for various penalties which may extend to the death sentence.

By the end of 1972 no foreigner had yet faced the firing-squad. But several dozen of them were languishing in Meshed prison chained to the walls of unspeakable cells. The efforts of their respective governments to obtain their extradition have so far proved unavailing. For this reason the American Embassy has finally decided to organize a special service to provide them with food and medicine. These facilities are sometimes extended to the nationals of other countries who have been more or less callously abandoned by their own, less wealthy, diplomatic missions. But not all consumers and traffickers suffer this fate. Far from it.

As we were told by a diplomat serving in Teheran,

'It is common knowledge that there's one law for the rich and another for the poor. Your small-time trafficker is shot, but at any big reception in Teheran there's sure to be someone or other smoking opium or hashish. And it's by no means rare for trays with pipes and lamps to be laid out in the middle of the drawing-room. This habit is even more widespread among provincial notables. Even at court, opium has long since taken the place of Turkish delight.'

So common is the use of opium in Iranian society that dainty little travelling pipes can be found in the bazaar in Teheran, along with a special type of charcoal for those who wish to smoke in their hotels.

'Iranian officials of all ranks are exceedingly corrupt,' our diplomat friend went on.

'If Iran ever comes to play a leading part in the traffic you won't find the operators among the lesser smugglers but among the government high-ups. Many of them are extremely unscrupulous men who will stop at nothing when it comes to feathering their own nests.'

In March 1972 there was something of a scandal in Switzerland when Prince Dawalouh of Iran claimed diplomatic immunity after he had been accused of smuggling opium into the country. He flew back to Teheran in the company of no less a personage than the Shah, and it was as a member of His Imperial Majesty's suite that he was able to take advantage of a privilege normally reserved for career diplomats. The Shah, always very sensitive to Iran's image abroad, was much irritated by the comments of the European press. Though not, of course, personally involved in the traffic, he seems quite prepared to tolerate the indiscretions of certain members of his entourage whose loyalty is essential if a proper balance is to be maintained among the supporters of his regime.

According to the Iranian authorities the selling-price of opium has been fixed at a high level in order to discourage addicts and, more important still, to deter potential ones. In France each successive government has used the same pretext to raise the

227

duty on alcohol which, while having little effect on alcoholism, indubitably provides additional revenue for the State. Teheran counters allegations of this nature by citing the enormous expense involved in operating the stringent controls demanded by the international organizations. These controls, the authorities maintain, ensure that not a single gramme of Iranian opium finds its way on to the black market.

No one in Iran may grow the poppy without a permit. These are granted for preference to the cooperatives and agricultural combines which have proliferated since the introduction of agrarian reform. Any individual issued with a permit must submit to the authority of the manager of the village cooperative who is thereafter answerable for him. No one may farm an area of less than five hectares, and peasants who are members of a cooperative are encouraged to pool their land so that one large poppy field serves the whole village.

The inspectorate moves into action at harvest-time. Police squads pitch camp close to the growing areas and are thus able to maintain a twenty-four hour watch. They are personally responsible for conveying the opium to a local collection point where it is weighed before being removed to a central depot in Teheran.

At Garmsar, situated on the fringe of the torrid, desert region of Dasht-i-Kevir, we watched a crop being harvested by one of the agricultural combines set up in 1967. These combines are limited liability companies, in which the peasants, having sold their land, are simply shareholders. So much does the climate vary from district to district that, on the day before our visit to Garmsar, we had been able to feast our eyes on vast stretches of country where the poppy was still in bloom. Having turned off the Isfahan road at Delijan we headed for Khomein. Suddenly we found ourselves in a pleasant, winding valley with field upon field of pale mauve poppies contrasting exquisitely with the surrounding verdure. Not one of the fields was smaller than ten hectares and we could easily have lost ourselves in the vast expanse of poppies, some of which stood nearly five feet high. It would be another two weeks till harvest-time, the peasants told us. So we were greatly surprised the following day to find

228

that the harvest was almost over at Garmsar, less than 250 kilometres away as the crow flies.

The Garmsar agricultural combine farms 5,000 hectares, of which eighty are put down to the poppy. On a basis of ten men per hectare, seven hundred are needed to harvest the crop. The majority of the labourers came from other districts, many of them from Meshed on the Afghan frontier. These are the old hands who grew opium before 1955 and are more knowledgeable about its cultivation than the local inhabitants. Armed with a small brush fitted with eighteen steel bristles they go out into the fields in the early evening. Gently taking hold of each poppy head in turn, they scarify one side of it. The next morning at four o'clock the latex which has seeped out during the night is removed with a crescent-shaped scraper. From time to time the labourers deposit the opium in a bucket standing at the edge of the field under the vigilant gaze of five inspectors – the combine's assistant manager, a retired colonel and three orderlies. In addition to these there are eleven overseers. The operation is repeated four times in twenty days, when each poppy head will have been scarified all over.

The men have to get through their work by nine in the morning, before the heat becomes unbearable. On leaving the field, they form up in line. As in the South African diamond mines, inspectors search them one by one, examining their pockets and the insides of their shoes and headgear. Known smokers are drawn up separately and searched with particular care. One man, his face wizened by age and sun, exclaimed indignantly: 'We've done our whack. Why can't you let us have a bit on the side?'

The buckets of opium are then taken to the combine's store where, on the day of our visit, we saw a row of some thirty pails, each containing as many kilogrammes of fresh opium. At first resembling pale yellow clay, opium gradually turns black as it dries out. Every day a wax seal is placed on the entrance to the store, no one being allowed in except the inspectors and then only in groups. When the harvest is over, the pails are loaded on to a truck, covered with a tarpaulin and taken to Teheran under police escort.

229

Obviously these checks cost a great deal of money. Moreover, to deter the peasants from selling their produce on the black market, the government deems it advisable to pay them a reasonable price. For good quality opium the rate has been fixed at about a hundred dollars a kilogramme, which represents an overall cost to the State of 120 dollars. Since this is almost ten times as much as is paid on the legal world market, Iran is no longer able to export her opium.

'No one can accuse us of failing to respect our international obligations,' a senior Iranian official told us. 'In order to abide by all the agreements on narcotics control aimed at stamping out illicit trafficking, we have been compelled to abandon a source of foreign exchange which was formerly of great value to us.'

When requesting Iran not to resume opium production, the U.N. argued that it would cost her less to obtain supplies for her addicts elsewhere. The Iranian authorities refused to be dissuaded. To import the drug would mean spending foreign currency and, once again, the beneficiaries would be Iran's neighbours. Domestic production, on the other hand, could be paid for in rials.[1] Although they will not officially admit it, the authorities were also swayed by the discontent prevailing in the former producing regions where alternative crops had proved to be very much less remunerative than opium.

The inevitable, so much dreaded by the United Nations, has happened. Far from being concentrated in prescribed regions, poppy fields have sprung up all over the country, while the area under cultivation has steadily increased since 1969, attaining 20,000 hectares in 1972 as compared with 5,000 or less in 1955.[2] 'It's rather more than we need to supply our opium addicts,' a senior official in the Rural Affairs Ministry confessed. The authorities admit to an annual production of some 250 tons, which implies an average yield of 12·5 kilogrammes a hectare. This would seem to be a gross underestimate, for according to officials in the Ministries of Health and Rural Affairs,

1. 1 dollar = 76 rials.
2. In 1969, the year in which production was resumed, 1,011 hectares were sown. In 1970 the area had increased to 6,200 hectares.

the average yield in Iran is somewhere between 15 and 26 kilos a hectare. In other words, the 1972 harvest must have amounted to between three and five hundred tons.

In 1954, with 25,000 hectares under poppy cultivation, Iran produced at least 750 tons of opium. The then Minister of Health, Dr Salleh, in a note addressed to the United Nations, admitted to 'an annual production since 1945 of 700 to 1,200 tons, of which 100 tons were exported'. This statement would seem to confirm the suggestion that current production is at least 300 tons. Hence it seems pertinent to ask what happens to the fifty to two hundred tons which the government fails to declare to the international organizations.

A similar question might have been asked prior to 1955. At that time Iran was reporting a bare two hundred tons to the United Nations even though the Minister of Health had offici-ally conceded a figure of 750 tons. In fact the two hundred tons represented State purchases, the remainder of the crop being either freely sold by the producers to domestic consumers or diverted on to the international black market. Since these two outlets were theoretically eliminated by law in 1969, it can only be concluded that the Iranian government is hoarding stocks. For this there would appear to be at least two reasons. Firstly, if she is to clamp down effectively on the traffic with neighbouring countries, Iran must be in a position to supply all her addicts, whether registered or unregistered.[3] Secondly, she must have sufficient opium in reserve to tide her over a poor harvest.

The officials of the U.N's Narcotics Division are perturbed by the steady increase of the area under cultivation, since they find it difficult to believe that strict controls could be maintained over twenty thousand hectares or more. As pointed out by Mr El Harim, Egyptian delegate to a conference at Geneva, 'experience has shown that once the expansion of licit production is legally authorized, illicit production inevitably increases.' This observa-tion is borne out by what has happened in India where, despite

3. Half a ton a day, or 182 tons a year, are needed to meet the demands of the 100,000 card-holding addicts.

the most rigorous controls at production level, twenty per cent of the crop evades the authorities.

It is still difficult to gauge the exact extent of leakages in Iran, which would seem to take place not so much in the fields as at the depots, and then on only a very limited scale. A European pharmaceutical firm, for example, which had bought a consignment of opium previously seized by the Iranian government, found, on opening the well-secured cases, that some of the opium had been removed and replaced with pieces of wood or metal.

Small amounts frequently disappear from the store-rooms of the cooperatives and combines. The technique, the peasants told us, is to hide a small jar under a brick or a piece of rag and to put a morsel of opium into it each day, the jar being retrieved when the harvest is safely over. Again, provided the necessary palms are greased, one of the buckets may be 'forgotten' during the loading of the truck for Teheran. But obviously this kind of traffic can never assume serious dimensions.

However at the end of 1972 the international organizations and the United States were alarmed not so much by possible leakages as by the indirect consequences of the resumption of opium production in Iran. For as Iran came to supply the needs of her own addicts, the three hundred tons or so of opium hitherto smuggled into the country for that purpose would have to find an outlet elsewhere.[4] To some extent the problem will of course be solved by the drying up of supplies from Turkey. But the Iranians calculate that, up till 1969, the quantity of contraband opium arriving from Afghanistan and Pakistan averaged at least a hundred tons a year. Where this will now go, no one can say. The American Bureau of Narcotics fears that there may be a link-up between the rings which have previously operated independently. One pipeline ran from Turkey to Europe and from Turkey to Iran, and another from Afghanistan to Iran. If the Afghan and Turkish rings decide to cooperate, there will be a continuous chain of racketeers between Afghanistan and Europe,

4. If each of the 300,000 opium addicts officially admitted by the Iranian authorities consumes 3 grammes of opium a day, total annual consumption will be 328 tons. This is a minimum figure.

and Iran will become an entrepôt for the traffic in opiates. The country already straddles the route, commonly used by hashish smugglers, that runs from Kabul to Munich by way of Teheran, Istanbul, Sofia and Belgrade. The same individuals could very well undertake to transport another kind of drug.

While the traffickers are well aware of the risks they run in Iran – the more so since many of their colleagues have already been shot – this has not deterred a number of Iranians from continuing to manufacture heroin illicitly. In 1971 the police discovered three laboratories, and it is suspected that there may be others in Azerbaijan, a province immediately adjoining Turkey. It is from that country that the laboratories draw their supplies of morphine.

The introduction of more stringent enforcement measures in 1972 led to higher black market prices in Iran. Opium bought at 2,500 rials (about £13) a kilo on the Afghan side of the border, cost three and a half times more (or some £40) on arrival in Meshed. In Teheran it fetched the equivalent of £62 a kilo. A dose of heroin which could be had for 70 rials (£8) in 1966, now costs more than twice that sum. But the severity of the law has failed to reduce the traffic across the Irano-Afghan border, some eight hundred kilometres long and almost impossible to control. Although devoid of vegetation the district is extremely rugged, with mountains, wadis and gorges in which a caravan is very difficult to intercept. Once, when the Meshed gendarmerie had been notified of a serious clash between smugglers and the forces of law and order, the helicopter sent to the latter's assistance never succeeded in locating the affray, because of the enclosed nature of the battle-ground. Between March and October heat and dust keep the police helicopters grounded. This, then, is obviously the busiest season for the traffickers, the more so since they may be held up by snow between December and March. In Iran as in any other country a consignment of opium is almost impossible to track down once it has crossed the border.

The Iranian frontier might, perhaps, be more effectively controlled if there were better coordination between the bodies responsible for suppressing narcotics – customs, gendarmerie, police, the military tribunals and the Ministries of Health,

233

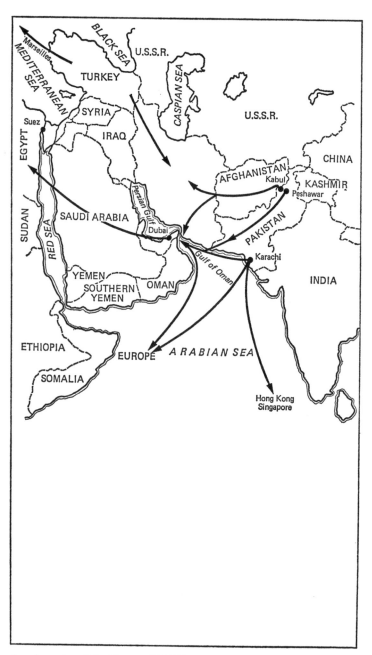

Supply routes of the Near and Middle East

Rural Affairs and Justice. But in fact the authorities are concerned not so much with putting a stop to the traffic as with combating its effects on the country's economy. They take the view that an assured supply of home-grown opium for their addicts would provide a more effective solution than the deployment of extra police along the country's borders. Hence the government is clearly more intent on preventing opium coming into the country than on seizing what may be smuggled out. Nor does it show an excess of zeal in its surveillance of the small ports in Baluchistan, the country's poorest and least patrolled province whose largely nomadic population themselves take part in the traffic. For some of the opium from Afghanistan and Pakistan passes through this territory, to be shipped across the Persian Gulf to the Emirates and thence to Europe. With the suppression of opium production in Turkey, this supply route will gain in importance.

The attitude of the Iranian authorities is understandable. In the first place they feel they are already doing enough for the international community, having been credited with sixty-seven per cent of the total tonnage of opium seized throughout the world in 1971. Secondly, opium is neither their sole nor their prime concern. Iran has five frontiers, that with the U.S.S.R. being 1,500 kilometres long, a circumstance Teheran must take into account when deploying its manpower and material, neither of which is inexhaustible. The Iranian police also have one overriding priority – internal security and the fight against subversion in the shape of anyone who casts doubt on the Shah's methods of government.

The resumption of production in Iran underlines one of the basic laws that govern the production and sale of opiates, namely that the problem of addiction cannot be solved by cutting off the sources of raw material used in the manufacture of narcotics unless concerted action is taken by all producer countries. The poppy-fields, which have once again become a feature of the Iranian landscape, will undoubtedly relieve the country of considerable economic losses. But the tons of Afghan and Pakistani opium previously absorbed by Iran have now become generally available. Traffickers whose supplies were formerly drawn from Turkey will be able to take advantage of this state of affairs. Thus the comparative shortage of opium resulting from the Turkish ban on poppy cultivation as from 1972 will be immediately made good.

The case of Iran also goes to show that neither an individual country nor the world as a whole can gain acceptance for humanitarian arguments when any one nation's economic interests are at stake. In 1969, at the twenty-third session of the Narcotics Commission, Dr Azarakhch justified Iran's national self-interest in the following terms:

'When my government decided to resume cultivation of the poppy after an interval of thirteen years, it did not do so with a light heart. But our situation had become so disturbing and the inefficiency and sluggishness of international measures so apparent that we found ourselves compelled to have recourse to unilateral action. When we prohibited the crop in 1955, thereby committing ourselves to a revolutionary and humanitarian course, we did so in the hope that the United Nations would not leave us to carry on unaided our enlightened struggle against the world-wide scourge of drug addiction. The Iranian government hoped that the United Nations Organization would have at its disposal sufficient means to put a stop to illicit trafficking. Unfortunately experience has shown that, despite goodwill and countless sacrifices on the part of the members of the Narcotics Division, the United Nations have not been able to work out the requisite solution and are unlikely to do so within a reasonable space of time. While we understand that satisfactory solutions cannot readily be found for the complex crises by which the world is beset, we had hoped that, in a technical domain such as that of narcotics, action by the U.N. would have proved more effective.'

In fact Dr Azarakhch was wrong, and Iran should have been the first to realize that the suppression of the production and sale of narcotics, far from being merely a technical question, is primarily an economic and political one. This has been amply demonstrated, not only by the difficulties encountered in formulating agreements that would permit of effective international cooperation, but also by the recent misfortunes of the United Nations Fund for Drug Control.

236

14   Humanitarianism and State Interests

The first attempt to set up an international system for the control of drug abuse dates back to the early years of this century. When, in 1900, Spain was driven out of the Philippines, the islands came under the control of the United States. Opium addiction was rife in this former Spanish colony which, however, did not itself produce the drug but imported it from Persia, Turkey, Siam and China. Even at that time Washington realized that nothing could be done to put a stop to opium consumption unless the producer countries could be induced to cooperate. At President Roosevelt's request the representatives of thirteen nations met at Shanghai in 1909 to consider how best to stamp out 'the deplorable habit of opium smoking' so prevalent not only in the Philippines but throughout the Far East. The delegates concluded that 'close and effective international cooperation was indispensable if the opium problem was to be solved'. And there the matter rested.

A big step forward was made at a conference which met at The Hague in 1912 and resulted in the signature of a convention providing for the control of opium production and prohibiting its use for non-medical purposes. No provision was made, however, for the creation of permanent national or international bodies responsible for enforcing these decisions.

Then came the First World War. The countries concerned had other things to think about and the agreements were placed in cold storage. Throughout the whole of Asia the 'deplorable habit of opium smoking' continued unabated. Moreover Europe and the United States were experiencing an upsurge of morphine and heroin addiction. Both drugs had been used indiscriminately in the treatment of the war-wounded, a number of whom had consequently become addicts. And, after four years of internecine strife, the western countries were

237

passing through a cultural crisis, later aggravated by the great economic crisis of 1929.

Soon after the Armistice the League of Nations appointed a committee whose task was to enforce the decisions made in 1912. But it was not until 1925 that its efforts resulted in the signing of a convention at the International Opium Conference in Geneva. This convention, which went considerably beyond the objectives set in 1912, provided for:

1. The obligatory assignment of licences to growers for the better control of production;
2. The registration of international commercial transactions relating to opium.

By accurately establishing the opium requirements of the world pharmaceutical industry and adjusting production accordingly, it was hoped to eliminate the surplus output that went to supply the black market. An organization known as the Central Bureau was set up to ensure the observance of international limitation regulations.

A further convention, signed in 1931, gave added weight to the decisions taken in 1925. This laid down that every country must supply the Central Bureau with an estimate of the opium it needed for medical purposes. By adding up these estimates the Bureau could arrive at the over-all total of opium to be produced throughout the world. It was further decided that, in the case of countries which refused to adhere to the convention the Central Bureau should draw up and publish its own comparative tables of their domestic requirements and production, thereby revealing exactly who was supplying the black market in narcotics. In thus taking recalcitrant countries to task, the League of Nations made use for the first time of a weapon which was to assume considerable importance – public opinion.

In 1936 an attempt was made to mount a more direct attack on the traffic by requiring the signatories of a fresh convention to introduce legislation providing for the 'extradition of the most dangerous traffickers' and more especially of those who, while not directly involved in the traffic, were responsible for instigating, coordinating and financing it, in other words the notorious 'Mr Bigs'. These provisions achieved nothing, except the regular publication of a confidential list of sailors known to deal in contraband, and of vessels aboard which narcotics had been seized. Though falling far short of the ambitious targets set by the 1936 Convention, this measure was not without its uses at a time when opium and its derivatives were largely transported by sea.

In fact, up till the Second World War these conventions remained largely inoperative. For though each signatory had undertaken to enact laws prohibiting the production and use of opium for non-medical purposes, the decrees enforcing them had not been promulgated. Again, legislation might provide for the suppression of opium production, but only by stages. Thailand, however, did not legislate in this sense until 1959, and Laos not until 1971. Iran, after banning poppy cultivation and opium consumption in 1955, went back on both decisions in 1969. Like many another, she had come to realize that addiction cannot be eradicated merely by prohibiting it on paper. And whereas it is one thing to determine the quantity of world opium production on the basis of licit requirements, it is quite another to ensure that those limitations are respected. In order to do so the Central Bureau would have to be invested with supranational powers enabling it to plan production on a global scale and to apply sanctions to such countries as failed to adhere to their quota. This further presupposed that the contracting nations would be able to exercise effective control over poppy cultivation within their own borders – which, as we have seen, is very far from being the case. The sorry tale of the 1953 Protocol and the 1961 convention clearly illustrates the kind of difficulties likely to be encountered in implementing international agreements.

In 1944 the United States had approached some hundred countries with a view to exploring the possibility of drawing up a fresh agreement which, rather than simply collating all the provisions of the various treaties then in force, would facilitate the adoption of more effective measures to limit the world's opium production.

It very soon became apparent that such a project would take a long time to come to fruition. Attention was therefore concentrated upon producing a document having limited geographical scope but extremely rigorous provisions.

The United Nations scheme stressed the need to set up a world duopoly in which the opium consuming countries would confront a limited number of producer countries. An initial attempt came to nothing in 1950, after negotiations had been brought to a standstill by a failure to agree on prices.

The interests of the two parties were obviously incompatible. The producer countries, wishing to obtain the highest possible return, pointed out that, should they agree to set up strict production controls to obviate leakages on to the black market, the rise in costs would have to be offset by higher selling prices. These, they maintained, would help to discourage the traffickers, an aim shared by both parties.

The consumer countries, on the other hand, had no desire to find themselves confronted by a 'producer bloc'. Any increase in the selling-price of opium would inevitably affect the cost of pharmaceutical products and thus rebound on the producer countries. For if opium were to become too expensive, the industry would be compelled to look for substitutes in the form of synthetics. True, the maintenance of a relatively low world market price for licit opium would encourage leakages on to the black market where rewards were far higher. But the traffickers' profit margins were so great that they could always compete with the official market by raising their buying prices. In such circumstances the rings were never the losers.

Another reason for the failure of the 1950 negotiations was the refusal of most of the participants to invest an international body with powers of control over the production and distribution of opium within their territory.

In 1953, when all idea of a duopoly had been abandoned, discussions were resumed with rather better success. The resulting Protocol[1] stipulated that the production of opium should be limited in accordance with demand. To that end the number of countries entitled to produce opium for export was reduced to seven – Bulgaria, Greece, Iran, Turkey, the U.S.S.R.,

1. Its provisions are not only still in force but are the most rigorous extant.

India and Yugoslavia. Other countries were permitted to produce the drug, but solely for domestic consumption.

Under the terms of the 1953 Protocol there was to be no international control as such. The United Nations would do no more than calculate the quantity of opium needed by the world pharmaceutical industry and express an opinion on the area to be sown and the yield to be expected. If any serious problems arose, the Bureau might institute inquiries, but only with the express permission of the country or countries concerned. It might also advise consumer nations – under seal of secrecy – to place an embargo on exports from recalcitrant countries.

Although drafted in 1953, the Protocol was not put into effect until ten years later, or two years after the publication of another convention, that of 1961! For hardly had the scheme been approved than it began to run into difficulties.

Under the terms of the Protocol the 'seven' did not enjoy a complete monopoly of production, since other countries were also permitted to cultivate the poppy in order to meet their domestic requirements. It soon became apparent that this left the door wide open to a number of abuses by providing justification for the existence of numerous uncontrolled producing regions and even for the appearance on the market of new producers. Japan, for instance, which had had no more than four hectares under poppy cultivation before the publication of the Protocol, subsequently put down 147 hectares to this crop so as 'to meet her internal needs'. Several countries, among them Afghanistan and Burma, made the terms of the Protocol a pretext for omitting to place an out-and-out ban on poppy cultivation in their territory. Accordingly, at the Eleventh Session of the Permanent Council of the U.N. Commission on Narcotic Drugs,[2] all governments outside the 'group of seven'

2. The Commission on Narcotic Drugs meets annually to draft international agreements and coordinate the campaign against the abuse and sale of narcotics. Its executive organ is the Narcotics Division based on Geneva. The International Narcotics Control Board (I.N.C.B.) is responsible for monitoring the development of the production and consumption of narcotics for licit purposes. It is also responsible for ensuring the observance of international agreements.

were asked to discontinue opium production and to obtain their future supplies from the internationally authorized exporting countries.

It was then that the problem of Afghanistan came to the fore. This country, which had not been a signatory to the 1953 Protocol, had in 1955 formally requested to be admitted to the group of official opium exporters, pointing out that ninety per cent of the population in certain parts of Afghanistan depended for their living on poppy-growing. Consequently, the Afghans maintained, if their country was to conform to international regulations, she must be authorized to produce for export.

This request threw the Commission on Narcotic Drugs[3] into a state of confusion. For Iran had just taken the 'great historic decision' to place a total ban on the cultivation of the poppy. It was the first concrete step towards reducing world opium production and the Commission could not, without loss of credibility, have followed up its hard-won victory by admitting another country to the exporting group.

For their part the Iranian leaders were not disposed to see Afghanistan, a neighbour with whom they were on far from easy terms, move into the place they had vacated as a result of their 'courageous gesture'. They also maintained that Afghanistan's lack of experience in controlling production would encourage illicit trafficking, and that Iran would be the first to suffer since Afghan opium would be smuggled in to supply Iranian addicts. The admission of another member to the group of seven was also opposed by India, the western world's largest opium supplier, who had been no less delighted by Iran's withdrawal from that group.

The Afghan question dragged on from session to session and was never resolved. Afghanistan's representative, wearying of the struggle, declared in 1958 that his country, 'in the interests of humanity and out of concern for international cooperation, has decided to place a total ban on the cultivation of the poppy and on the sale, import, export and use of opium'. No one really

3. This organization replaced the Opium Advisory Committee after the Second World War.

believed that this decision would be put into effect and time has proved them right. Consequently the 1953 Protocol has remained both unratified and inoperative.

In the meantime work had been proceeding on the preparation of the Single Convention on Narcotic Drugs. The intention was to collate the provisions from all the various agreements published since the turn of the century 'in order to unify and simplify existing instruments'. This *tour de force* proved impossible, for the problems which had hampered the implementation of the 1953 Protocol obtruded once again. The Single Convention, adopted in 1961 after a number of stormy encounters, is an unsatisfactory compromise. In many respects it is a good deal less bold than the 1953 Protocol, for which reason it was also more easily ratified.

At the very start, the Afghan question was again tabled. Article 32 of one of the drafts laid before the members of the Commission on Narcotic Drugs listed the countries authorized to export opium, among them not only the original seven but also Afghanistan which, having been thrown out at the door, had now returned through the window. This gave rise to some furious arguments, as may be seen from the detailed report of the U.N. Conference's plenary sessions.

'At our 1958 session' [exclaimed the Iranian representative, Dr Azarakhch] 'the representative of Afghanistan declared that his country no longer intended to figure among the exporters of opium, thus resolving a problem which had been a grave cause of concern to Iran. But now that problem has once more raised its head. With much regret the Iranian delegation finds itself compelled to request that the name of Afghanistan be deleted from Article 32 . . . In the interests of the world at large Iran assented to great sacrifices in order to reduce the amount of opium produced in the world. But we are encountering tremendous difficulties in closing our frontiers to clandestine imports. If Afghanistan is to be regarded as an exporting country, Iran will be faced with a very difficult if not an impossible task.'

Replying to Iran's barely veiled threat to resume production, the Afghan delegate, Mr Tabibi, said:

243

'If Afghanistan declared, in the course of the Eleventh Session of the Commission on Narcotic Drugs, that she would not insist on her name appearing in the 1953 Protocol among the countries authorized to export opium, it was because that Protocol was not in force. In any case the procedure required to modify it was too complicated. But subsequently my country made no secret of her wish to figure among the exporters agreed under the Single Convention. Contrary to Iran's allegations, we have never renounced our intention of joining the "exporters' club". Afghanistan has a long tradition as a producer of opium – opium of excellent quality, moreover, since its morphine content ranges from eighteen to twenty per cent. In opposing Afghanistan's wishes, Iran has cited the risk of contraband entering her own territory. It seems hardly logical for Iran to be concerned about this problem in respect of just one of her frontiers. Turkey, a very large opium producer, is also a neighbour of Iran's. Has it not occurred to the representative of the government in Teheran to ask that Turkey be deleted from the list of exporting countries? There can be no control over the world trade in narcotics unless this is founded on good faith and mutual cooperation between members of the international community. Failing that, no convention can ever hope to be properly implemented.'

The U.N. eventually fell back on half-measures and simply abolished the list of exporting countries. The 1961 convention stipulates that only such countries as traditionally produce opium for export may continue to supply the world pharmaceutical industry, and that others wishing to enter the market must first be approved by the International Narcotics Council Board. None of these restrictions, however, applies to exports of five tons and under.

By her stubbornness, Afghanistan succeeded in preventing the emergence of a closed shop of opium exporters. Nevertheless, the fact that would-be suppliers to the world pharmaceutical industry must first be cleared by the I.N.C.B. has since enabled the United Nations to withhold this privilege from countries applying for authorization, as did Burma in 1964. If Afghanistan or Burma had been granted permission to grow opium for export, the same privilege could hardly have been denied to Thailand and Laos, both of whom were equally insistent. For any poppy-growing country would far sooner be recognized as a 'traditional opium-producer' than be forced by international pressure to impose a ban.

Another of the Single Convention's half-measures related to the U.N's powers of embargo on such opium producing countries as failed to abide by the decisions made at Geneva. While the *de facto* members of the exporters' group looked kindly on this move, the countries who found themselves excluded were obviously somewhat less enchanted. Finally it was decided that the Commission on Narcotic Drugs could recommend an embargo but would not be empowered to impose it.

This convention, by trying to please everybody, left much to be desired in terms of effectiveness. Such were its imperfections that in 1961 the United States felt impelled to put forward a number of amendments. In justification of this initiative John Ingersoll, head of the B.N.D.D. and leader of the American delegation at Geneva, made a number of points in a speech in June 1971.

A glance at the 1969 I.N.C.B., he said, report would show that the situation had not developed in accordance with the hopes engendered by the Single Convention. The report revealed that the legal production of opium had continued to fall – from 1,700 tons in 1930 to an average of approximately 800 tons between 1963 and 1968. This could indicate some progress, even taking into account the fact that in 1969 declared production was as high as 1,200 tons. But in the same period the quantities of opium escaping into the clandestine market were more significant than before. As the pharmaceutical quota diminished, so the quantities offered to traffickers increased. The I.N.C.B's estimate of annual illegal production at more than 1,200 tons was, in Ingersoll's opinion, a modest one. The United States had good reason to believe that this figure barely covered illegal production in south-east Asia alone – proof of the inadequacy of the Single Convention. Its object had been to reserve opium for scientific and medical use only, but this had not been achieved.

The United States proposed to remedy this situation by conferring coercive powers on the International Narcotics Control Board. Their suggested amendments came under five headings.

Firstly it was proposed that the I.N.C.B. should be authorized to procure and make use of information other than that provided by any particular government. Should the I.N.C.B. suspect a country of not complying scrupulously with the provisions of the Single Convention of 1961, it might make use of information from private sources, treating it as though it were official information. Had this amendment been carried, it would have enabled all the American intelligence agencies, not least the C.I.A., to extend their activities to the field of narcotics. A further amendment followed much the same line in proposing that the I.N.C.B. be permitted to send a committee of inquiry to a given producer country on the understanding that its government consented to receive the said delegation. The third amendment proposed that the I.N.C.B. should be empowered to make use of its own sources of information to correct the estimates of production and consumption provided by any one government. It might also enjoin that government to conform to the figures so adjusted. The United States further hoped that the I.N.C.B. would be given the power – withheld in 1953 and 1961 – to impose an embargo on any country failing to abide by the Single Convention. Finally, Washington called for stiffer provisions governing the extradition of traffickers.

These suggestions stirred up a veritable hornets' nest. It seems difficult to believe that the United States could seriously have expected to gain acceptance for such proposals merely on the strength of the growing concern felt about the world-wide spread of drug addiction. For in fact these amounted to the creation, for the first time in history, of an organization with supranational powers in which America's influence would be decisive by reason of the dominant position she occupied on the various international bodies. In effect, the opium-producing countries were being asked to relinquish part of their national sovereignty. Their attitude was neatly summed up by the Mexican representative to the Commission on Narcotic Drugs when he said:

'The Mexican delegation could not agree to a system of rigid controls being substituted for goodwill and mutual trust between nations.

246

This would place the member countries of the United Nations in a state of dependence *vis-à-vis* the International Narcotics Control Board, since that organization would be able to impose controls, inquiries and other formalities prejudicial to their sovereignty.'

The Hungarian delegate inquired sarcastically whether the proposed amendments applied to synthetic drugs such as methadone and pethidine, of which the United States were the chief producers. The view taken by the Soviet representative was that if the American proposals concerning the collection of information were to be adopted, the I.N.C.B. would become not so much a supranational as a police organization.

It is hardly surprising that the American amendments, whereby an international body would in effect have been placed at the beck and call of the United States, should have been unanimously rejected by the plenipotentiaries foregathered at Geneva in March 1972. At this meeting a few minor changes were made to the Single Convention, but generally speaking it remained the same 'inefficient' instrument denounced by John Ingersoll when seeking to justify his country's initiative in 1971. The fact is that international organizations, whether concerned with drugs or other problems, are no more than forums for the ventilation of opposing views. The decisions taken there are determined by the interplay of political forces. Since the contents of international treaties represent the lowest common denominator on which the various member countries are able to agree, the scope of such agreements becomes inevitably circumscribed once a nation's political and economic privileges enter the equation.

Yet some explanation is, perhaps, required for the lukewarm reception accorded the American proposals by the developed nations, especially those in Europe who were themselves no strangers to the problem of addiction. Undoubtedly their attitude was in some measure determined not only by the Utopian nature of the amendments but also by reluctance to alienate the underdeveloped countries without good reason. But other considerations were almost certainly involved. For behind Washington's avowed intention to suppress or reduce the illicit production of opium there looms a more ambitious objective, namely the total suppression of poppy cultivation, whether legal or illegal, throughout the world.

As things are now, the European pharmaceutical industry has need of opium from which to extract the ten or so alkaloids commonly used for medical purposes. Even though a number of synthetic substitutes have been found for morphine, this drug remains indispensable. Codeine, one of its derivatives, is a powerful cough suppressant for which no really reliable or economic substitute has yet been found. The manufacturing costs of possible alternatives for codeine are very high and, in view of the comparatively low price of opium on the legal international market, it is therefore more advantageous to manufacture codeine from the opium derivative, morphine, than it is to produce a synthetic drug. Today more than ninety per cent of the morphine manufactured by the pharmaceutical industry goes into this product.

After the Second World War almost all the opium used for medical purposes was supplied by four countries: India, the Soviet Union, Iran and Turkey. India is far and away the largest producer of licit opium. In 1971 she herself accounted for 1,200 tons of the combined tonnage of 1,616 produced by all four countries.[4] Moreover India now enjoys what amounts to a monopoly in the export of licit opium. The U.S.S.R. has virtually ceased to export, Iran reserves her entire output to supply her own addicts, and Turkey undertook to withdraw from the international market as from June 1972.

This, the very situation the consumer countries had sought to guard against in 1953, is currently reflected in the higher selling price of opium on the legal world market. Whereas in the sixties a kilogramme of opium with a ten per cent morphine con-

4. These figures relate to opium of varying moisture content. The production figures published by the United Nations are rather lower, being based on a standard unit, namely one kilogramme of opium at ninety per cent dry weight. Most of the producer countries express their output in terms of a lower dry weight. Calculated on the basis of ninety per cent dry weight, the 1970 production figures read as follows: India, 794 tons; Iran, 78 tons; Turkey, 51 tons; Soviet Union, 226 tons.

tent sold for between 12 and 14 dollars, its price in 1972 had risen to at least twice that amount. In 1968 alone the price of Indian opium went up by 25 per cent.

There are several ways, none of them as yet particularly effective, in which the consumer countries can exert pressure on prices and generally mitigate the disadvantages deriving from the monopoly situation enjoyed by India. One of those ways is the exploitation in the developed countries of the black poppy.[5] Though its morphine content is no more than two parts in a thousand, the whole plant, when processed industrially, may be used for the extraction of this alkaloid.

A country that encourages the expansion of black poppy cultivation will benefit in two respects. First it will attain some measure of self-sufficiency as regards morphine supplies so that, at times of international crisis, it will not be so immediately dependent on the countries exporting licit opium. Thus, during the Second World War, France put down 35,000 hectares to this crop, thereby securing supplies of both morphine and oil. Secondly, unlike the opium poppy, the black poppy cannot be used as raw material for the illicit manufacture of narcotics, since fifty tons of this plant – as compared with one ton of opium – are required to produce a hundred kilogrammes of morphine. Moreover its processing calls for highly sophisticated industrial equipment.

At the end of 1972 the cost of morphine extracted from the black poppy was still much higher than that of the opium based product. But as the price of opium rose on the world market the gap began to narrow, reducing in France from sixty per cent to thirty per cent between 1970 and 1972. France has invested large sums of money in research on the black poppy; geneticists are constantly at work in an attempt to isolate more productive strains, while manufacturers are seeking to improve their extraction processes. Between 1968 and 1972 the area under culti-

5. *Papaver somniferum*, var. *nigrum*. The black poppy has long been grown in Europe for its oil. Circa 1870 40,000 hectares were devoted to this plant in France. It was then gradually abandoned in favour of more productive oilseeds. In 1935 a Hungarian, Kabay, was perfecting a technique for extracting morphine from the black poppy.

vation increased from a few hundred to two thousand hectares, and by 1975 the total area is expected to extend to 5,000 hectares. For several years a similar policy has been pursued by other countries, notably those in the communist bloc, including the U.S.S.R., Czechoslovakia and Hungary. Australia and Argentina are also experimenting with this crop.

But the development of the black poppy has as yet made little impression on India's position of strength. Indeed the world demand for morphine is growing appreciably, at a rate of around five per cent per annum. And though India is continually stepping up production she cannot, for technical reasons, keep pace with that demand.

The present world situation is therefore altogether paradoxical, for whereas illicit production of opium is continually going up, the world pharmaceutical industry is short of supplies.

The United States would appear to be little concerned about the comparative shortage of opium and still less by the ever-rising price of the drug. While not admitting as much, they would probably like to see the total suppression of world opium production, since this would permit them to reconcile humanitarian considerations with certain of their economic interests.

Indeed, if morphine derived from opium were to disappear from the market, American drug companies would be able to thrust on to the rest of the world the synthetic preparations they now manufacture or hope to manufacture at some future date. Today American firms hold the patents for every synthetic product capable of replacing morphine and codeine. Admittedly no real substitute has yet been found that can compete with natural codeine, whether in terms of cost or safety, but research is still going on. In his speech of 17 June 1971 President Nixon made no bones about what he deemed to be the best solution. 'The development of effective substitutes for morphine and codeine,' he said, 'would eliminate any valid reason for opium production.'

Things do not appear in quite the same light to European industrialists who, in veiled terms, accuse the United States of hypocrisy. It is no coincidence, they point out, that Turkey, a major exporter of licit opium, should be the first victim of America's policy of total war against illicit opium. And, while admitting that the elimination of Turkish opium production has cut off one of the traffickers' sources of supply, they argue that it has also exacerbated the world shortage of licit opium. 'Why not,' they ask, 'apply equal pressure to countries such as Thailand and Laos, whose whole output finds its way on to the black market?' Today the European pharmaceutical industry is quietly looking out for potential opium exporters. Iran, for instance, has been approached by drug manufacturers anxious to purchase part of her stocks. Negotiations have been held up by the question of price, but one manufacturer told us that an agreement was still on the cards. Turkey has been officially notified by representatives of European countries that, should she ever resume production, they would be willing buyers. More important still, representations of an equally official nature have been made to the Chinese People's Republic, urging that country to apply for formal permission to export opium. The objections upon which the United Nations based their refusal of this privilege to Burma, Afghanistan and Pakistan cannot be invoked against China which possesses all the qualifications demanded of a licit exporter of opium. Not only is the country a traditional producer but it is also in a position to exercise stringent controls over the growers.

The United States may be expected to bring all their influence to bear in order to block such a decision. The consumer countries on the other hand, are growing ever less inclined to support a restrictive policy with regard to opium production, the more so since its only effect so far has been to reduce the amount of opium on the licit market while increasing the quantity available to traffickers. They further point out that the fight against drug addiction must not be confused with the protection of the interests of the American pharmaceutical industry. All this explains why, in their crusade against poppy-cultivation, the United States have fewer allies than might have been expected.

Even supposing no part had been played by these economic considerations and the American amendments had been carried, it may be doubted whether the scope of the international agreements would have been any wider. It is one thing to draft or strengthen legislation and quite another to impose it. For

251

though there may be ample proof that Thailand, Burma, Laos or Pakistan is producing such and such a quantity of opium in such and such a district, and that the output is finding its way on to the black market, there is no means of compelling any of these countries to put a stop either to production or to trafficking.

Had the Single Convention of 1961 been amended in accordance with America's wishes, the only tangible result would have been the refusal of many countries to ratify it, with a corresponding increase in the number of non-contracting nations. Indeed, the Yugoslav delegate said as much when he recalled that, of the eighty countries who had signed the Single Convention in 1961, only fifty-three had subscribed to the 1953 Protocol, since 'the terms of this treaty were unacceptable to a great many countries'. This is particularly true of the producers, nor is it surprising that Thailand, Burma, Laos, Afghanistan and Pakistan should have refused to adhere to the Protocol. U.N. experts and technical advisers were aware of these difficulties when they decided not to limit the activities of international bodies to the field of international law, but to extend them to include economic aid to the opium producing countries.

Anyone in search of opium, whether licit or illicit, invariably looks to the underdeveloped regions, for it is there alone that all the conditions combine to make this crop possible, if not inevitable: cheap and plentiful labour, a remote situation, few, if any, roads, limited home demand, deficient administrative machinery.

A study of the conditions governing production in Thailand[6] reveals that the problem of eliminating poppy cultivation is closely bound up with a country's development as a whole. There can be no instant panacea, for the solution lies in massive investment coupled with a great deal of hard work. A case in point is Yugoslavia whose annual production of opium prior to the Second World War was sixty tons as against two and a half tons

6. See Chapter 6.

today. From this it may be seen that regional development leads to the disappearance of the poppy, as soon as there is a stable market for alternative crops.

It is not for climatic reasons alone that the French government, in an attempt to become independent of the traditional morphine and opium suppliers, has chosen to grow the black rather than the opium poppy, even though its morphine content is no more than two and a half parts in a thousand. In France, as in all developed countries, labour costs are so high that, assuming the opium poppy were to be grown there, one kilogramme of opium collected by hand would cost as much as its equivalent in caviar. The black poppy, on the other hand, can be harvested by machine and industrially processed. Though it still costs more to extract morphine from the black poppy than from opium produced in the Third World, prospects are promising enough to justify the strategic considerations which have led a number of countries to seek self-sufficiency in this field.

Opium is the 'mongol child of underdevelopment' not only from a strictly economic point of view, but also in a wider and more political sense. It has generally been noted that illicit opium is produced by alien populations and ethnic minorities, as is the case in Thailand, Laos and Burma where the poppy is grown by the Meo, Lahu, Akha, Shan, Kachin and Wa tribes. In Pakistan the growers are Pathans and in Afghanistan, Kafirs or Tajiks. This anthropological aspect of opium production can be readily explained. It is not because a people belongs to such and such a minority that it traditionally engages in poppy cultivation. Rather it is because these minorities have, for historical reasons, been herded into the remote fastness of the country they inhabit – into regions, that is, where opium is technically and economically more advantageous than any other crop.

These same minorities are also relegated to the political fringe and, indeed, the two aspects of this problem must be seen as related in terms of cause and effect. Today most of the peoples who grow the poppy illegally have no political power in the countries where they live. In so far as their interests are represented at all at government level, their spokesmen carry little or no weight. Most of the time the tribes are exploited by the dominant ethnic group which at best despises and ignores them when not actually attempting to seize their lands. But by a curious twist of fate, their position on the geographical, economic and political fringe has for its corollary not only under-representation but also virtual freedom from supervision by the central power. This explains why the producer countries find the production and distribution of opium almost impossible to control inside their territories. Hence opium production cannot be stamped out by spending millions of dollars exclusively on 'technical' measures. It is also necessary to strengthen the socio-political cohesion of the underdeveloped nations, which in turn presupposes their attaining regional integration. In this respect the specific projects of the United Nations could only make sense if they aimed at promoting the over-all development of the opium producing regions – development, that is, embracing not only the economic and technical but also the adminis-trative, social and political aspects. This being so, there is one crucial question which arises out of any U.S. or U.N. proposal to solve the problem of drug addiction by striking at the source of the raw material for opiates, and that is the question of the priority to be accorded to aid for the countries of the Third World. Everything depends on what sacrifices the countries afflicted by addiction are prepared to make in order to attain their end.

On 11 November 1970, at the instigation of the United States, the U.N. Economic and Social Council's Commission on Narcotic Drugs passed Resolution no. 1559 requesting U Thant, the then Secretary-General, to set up the Fund for Drug Control. In a letter addressed to all the governments concerned, the secre-tary of the Commission emphasized the 'extreme urgency' of this step. By 25 December the General Assembly of the United Nations were able to vote Resolution no. 2719, congratulating themselves on the 'implementation of Resolution no. 1559'. In their customary inimitable style the United Nations went on to announce that they were launching an attack on opium produc-tion by tackling the problem from the economic angle. When the fund was set up on 1 April 1971 its first (Dutch) director, Mr Schurmann, set about searching for backers.

A year or more later he was forced to admit that the Fund's financial situation left a good deal to be desired. By this time his organization had already worked out a concerted plan of campaign, both short- and long-term, to combat drug abuse, and had drawn up a provisional list of 160 major projects and numerous minor ones. These were concerned both with the medical aspects of addiction and with the economic and technical problems posed by the substitution of crops and the coordination of enforcement measures in the opium producing countries. The plan's implementation would necessitate an expenditure of ninety-five million dollars over the first five years. Unfortunately the total amount paid or promised by the member countries of the Commission on Narcotic Drugs did not come up to the expectations of the Fund's original promoters. The United States, worse hit by addiction than any other country, contributed two million dollars; Saudi Arabia, the Holy See, Turkey and South Vietnam between them raised eleven thousand dollars, and Iran promised five thousand. Finally, the Director of the U.N. Narcotics Division handed over the five thousand dollars he had received the previous year as winner of the Edward W. Browning Award. Having added together these modest sums, the Fund found itself possessed of 2,021,000 dollars – a far cry from the ninety-five million called for in the plan.

The proposal for an international fund to combat the production and abuse of drugs had been unanimously acclaimed by the delegations of the member countries of the Commission on Narcotic Drugs.[7] But as soon as it came to deciding how much each country was to contribute, serious difficulties arose. A study of the minutes of the Twenty-fourth Session of the Commission on Narcotic Drugs (29 September–21 October 1971) reveals that while the representatives of the developing countries such as Ghana, India, Mexico, Peru and the United

7. Report on the 24th session of the Commission on Narcotic Drugs, 29 September–21 October 1971, Geneva.

Arab Republic, did not hesitate to give the Fund their moral support, they were in most cases precluded by their financial situation from providing support of a material nature. Some, however, were prepared to offer the U.N. certain facilities to enable experimental projects to be carried out in their respective territories. The report records the Indian representative as saying that his country could only agree to cooperate with the Fund in return for the latter's financial assistance. Indeed, far from proposing to help finance the Fund's projects, the under-developed countries expected to be helped themselves. According to the 'poor' nations, responsibility for financing the world-wide campaign against narcotics lay with the developed nations which, after all, were the chief sufferers from drug addiction.

This point of view was implicitly accepted by the developed countries. They knew that there was no real prospect of compelling the producer countries to improve their control over production unless they were given material aid. Yet this prospect aroused little enthusiasm. Prevarications and excuses abound in the minutes of the debates that took place during the Commission's Twenty-fourth Session. The Belgian representative, for instance, pointed out that, because of the dissolution of Parliament, his country had not yet been able to examine the question nor, though elections had since been held, had there been any further mention of a possible contribution to the Fund. The German delegate promised a million marks, with the proviso that this sum must come out of the national budget and be approved by the Bundestag. Great Britain, on the other hand, objected to the creation of yet another United Nations agency and suggested that anti-drug measures be financed out of the regular funds of the United Nations Development Programme (U.N.D.P.).[8] This was clearly unacceptable to the underdeveloped countries who believed it would eat into the sums already allocated to specific development projects regarded by them as having higher priority. In their eyes the campaign against the illicit production and sale of opium called for the tapping of

8. All member countries regularly contribute to this Programme. The subventions are planned in such a way that the main financial burden falls on the developed countries.

new sources of finance. But the British representative took the view that, before the United Kingdom could commit herself to a possible contribution to the Fund, she must first be in a position to assess the extent to which that new agency was helping to improve the U.N's capacity to eradicate drug abuse. To this Schurmann replied logically enough that such an attitude would give rise to a vicious circle. If everyone waited to see results before giving the Fund the wherewithal to operate, all action would be inhibited from the start.

But the most stubborn opposition to the very principle of such a fund came from the Soviet Union. In vindicating his country's attitude the representative of the U.S.S.R. based his argument on administrative and financial premises.

'We do not contest the need' [he said in effect] 'to dispense technical and financial aid to certain countries to help them maintain tighter controls over their domestic production, distribution and consumption of opiates. But we are opposed to the principle of voluntary contributions, for either these are insufficient – and as often as not too quickly exhausted to produce any worthwhile results – or else they rapidly turn into compulsory contributions.'

He went on to recall that at one time the International Labour Organization had set up a further education centre at Turin, theoretically financed by voluntary contributions. To avoid being hamstrung by lack of funds, the centre had very soon had to draw on the U.N's regular budget. Exactly the same thing had happened in the case of the W.H.O's world-wide anti-malaria programme and a similar fate would inevitably befall the Fund for Drug Control. An enterprise of this nature, he held, would not only lead to the dissipation of U.N. funds and constitute a perpetual hazard to the financing of programmes already adopted and in course of realization, but would upset the order of priorities for projects planned within the framework of world aid to underdeveloped countries. The creation of bodies dependent on voluntary contributions was all the more inopportune, Moscow's spokesman went on, in that even compulsory contributions could be cancelled from one day to the next. In this connection he recalled that, in 1970, the United States had withdrawn financial support from the I.L.O. after that organization had appointed a chairman whose political opinions conflicted with their own.

Although the reasons underlying the attitude of the U.S.S.R. were never precisely spelled out by its representative, the political motivation was quite unambiguous. For the Soviet Union and her satellites could hardly be expected to finance a fund whose first and chief beneficiary would be the United States. In other words, it was a question not so much of helping the underdeveloped countries as of combating the spread of addiction in North America. Thus the creation of a fighting fund would mean in effect that the world would be asked to contribute to the solution of the cultural crisis then developing in the United States. In the circumstances neither the Soviet Union nor, for that matter, any other socialist country, could be expected to go out of its way to provide financial support for the struggle against the illicit production and sale of narcotics.

The chief editor of Hong Kong's important Communist daily, the *Takun Pao*, discussed this subject with us in March 1972, declaring,

'Although I have no mandate from my country to comment on this question, I can give you my own personal opinion.[9] The People's Republic is indubitably opposed to the use of drugs. Moreover after 1949 the government in Peking took energetic steps to stamp out opium addiction, which the British had imposed upon our country by force of arms. But the drug problem is essentially the concern of the United States and their lackeys. Hence my country will scrutinize closely, project by project, the use to be made of the contributions that it might eventually contemplate making to such a fund. Consider, for instance, that today a large part of the resources already at the Fund's disposal are to be spent in Thailand, in effect a rear base for the American imperialists in the Vietnam war.'

There can be no doubt that the People's Republic will lose no opportunity of unmasking the stratagem employed by the

9. The 'personal opinions' of the chief editor of the *Takun Pao* are generally regarded by political observers in Hong Kong as reflecting the official views of the Chinese government.

United States in seeking to solve their own problems by an indirect international financing operation. Hence China cannot be counted on to make any sizeable contribution.

Again there would seem little likelihood that other specialized international bodies will release a portion of their credits to the Fund for Drug Control. Paragraph 392[10] of the report of the Twenty-fourth Session of the Commission on Narcotic Drugs reveals that, though F.A.O. (Food and Agricultural Organization), UNESCO and the W.H.O. came out strongly in favour of the Fund and were fully prepared to participate in a concerted plan of action against drug abuse, their existing budgets would not permit them for the time being to finance such participation.

While most countries have given their approval – an inexpensive item – to the creation of the Fund, they are unable, unwilling or reluctant to provide the wherewithal for the realization of its various projects. This being so, it is easy enough to predict that the effectiveness of the Fund will, in practice, be severely limited. In 1972 eighteen priority schemes, chosen from among the 160 initially adumbrated, were under study in some dozen countries. Their total cost was not to exceed two and a half million dollars, or slightly more than the over-all resources then at the Fund's disposal. One of the main beneficiaries was Thailand where, in March 1971, work began on a specific project elaborated by the Commission on Narcotic Drugs.[11]

The history of this Fund illustrates one of the great truisms applicable to the workings of international organizations, namely that the sum a country contributes is most often proportionate to the advantages that country hopes to gain from the recipient of its contribution. By way of example we need only compare the two million dollars so laboriously collected by the Fund for Drug Control (and largely earmarked for the underdeveloped countries) with the amounts promised at an international conference at Stockholm in response to a decision to set up a Fund

10. Report on the Twenty-fourth Session of the Commission on Narcotic Drugs, Geneva, 29 September–21 October 1971.
11. See Chapter 6.

259

for the Human Environment. Even before the launching of the Fund several of the industrialized countries had already offered substantial contributions. Canada promised nearly six million dollars, the Netherlands a million and a half and the United 'States no less than forty million. Germany, Japan, France, Austria and Spain, who had not seen fit to subsidize the Fund for Drug Control, decided to contribute as yet unspecified amounts to the new Fund. It could, of course, be argued that this difference in attitude is attributable to the lesser magnitude of the drug problem as compared with that posed by the destruction of the environment. But there is another, more plausible explanation. Whereas the monies passing to the Fund for Drug Control will be spent in the underdeveloped countries and hence will generate little or no industrial or commercial activity in the donor country, such is by no means the case with the contributions made to the Fund for the Human Environment. We may be perfectly sure that the forty million dollars guaranteed by the United States will not lie idle in Africa, Latin America or Asia but will, for the most part, return whence they have come, to swell the order books of industrial firms which even now are already preparing to supply what promises to be a lucrative market. In the circumstances they have had little difficulty in finding complaisant U.N. delegates, prepared to stigmatize in tones of fashionable protest 'the unprincipled scramble for increased productivity'. Meanwhile Schurmann's appeals have failed to elicit anything like the same enthusiasm.

Hence not too much reliance should be placed on the ability of the United Nations to conduct an effective campaign against opium production in the underdeveloped countries. For it seems all too probable that the few hundred million dollars required to implement the programme envisaged at the Fund's inception will never be found. Senior U.N. officials admit in private that they would be happy to settle for ten per cent of that sum. As it is, the better endowed nations are not prepared to make the necessary sacrifices for the benefit of the underdeveloped countries even though, in the long term, this would be the only way of solving their own addiction problems.

Conclusion: the Search for Scapegoats

The prospects for the campaign initiated by the United States in the endeavour to 'stem at source the flood of heroin flowing into the veins of Western youth' are far from encouraging. The internal contradictions of U.S. policy, America's comparative or total lack of influence in certain parts of the world, the precedence accorded national self-interest over humanitarian considerations, the impotence of the United Nations and the patent refusal of the more prosperous nations to modify their policy of assistance to underdeveloped countries – all these combine to hamper that campaign at production level, the level, that is, at which the raw material for narcotics is produced. The international anti-drug crusade launched by the United States in June 1971 holds out no hope whatever of victory. Moreover the chances of winning even one individual battle are very remote, as experience in Turkey has already shown.

It may therefore be asked why Washington has deliberately chosen to fight the growth of drug addiction on what would seem to be the worst possible ground. Behind the humanitarian arguments employed to vindicate that policy may be discerned the deeper reasons for America's anti-drug strategy whose roots, while of course partly economic, are first and foremost political.

By blaming other countries for what is one of the gravest problems confronting the United States today, the authorities can divert attention from the fact that the cause of the evil is essentially indigenous. At the same time, while pandering to national self-esteem, this approach offers a cheap and politically expedient way of convincing the public of their leaders' determination.

Any success can thus be credited to the efforts of the Republican administration and inflated accordingly, as the wide publicity given to the Turkish affair testifies. Even if the suppression of

261

the poppy in Turkey has no decisive effect on the level of heroin addiction throughout the world, it will at least have permitted the Nixon administration, on the eve of re-election, to divert attention from the corrupt regimes in south-east Asia and their responsibility for the spread of drug addiction in the United States and the Far East. When, in November 1971, President Nixon announced the launching of an aggressive anti-narcotics campaign, he did not hesitate to pat himself on the back for having secured the collaboration of five countries, among them Thailand, Laos and Paraguay!

Any setback, on the other hand, can easily be explained away by citing America's inability, on moral and objective grounds, to intervene in the domestic affairs of certain States. If Richard Nixon is ever asked to account for the policy he has pursued in his anti-drug campaign, he can always say: 'The reason why it has been so difficult to suppress opium production in Afghanistan or Burma is that, as things are right now, we have no means of applying sufficient pressure, nor do we have the moral authority to ensure that our problem receives due attention.' This is no mere conjecture on our part, for such arguments are already being advanced by B.N.D.D. agents in Asia.

This strategy is not without its dangers and may rebound on the government now in power in Washington should its opponents begin to delve really deeply into the reasons why, despite the close links which bind the United States to Thailand, South Vietnam and Laos, Nixon's war on drugs has already been lost in advance in south-east Asia. But embarrassing though they may be, the charges of corruption levelled against certain of the Republican administration's Asian allies weigh little by comparison with the advantages to be gained in the field of home politics from having scapegoats on whom to blame the drug problem, a problem accorded high priority by American public opinion.

In an all-out war on heroin the specifically international aspect cannot be ignored. But it would seem clear that henceforward the primary object of attack will have to be the national roots of the evil.

Like many another anti-social activity, heroin addiction is the by-product of an unprecedented cultural crisis. If the author-

262

ities were to decide to attack the causes rather than the effects of the evil, they would have to acknowledge that a proliferation of electronic gadgets, undercover agents, or even disintoxication programmes would not be enough. This would mean embarking on a course so disruptive of existing social and political *mores* that no one would think of arrogating to himself the powers necessary to that end. It is by no means fortuitous that, sooner than promote a policy of full employment, the American government should prefer to hand out the dole to the unemployed ghetto-dwellers, knowing full well that these underprivileged people will squander the better part of it on drugs.

Today only a few peripheral protest groups, whose lucid thinking fails to make up for their lack of political influence, are denouncing heroin addiction as the inevitable by-product of a decadent capitalist system which must be called in question in its entirety. Since this point of view is unacceptable to the leaders of the countries afflicted by addiction, their entire energy is devoted to containing the scourge within limits compatible with the functioning of the social system. Such being the case, there can be no doubt that heroin addiction is here to stay and that it will take its place alongside poverty, racism and social injustice on the list of insoluble problems which, though ceaselessly deplored, are finally accepted by the majority as necessary evils.

Index

Index

police: Afghan (*cont.*)
Narcotics Squad, Interpol, narcotics agents
Politics of Heroin in South-East Asia, The (McCoy), 140n
poppy, black, 249–50, 253
poppy cultivation, 14–15
in Afghanistan, 191–2, 197; and 1953 Protocol, 241, 242
in Burma, 156, 166–7, 241; in Burmese Shan States, 99, 156, 160–3, 253
difficulties of, 116, 118–19
and ethnic minorities, 253–4
in Iran: banning of, 200, 222, 236, 242; control of, 228; resumption of, 200, 222, 224, 228–31, 232, 235–6
in Japan, 241
and land degradation, 85
in Laos, 116, 118–19, 253; legislation against, 146; Pathet Lao and 128; and secret war, 120, 122–3
in Mexico, 14, 57–8, 218
and 1953 Protocol, 241
in Pakhtunistan, 180, 191
in South America, 57–8
in Thailand, 82–6, 88–9, 91, 252, 253
in Turkey, 14, 84, 202, 205–6; U.S. campaign against, 34–5, 200, 201–2, 203–5, 209–10, 213, 215, 218, 220
world, U.S. campaign against, 247–8, 280–1
Praphas, Gen. Charusathien, 110, 112
Prasong, Charasdamrong, 112
Protocol of 1953, 239, 240–3, 244, 252
psychiatric disorders and addiction, 4
Puerto Ricans, 7–8, 22
Puerto Rico, 51, 64
'pushers', 13, 70–1
Puzo, Mario: *The Godfather*, 21n2

racketeers *see* gangs and racketeers
Ramparts, 140n
Rangel, Charles B., 71

Rangoon, 159, 170–1, 174; government at, 155, 157, 158, 164, 167–8, 176; opium traffic in, 171, 172–3
Readers Guide, 8
'Red Flag' group, Burma, 158
Richard, Rafael, 54–5
Ricord, Auguste, 52–3
RO (Régie le l'opium, French Opium Administration), 116, 119
Roosevelt, President Franklin D., 237
Rosario, Del, 140–2, 145

SAC (Service d'Action Civique), 29, 30
Saccomamo, Eugène: *Bandits à Marseilles*, 29n11
Saigon, 48, 49, 150
Saint Lucia, 51
Salleh, Dr, 231
Sananikone, Phoni, 150
Second World War, 30–1, 204, 239, 248, 249; increase in addiction after, 7, 7n, 21, 56; opium traffic during, 133
Service d'Action Civique (SAC), 29, 30
servicemen, American, in South-East Asia: and heroin, 37, 39, 46, 48, 65, 79, 118, 139, 143, 145–6; and opium traffic, 132, 135, 143
Shan Liberation Armies, 100, 156–7, 160, 175
Shan State Army, 159
Shan State Progress Party, 159
Shan States, Burmese, 94, 96, 99, 189, 155–67; opium production in, 99, 100, 156, 160–3, 166–7, 253; and opium traffic, 101–2, 161–7
Shan tribes, 94, 103, 153; *and see* Shan States
Shanghai conference (1909), 237
Sicilians, 22; *and see* Mafia
Singapore, 37, 38, 40, 186
Single Convention on Narcotic Drugs (1961), 203, 205, 212, 241, 243–5, 252

274